ANDREA PALLADIO
UNBUILT VENICE

ANTONIO FOSCARI

ANDREA PALLADIO UNBUILT VENICE

LARS MÜLLER PUBLISHERS

for Barbara

AN INTRODUCTION TO MY PALLADIO

A friend once told me that I was destined to write about Palladio because I am an architect, because I have taught architectural history at the *University Institute of Architecture* in *Venice* (IUAV), and because – at least for part of the year – I live in a house built by Palladio.

Perhaps he was right. But that was not why I finally put pen to paper at the end of the year marking the fifth centenary of Andrea Palladio's birth. Instead it was the sight of thousands, even tens of thousands, of people gazing with lively curiosity and intense pleasure at Palladio's drawings – in Vicenza, London, Madrid and New York – that rekindled my fascination for an art based on the exercise of a *virtù*, a virtue both ethical and intellectual, that is rare – indeed I would say exceptionally rare – to find in the form it takes in Palladio's work. I, too, was surprised – yet again – by the clarity of line in every drawing, and I admired the completeness of each project. It prompted me to reflect on how this architect was always conscious of the importance of his work; so much so, in fact, that he took the trouble to gather it together and (miraculously) bequeath to future generations a documentation abundant in projects attesting to his remarkable, and natural, creativity.

I could have taken my notes for a lecture series I gave on Palladio in 2008 and reworked and extended them for publication. One lecture focused on how his method of composition was based on analogy; another on the distinction that clearly transpires from his work between the concepts of *fabbrica*, *ragione* and *forma*; another examined the intriguing meaning of the term *invenzione* – in the sense of "finding again" – which he used to define his projects; yet another discussed the "peripteral dream" that fired his imagination during the last years of his life, and so forth.

But the outcome would have been a collection of essays. Once again the figure of Palladio would have been seen refracted through the prism of just one specific facet of his extraordinarily rich and complex personality. The whole would only have been accessible to those specialists capable of piecing together these facets and understanding the structure of the pure gemstone before it is cut.

Therefore, instead of focusing on individual themes, I have tried to follow the traces left by his work as it developed with unwavering consistency for over half a century. But with one note of caution: I wanted to free Palladio from the human and social isolation in which a certain historiographical tradition has tended to place the artist, and I also wanted to liberate him from the context of a specific setting – such as Vicenza, for all its fascination – lest it come to be seen as representing his entire field of action.

While being fully aware of the pitfalls facing an approach of this kind, I followed my conviction, perhaps somewhat outmoded but nonetheless deeply felt, that architecture – the profession Palladio exercised with such natural élan – can only be produced in the context of a society that is completely in tune with its time. Luckily, this does occasionally happen, in some corner of the world. When it does, when a society acts with an awareness that history serves as both the premise and the consequence of its actions, the form in which it expresses its most profound convictions through building, through architecture, becomes an historical event itself. It is, quite literally, history in the making.

I have, on occasion, compared this situation metaphorically to the fact that water, no matter how many practical and even vital uses it may have at lower temperatures, only takes on the vigour and energy of a rolling boil when it reaches a temperature of one hundred degrees.

By removing architecture from the specialised and somewhat restrictive ambit of a "history of architecture", understood as a self-referencing and circumscribed world, and instead exploring it as history does not mean that its autonomy as a discipline is limited, or worse still denied. It means explaining the reasons why that autonomy is an inevitable outcome of intellectual endeavour at a given historical moment, and therefore a necessary form.

Returning to Palladio, there is no question that his work is enmeshed with the history and reality of Venice, whose lure proved irresistible at the time. This was a state that experienced a period of splendour in the sixteenth century, as well as a time of crisis, and which now, in the autumn of its centuries-long evolution, produced extraordinarily sweet fruits.

Reconnecting Palladio to history, and in particular to the history of Venice, does not mean cutting him off from the city of Padua where he was born, or from Vicenza where his talent matured, just to immerse him in the salty waters of the Venetian lagoon. Instead, it means following or trying to follow the path that he himself took when he decided to leave the prestigious work on the loggias of the Palazzo della Ragione in Vicenza only a few months after he had been appointed to supervise their construction.

It is almost impossible to understand a decision that entailed so many implications and consequences unless we start from the assumption that Palladio, first and foremost, knew full well his cultural message could only gain historical legitimacy, and therefore a recognised normative value, if it were elaborated and put into practice at the political epicentre of a state that played a leading international role – whatever the cost, even at a personal level.

For Palladio, Venice was not merely the nerve-centre of peoples and buildings in which the destinies of East and West had become so closely intertwined, producing a civilisation fuelled by cosmopolitan impulses and unusually high tensions.

For Palladio, Venice was an *idea* rather than a physical entity. To his way of thinking, it was the only surviving testimony of the "virtue and greatness of the Romans." Palladio used this idea, which was based on an ideology imbued with lay and republican principles, to trace a *romanità* or Roman-ness that was no less ideal than the *venezianità* or Venetian-ness that had become such a distinct element of his imagination.

In short, Palladio joined together two utopias. He set aside the centuries of Byzantine tradition that had shaped the life of Venice and forged its unique identity, as well as the Christian tradition that had pervaded the last fifteen centuries of Rome's existence.

The essence of Palladio's legacy is the synthesis of these two utopian traditions, purged of any trace of the past: the vessel that contains all the paradigms that would allow an autocratic ruler, like the Tsar of all the Russias, or – equally – a democratically elected President of the United States of America, to tap into history, seen as the *archaeos* of every form of modernity, without it being tainted in any way by the past.

Palladio is therefore not "Venetian" in the sense that he tried to interpret the circumstances, let alone the building requirements of this unique city or its governing class. He succeeded in interpreting the Venetian aspiration to become the "third Rome" in the only way in which an abstract notion of this kind could ever be expressed with intellectual vigour: namely, by requiring Venice to renounce its past; to become, as it had been on many earlier occasions, wholly of its time and in synchronicity with historical events as they occurred day after day during the course of the sixteenth century. Even, when the need arose, to be prepared to deny its own identity.

Palladio would never have put forward a proposal in such a radical format: it is not in that sense that he was a "modern" man. However, just by looking at the projects he drew up with impressive consistency, one after the other, on Venetian themes, it is clear that his thoughts were leading in this direction. They culminated in his proposal to give a new form to the palace that symbolised the power and sovereignty of the Republic that continued to call itself *La Serenissima* notwithstanding the contradictions that still beset it in the mid sixteenth century.

Venice, the great port where ships docked from all over the world, received the Palladian message with a detachment that characterised the collective psychology of its ruling class. In the same way that it had taken in the Humanists' pagan teachings, the Reformist tensions from north of the Alps, and the news of new maritime routes capable of revolutionising world markets: not as a warning, still less as a prophecy.

It is not surprising, therefore, that as the history of Venice slowly began to dim over the years after Palladio's death and its image faded, the paradigmatic idea of the *antique* which he had formulated gained ground, indeed was almost imposed, as a collective *archaeos* in vast areas of the "new worlds", from St Petersburg to Washington.

It was an idea that would not be superseded until the advent of another "Venetian": Piranesi. Like Palladio, Piranesi, too, was committed to the unique way in which Venetian culture had imitated the model of the Roman republic over the course of the centuries, and he offered the world a dazzling and, by then, ineluctable image of Rome's grandeur: its ruins. This shift in the perception of the *antique,* a prelude to the advent of Romanticism, was the sign that Venice and Venetian history were coming to an end.

Work undertaken in this spirit requires the mindset of an explorer rather than a researcher: someone who might encounter an unexpected vista by taking a different route instead of following the clearly marked paths created by centuries of studies and research.

It might perhaps seem foolhardy to venture into such a vast territory with an attitude of this kind, but before she left for Hong Kong Giulia said that we would meet on the other side and, although I knew I would arrive with muddy shoes and looking slightly bedraggled, I did not want to disappoint her.

I also took a conscious decision to leave the work at this stage of its elaboration. I do so in memory of Manfredo Tafuri to whom I outlined my thoughts in this form. The discussion that followed was a very fervent one. Sometimes it lasted for weeks. When we had convinced ourselves that these thoughts deserved to be elaborated in greater detail, we started to work on each statement with academic rigour. Manfredo then gave it the refinement, also in conceptual terms, that made his work masterly in so many ways.

It would be remiss of me not to acknowledge my debt to the others who have enriched Palladian studies over the past decades, to James Ackerman, Lionello Puppi, Howard Burns, Guido Beltramini and Tracy E. Cooper. Without their scholarship, I would know so much less about Palladio. However, before thanking them again for the enormous gift they have given us, I must apologise to them all if I have strayed too often from the beaten path left by their essential contributions to the almost endless field of Palladian studies.

Antonio Foscari
April 2010

Andrea Gritti

Francesco Maria della Rovere

Leo X

Charles V

Francis I

Paul III

Jacopo Sansovino

Pietro Bembo

Giangiorgio Trissino

Baldassarre Castiglione

Niccolò Ridolfi

Ercole Gonzaga

Giulio Romano

Francesco Donà

Iseppo Porto

Daniele Barbaro

Francesco Venier

Giovanni Grimani

Reginald Pole

Giorgio Vasari

Alvise Cornaro

Emanuele Filiberto of Savoy

Henri III

Alvise Foscari

Alvise Mocenigo

Marcantonio Barbaro

Antonio da Ponte

ANDREA PALLADIO
UNBUILT VENICE

Venice, or the *Dominante* as it would have been referred to then, had been the epicentre of all the events that young Andrea had witnessed since childhood, and of everything that might fire the imagination of an alert young man such as himself, growing up in the Veneto during the early decades of the sixteenth century.

From his father, Pietro, he would certainly have learnt that a few days after he was born large swathes of the population in Padua had had no hesitation in hoisting the imperial flag – and lowering that of San Marco – when they heard that Maximilian of Habsburg's army was advancing across the territories of the Republic. [1] [2] Moreover, only a few weeks later, led by an energetic and determined patrician, Andrea Gritti [3] – who would later become doge when Palladio was fifteen – the Venetians had attacked the stronghold where the rebels had barricaded themselves and had recaptured the city under mortar fire. What's more, immediately after these dramatic events, a frenetic construction programme had started under the guidance of Fra' Giocondo, a man of outstanding humanist and technical learning, resulting in a defensive system around the city that would prove invincible over the coming centuries.

Working as a stonecutter in Vicenza with a building firm to which his father had apprenticed him, Palladio, even at such a tender age, would certainly have been aware of the rigorous punishment meted out by the Venetian magistracy – albeit by less draconian means than in in Padua – to anyone, especially from the

1

2

3

higher classes, who had betrayed the Republic after the Venetian forces had been routed at Agnadello (1509).

One by one the castles that stood on the hilltops around Vicenza (as seen in the landscape backgrounds of paintings by Cima da Conegliano, Bartolomeo Montagna, Giorgione and many others artists working in the Veneto on the cusp of the fifteenth and sixteenth centuries) were demolished. [4] [5] [6] [7] [8] Likewise, those members of the nobility who had chosen to side with the Empire – at a moment that might have been crucial for the fate of the Republic – had their estates confiscated.

In the Vicentine workshop of Pedemuro, these events would have been keenly felt, not only because many of the well-to-do nobility had been wont to commission works from the *compagni* who ran the business, but also because this social upheaval, ands the resulting changes in the landscape, triggered a sort of cultural depression that precluded any new initiatives, especially in terms of building projects. It was a depression that lasted for years, even after the 1529 Peace of Bologna that heralded the dawn of a relatively stable political situation in Italy, yet failed to satisfy Venice's expectations because of the high price the city had to pay to recover the territories in its *Stato da Terra* that had been lost under the threat of the joint forces of the League of Cambrai.

The Pedemuro workshop was a place that would have been buzzing with information among local tradesmen. While working there, young Andrea would also have heard of the determination with which the Republic of Venice, widely known as *La Serenissima,* had set about dismantling the defensive system comprising a network of castles commanded by noble fiefs that had proved so unreliable. In its place, the Republic's defences were being centralised under the command of Francesco Maria della Rovere, [9] a "man of arms" and a shrewd interpreter of Doge Gritti's plans, who had embarked on a series of fortifications that called for a massive investment of financial resources.

It was against the background of this decision, and with the help of the specialists in *all'antica* architecture who were promptly

4

5

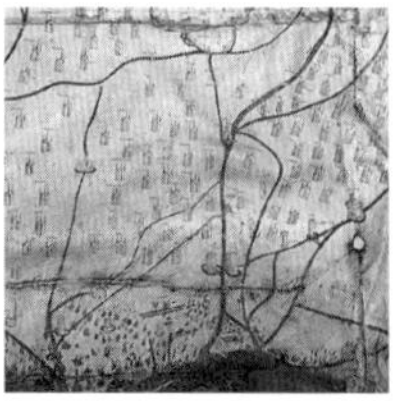
6

7

engaged, that Venice created works that eloquently expressed and openly demonstrated the ideological basis for this operation.

While huge walls were erected to protect the cities of the *Stato da Terra* from the enemy (but also to enclose them in a way that would assure civic control), massive *all'antica* gates were designed by Gianmaria Falconetto for Padua and by Michele Sanmicheli for Verona [10] that were emblematic of the political line taken by the *Signoria,* Venice's governing body, in the forbidding halls of the Doge's Palace.

Vicentine building firms were excluded from all these works because Vicenza had not been assigned a specific strategic role in the defence plan that the Republic had embarked on with such determination. In Vicenza all they could do was wait. Even the aristocratic members of the pro-Venetian faction (among them the Thiene, the Da Porto, the Caldogno and the Chiericati) were not sure how to react, even when it came to the architectural definition of their urban residences.

They were well aware that, in Venice, the architectural vocabulary of the *all'antica style,* which drew on Tuscan and Roman influences, was banned from the urban setting because it had been conceived and developed on the banks of the Tiber: it was the language used by such "enemies" of the Republic as as the della Rovere pope, Julius II, and by antagonists like the two Medici popes, Leo X [11] and Clement VII, whose political forebear, Cosimo, had not hesitated to provide financial backing for the *condottiere* Francesco Sforza's conquest of the duchy of Milan in order to block any further expansion by the Republic westwards across the Po valley.

In the mid 1530s, therefore, there would have been much talk in the workshop of Pedemuro when, after a self-imposed "silence" in the field of architecture that had lasted over twenty years, the Signoria decided to renew the image of the city itself by launching a process of *renovatio* that would transform the area in front of St Mark's, known as the Marcian *platea,* into a Roman forum *all'antica.*

8

9

10

This was a decision that came to a head surprisingly quickly – providing an outlet to tensions and expectations that had been smouldering for some time among some higher levels of the Venetian oligarchy – and coincided with the news of Charles V's unexpected victory against the Ottoman fleet off Tunis. [12] This military event disturbed the equilibrium of Europe's entire political class and excited those intellectuals (of whom there were many) who, hearing that the young Habsburg emperor had landed victoriously on African soil, saw as him as emulating the greatness of Scipio Africanus (to name just one eloquent figure from Roman history) and as the champion of a new cycle of world politics.

While the French king [13] weighed up the possibility of siding with the Sultan – Christianity's most dreaded foe – solely to counter the success of his European rival, the Farnese pope [14] showed a fine sense of political timing by using this intense wave of collective excitement to call for a crusade against the Turks and to convene an ecumenical council.

Both were goals that could not be achieved without the involvement of the Venetian Republic, the only western power with a fleet capable of transporting an army across the Mediterranean and the only State which – thanks to its geographical position and the secular nature of its political ideology – could act as a buffer and mediator between Rome and the central European states where the movement of religious reform that had started at Wittenberg some twenty years earlier was now widespread.

In view of this unexpected and disconcerting situation, the Procuratia di San Marco – Venice's highest political magistracy, second only to the doge in importance – convinced the doge, who was pro-French and pro-Turk, to persuade the Signoria to draw up a League with the pope and the emperor, heedless of the risk that Venice might find herself and her eastern outposts unprotected against any counterattack by the Ottoman empire against the Christian west. The Republic prepared to take this step based on a very clear ideological precondition: that the city should be acknowledged as the "Third Rome", a role it was entitled to claim

11

12

13

14

as the protagonist in the movement that in 1204 had led to the crusading conquest of the "Second Rome", namely Constantinople, and as the sole Italian guardian of that "virginity", or rather, "liberty" which, according to the political thinking of the time, Rome had lost in 1527 when the Landsknechts had violated its walls and sacked the city.

The ideological, as well as the political grounds for embarking on the plan for the *renovatio* of the Marcian *platea* can be fully understood if set against this background.

Of all the buildings, in this plan, it was a library [15] [16] that would provide the most eloquent expression of this sudden and daring volte-face in Venice's foreign policy. Such a building, sited opposite the Doge's Palace and with an impressive iconographical array of forms appropriated from Roman architecture, would also serve to evoke an eminent figure who had played a key role in the Ecumenical Council held at Ferrara in 1438. It was Cardinal Bessarion who, by symbolically bequeathing to the Republic the valuable collection of ancient codices that he had managed to bring with him from Constantinople before it fell to the Turks, had singled out Venice as the European power most entitled to take on the political heritage of Byzantium. Venice was also the only power capable of rallying the necessary forces to salvage for Christianity what little had survived of the Eastern Roman Empire by the mid fifteenth century.

Furthermore, the construction of a building with such explicit symbolic intent, as a strong rhetorical statement at the heart of a city whose only defensive system was the waters of its lagoons, also demonstrated Venice's superiority over Rome – which, in spite of its city walls, had undergone the humiliation of being overrun by enemy troops and had seen its libraries go up in flames.

It was no coincidence that to work alongside a Florentine architect like Jacopo Sansovino [17] on a project of this kind the Signoria summoned Pietro Bembo, [18] a *letterato* who was then the greatest interpreter of Francesco Petrarch's teachings. There was a clear awareness at the highest level of Republican government

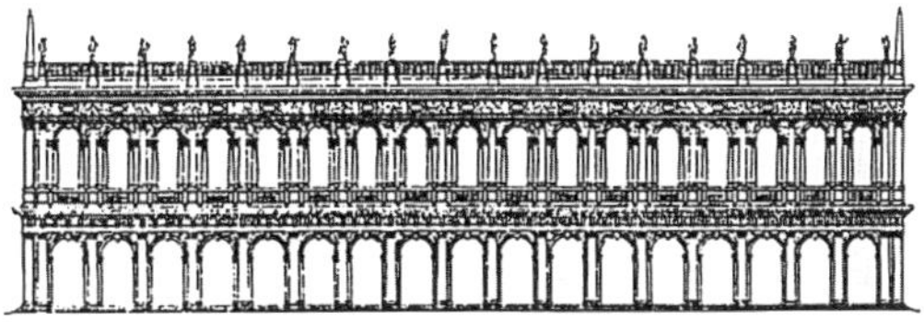

15

16

of the decisive importance, also in political terms, of the "question of language" that Petrarch himself had raised two centuries earlier, confronting it with prophetic clarity.

All these events would have been well known to Giangiorgio Trissino, [19] a Vicentine nobleman who had been exiled from the Republican territories during the troubled months of the War of the League of Cambrai for having had the temerity to express his pro-Imperial sentiments. Baldassar Castiglione [20] had also included him in an ideal dialogue with other exiled aristocrats, discussing the truly utopian view that Italy might witness the formation of a virtual court whose members – the *cortigiani* or courtiers – would represent a new and homogeneous ruling class, well versed in the latest cultural developments.

It mattered little that Trissino – anchored as he was, intrinsically, to the late medieval stamp of his cultural formation – opposed Baldassar Castiglione's figure of the courtier with that of an ideal *castellano*, the lord of a castle, and that he preferred Dante to the mastery of Petrarch invoked by Pietro Bembo. The "question of language" also carried weight and was of topical importance in the Veneto, over and above any ideological differences that distinguished and sometimes divided intellectuals from different backgrounds.

The events that were unfolding in Venice, in the urban setting of the so-called *platea marciana* that had, for centuries, been the preserve of political life, were so charged that they ignited, or rather inflamed Trissino's imagination. The idea of a political rapprochement between the Empire and Venice was, in his eyes, a sign that the dramatic events that had so radically altered the fate of his family might at long last be over. What's more, it opened up a possibility that enabled him to settle, or at least attempt to settle, the divergent and, in many cases, irreconcilable ideological claims that had torn his life apart (after being exiled from the Republic, he had been Leo X's ambassador to Maximilian of Habsburg and, immediately afterwards, apostolic *nunzio* to the Venetian Signoria).

17

18

19

20

GIANGIORGIO TRISSINO AT CRICOLI

This was the state of mind in which Giangiorgio Trissino introduced a decisive change in the remodelling of a late mediaeval building at Cricoli, on a slightly raised site protected on one side by the fast-flowing river Astico, and on all the others by a high wall whose presence alone emphasised the fact that a *Signore*'s land should be both protected and set apart. [21] [22]

In the course of this project, he chose to introduce a modern feature – in the form of a loggia – at the centre of the new façade, but at the corners he included towers whose sole purpose was to confirm his family's feudal status and its continued right to the title of count assigned by the Emperor centuries earlier.

But there was also another particularly enlightened sense in which Trissino construed the transformation of his ancestors' late medieval *casa:* he used the vocabulary of architecture to define what it meant to be a *Signore* in the historical reality of the political scenario that followed the Peace of Bologna and the rapprochement between the Papacy, the Empire and the Republic.

This *Signore* was no longer the central figure in a community of families and servants, as he had been in the past and as he might have remained in a castle. An individual's requirements – no matter how elevated his social position – must be satisfied by an orderly series of (just) three rooms linked together to form an *appartamento.*

The *casa* of a *Signore* of this type would have consisted of two such apartments because this allowed him to maintain a suitable distance from the other members of the household who lived with him. Between the two apartments – and acting as a meeting place between them – was a central space (in many ways reminiscent of the typology of the *portego* in Venetian houses) that was also used to welcome visitors.

Andrea, the budding young architect from the Pedemuro workshop who was in charge of the building site opened by Trissino, absorbed this information without being influenced by the ideological or cultural predelictions that motivated his patron.

21

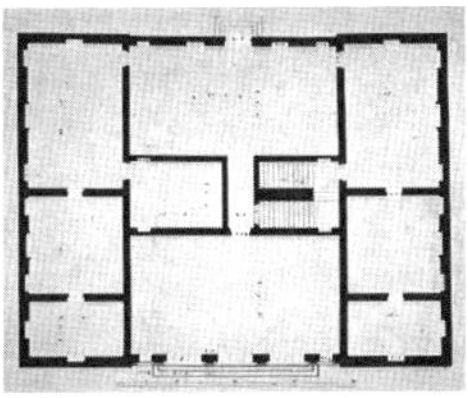
22

THE PAX VENEZIANA

The building project he worked on at Cricoli stood out, in his view, against a much broader and equally impressive panorama.

Venice was imposing a geographical, as well as a cultural and social transformation on the territories that the seafaring Republic had conquered in its Po Valley hinterland, amalgamating the maritime empire that it had ruled for centuries with a *Stato da Terra.* Major rivers like the Sile, the Piave, the Brenta and the Adige had been diverted from their natural course by major engineering works (just as the river Astico, running through the grounds of Trissino's own house would be some years later), providing the region with a hydraulic network unlike anything it had previously known. This meant that, having been liberated from the devastation wreaked by the passage of warring armies, the land and its inhabitants were also now freed from the no less devastating floods and the swamps that had been a lasting consequence.

During this period the Republic had invested in its own hinterland the financial resources that, earlier in the century – when it was still determined to find a way of securing the future of its maritime trade with the East – it had considered using to excavate a canal at Suez. Moreover, it had tackled the works with an entrepreneurial capacity that presupposes the availability of a group of trained specialists, above all in the field of engineering, unaparalleled elsewhere in Europe.

What's more, the Venetian Water Magistracy had been – and still was – responsible for these operations. Since the hinterland fell entirely under the control and administrative jurisdiction of the Republic, not only did it complete work on the larger rivers, but it also regulated all the minor waterways, creating a navigable network that boosted the circulation of goods throughout the area, flowing to and from the commercial hub of the Rialto.

What made Palladio immune to cultural ideas based on medieval topoi was precisely the contrast – too striking to escape his attention – between a heroic scenario, like the one imposed on its *Stato da Terra* through the *pax veneziana,* and the predicament of a Vicentine nobility unsure as to what might be the appropriate architectural language by which to affirm their presence in a territory where they had been pre-eminent for centuries. They could no longer build on high ground, on the hilltops occupied by their ancestors' castles or towers. No feudal forms or symbols could be used. Moreover, the persistence of a gothic figurative repertoire made it impossible for those who supported the political regime imposed by the Republic, either through conviction or for convenience, to distinguish themselves – in the city – from the pro-imperial faction that still existed, despite frustrating setbacks, among the Vicentine nobility.

THE CASA GODI AT LONEDO AND THE VILLINI GIOVANILI

The link, indeed the overlap, between history and architecture is so strong that architecture cannot exist in an environment of this kind where history is silent. Instead, any attempt at architectural expression in such a historical vacuum will produce a form so laconic as to appear almost entirely allusive. A clear example may be found in the *casa* built by the Godi in Lonedo [23] with the assistance of the Pedemuro workshop: it is closed, compact and makes no concessions to imagery. Other eloquent examples of this extreme form of prudence, verging on reticence, include the Palladian projects for the so-called *villini giovanili,* or youthful villas – minimalist works of immature quality: these are *fabbriche* whose spaces and forms seem more like hopeful expressions or projections of a dream, rather than an explicit desire to imprint the sign of a political presence on a territory using a syntax freighted with contemporary meaning. [24]

Even Palladio felt the weight of a political situation that allowed the Vicentine ruling class to exercise its exceptional entrepreneurial ability, but which, in practice, curbed all freedom of expression.

This situation was only resolved by an event of such an exceptional nature that it removed an obstacle which, for some time, had become more psychological than objective. It was an event that would bring the foremost members of the Vicentine nobility closer to the Venetian patricians, thereby sweeping away contradictions that had taken root so long ago that they had almost

23

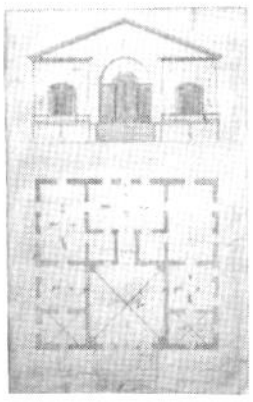
24

become embedded and fixed in the collective mentality, to the point of becoming anachronistic in view of the situation then taking shape in the early 1540s.

To explore the background to this event we need to return to the situation that had caused the Venetian Signoria to make a sudden and risky political turnaround in the mid 1530s, one that excited even Giangiorgio Trissino.

AN ECUMENICAL COUNCIL AT VICENZA?

While the programme for the *renovatio* of the Marcian *platea* was getting underway and architectural projects were being drawn up by the *proto* of the Procuratia di San Marco, Jacopo Sansovino, Pope Paul III decided to convene an Ecumenical Council. In 1537 he chose Vicenza as the place where it would meet.

The fact that the Farnese pope's decision was not followed through can be attributed to the Republic's lack of enthusiasm at the idea of hosting a meeting of Christian bishops and princes in a city within the *Dominio*. (Venice knew all too well that the Ottoman Empire had already amassed a huge fleet to fight off the crusade which it was widely known that the pope wished to launch.)

The boost to the city's pride at the thought that Vicenza might find itself, even temporarily, in the exceptional role of being at the hub of Christianity made the sting of disappointment even more intense when the Vicentine ruling class realised that the Farnese pope had elected to hold the Council elsewhere.

In 1541 Giangiorgio Trissino left for Rome, taking Palladio with him, and on his way he visited Nicolò Ridolfi (Leo X's nephew) [25] in Bagnaia. It seems likely that his decision to undertake such an arduous and hurried journey may have been to persuade the cardinal – who had been appointed Bishop of Vicenza by Clement VII (another Medici pope) – at long last to visit the diocese that had been assigned to his pastoral care in 1524. His arrival in Vicenza would, to some extent, have made up for the failure to convene the Council (at which Ridolfi would have acted as an inevitable point of reference as the city's bishop).

25

Moreover, it must have been Giangiorgio Trissino's influence that prompted Cardinal Ridolfi to make a point of visiting Cricoli to pay his respects to his prominent contact in the city on the day he made his triumphal entrance into Vicenza.

CARDINAL NICCOLÒ RIDOLFI'S ARRIVAL IN VICENZA

Unwavering in its lay and republican stance, the Venetian Signoria had no intention – even in this case – of becoming officially involved in an event that it regarded as exclusively ecclesiastical in nature; nonetheless, it did not fail to keep a close watch over the movements of such a high-ranking member of the Roman curia coming to take possession of the diocese of an important Venetian city.

As usual, it did so by discreetly collaborating with leading members of the patriciate, who, as a group, were regarded as an institutional body permanently at the State's service: in this case, also with the collaboration of a patrician who was not short of experience in the diplomatic world and who also knew the Medici sphere of which Ridolfi was an influential representative: Marco Foscari.

In 1522 it was Foscari who – as Venetian ambassador in Rome – had worked tirelessly on behalf of the Signoria to ensure that Adrian VI appointed Niccolò Ridolfi to the bishopric of Vicenza. Likewise, it was Foscari who, following Adrian VI's death, had put pressure on the Venetian cardinals to support the papal candidature of Giulio de'Medici, acting with added authority given that his cousin, Andrea Gritti, had meanwhile been elected to the highest office of the Venetian State.

Confirmation of the links between Marco Foscari and the Medici can be had from the fact that it was Foscari who organised a spectacular feast at his Venetian *casa* to welcome the young Cosimo, the future Duke of Florence (son of Giovanni dalle Bande Neri) when he came to Venice in 1530 accompanied by the daughter of Clement VII's main advisor and banker, Jacopo Salviati, and Pope Leo X's sister, Lucrezia de' Medici.

A closer analysis of this episode (without going into detail about the crisis of the Medicean government in 1527 when Foscari was in Florence, once again as ambassador for the Republic) reveals the early link between Marco Foscari and Giangiorgio Trissino. It was Trissino who acted as a sort of go-between to finalise an arrangement whereby one of Pope Leo X's nephews, possibly another Ridolfi, would marry the young Venetian noblewoman Elena Grimani, daughter of Marco Grimani, the future Patriarch of Aquileia. Some time later, in 1534, Elena would eventually marry Marco Foscari's son Pietro.

What prompted Foscari – now aged sixty-five – to throw his weight behind these events was his election as *Savio del Consiglio* for the first half of 1542, an appointment that strengthened his authority and freed him from the sort of political isolation he had found himself in following Andrea Gritti's death. However, there was also a personal reason: three days after Cardinal Ridolfi's triumphal entrance into Vicenza, on 16 December 1543, his daughter Paolina Foscari married Vettor Pisani, son of Zuanne, a Venetian patrician who had accumulated huge possessions in Bagnolo, which the Republic had expropriated from the Counts of Nogarola during the War of the League of Cambrai.

ZUANNE PISANI

One does not need to know much about the social customs of the time to realise that, during the negotiations leading up to his daughter's marriage with Vettor Pisani, Foscari would have had plenty of opportunity to learn every detail about what had happened in Bagnolo.

The castle belonging to the Nogarola had been razed to the ground – as had all the castles owned by nobles who had betrayed the expectations of the Republic; this act of *delenda memoria* aimed to ban any evidence of a feudal regime surviving in any corner of the *Stato da Terra* after the Venetian reconquest of the Terraferma.

Within the ambit of his properties, Zuanne Pisani – a man trained under Andrea Gritti's political teaching – had embarked on a series of operations with the sole aim of accomplishing the Republic's ambitious plans to re-route the rivers that had been carried out over the past few decades. He had reclaimed the marshlands and had introduced specialised crops that would increase the land's agricultural output. This activity was clearly economically motivated, but it was also backed by the conviction that the extensive practice of agriculture – such as Cato had undertaken on his estates – was a demonstration of *all'antica* Republican *virtù*.

While he was fully absorbed by this enterprise, Zuanne Pisani probably never even thought about building another house in the heart of his estates. He died in 1540 before the building work actually started. It was the wedding of one of his sons that prompted the decision to start building, a process that sanctioned the handover from one generation to the next and assured – as if by some ritual act – the family's continuity.

The event naturally took Vettor somewhat by surprise: soon after Zuanne Pisani's death, of the three brothers, and in spite of his youth, he was singled out as the candidate who would ensure the family's "posterity". It is at this stage that the figure of Marco Foscari, who loved his son-in-law "*come un fiolo*" (as a son, to use his own expression), appears behind him.[1]

In order to follow these events, it is necessary to make a choice that at first might not seem obvious: namely to view them against the background of Padua. Marco Foscari owned a large building complex in Padua (the magnificent residence that had belonged to the Scrovegni in the late Middle Ages) and Pisani also had a *casa* there, right in front of that complex. It therefore seems logical – at least until a building site was opened in Bagnolo – that the preliminary stages of the design for the *casa* to be built in the Vicentino took place here. It was to Padua, therefore, that the budding young architect from the Pedemuro workshop came, having almost certainly been recommended to the two Venetian gentlemen by Giangiorgio Trissino on the strength of his long acquaintance with Foscari.

The effect of Palladio's separation from Giangiorgio Trissino, whose base continued to be Vicenza when he was not in Venice, is palpable. If only because, from the outset of the design, he appears to have lost the train of thought that had brought him to such a rigorous definition of the building typology for a *casa* worthy of a perfect *Signore* and yet austere.

At the same time, Alvise Cornaro's influence on the compositional process also deserves to be acknowledged, as evidenced by Guido Beltramini's persuasive arguments in detecting his early *invenzioni* for the proposed *casa* in Bagnolo in two drawings (RIBA VIII, 13r and RIBA XVII, 1) by Palladio.

When establishing a connection between Alvise Cornaro and Marco Foscari (whom we continue to see as a sort of intermediary playing a specific role in this project), it is important to bear in mind that, years earlier, it had been at Foscari's house in Venice that Angelo Beolco had made his debut. After being expelled from Venice for his intemperance of speech, this extraordinary actor, known as *il Ruzzante,* continued to appear for years on the stage of the "theatre" built by Alvise Cornaro in the *corte* of his Paduan house. It was therefore probably Foscari, Andrea Gritti's cousin, who acted as go-between to persuade the Venetian Signoria to appoint Gian Maria Falconetto, the architect who lived in Cornaro's house in Padua, to build the modern city gates for Padua – Porta San Giovanni (1528) and Porta Savonarola (1530) – and later also the Monte di Pietà (1532).

Moreover, it should be borne in mind that in 1537 – just before the period we are exploring – Alvise Cornaro had given his daughter's hand in marriage to Giovanni Corner, from the *Piscopia* branch. As the son of Fantin Corner – Francesco Foscari's son-in-law and heir – Giovanni enjoyed considerable rights to the buildings around the Arena, including, most notably, its adjoining chapel whose walls had been so wonderfully decorated by Giotto. In this way, he too, to a certain degree, felt at home in the Arena.

The fact that two of Palladio's drawings, RIBA VIII, 13r [27] and RIBA XVII, 1, [28] can be seen as reflecting Alvise Cornaro's architectural experience in relation to the courtyard of his Paduan *casa,* and in particular to the construction of the Odeon, [26] thus

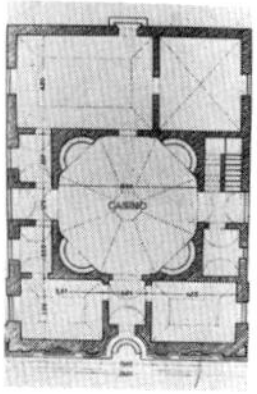
26

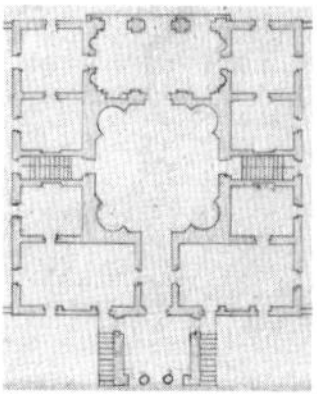
27

28

29

becomes more readily understandable. But this is not the time to pursue this further.

Rather, what is worth noting are the reasons why such a unique *exemplum* was not used – indeed, it was discarded – as a model that could be adopted for the Vicentine project at Bagnolo. An Odeon is a construction that cannot be thought of as a *casa,* since it is characterised by the presence of a central space, lit almost exclusively from above, that has no or very few openings to the outside. Clearly, it was a building intended for activities that, at the time, would have been described as "contemplative": namely, the cultivation of intellectual interests. For this reason, it would not have been a *fabbrica* that expressed the "political" significance of a Venetian presence on the Terraferma. In other words, it would have been regarded as an updated form of the humanist concept of the *villa* that saw the countryside as an alternative to the city and to the political tensions of city life.

If one tries to follow the process used by the *edificatore,* or patron, and the architect in designing this *casa,* and in abandoning the Odeon as an example, a highly specific suggestion seems to have emerged for the formal definition of the façade: a suggestion that appears, intentionally, to discard the solution of the loggia in the *corte* of Cornaro's house in Padua (an echo of which had returned in the *casa* built by Trissino at Cricoli).

The inclusion of an exedra was also the result of an external suggestion. [29] [30] [31] [32]

The teachings of Sebastiano Serlio may have played a significant role in the sense that they may perhaps have reminded Foscari of the excitement he had felt some twenty years earlier on seeing Bramante's *nicchione* being built in the Belvedere courtyard in Rome: according to contemporary diarists, his excitement had been such that he had immediately taken the other orators in the Venetian diplomatic delegation to visit the building site.

But such a daring experimental approach could also have been prompted by another factor: the knowledge that the architect who had managed the building site for the *fabbrica* subsequently

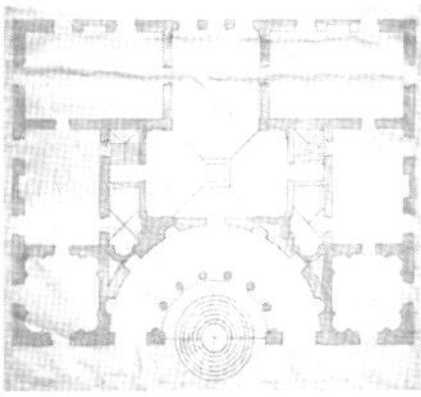
30

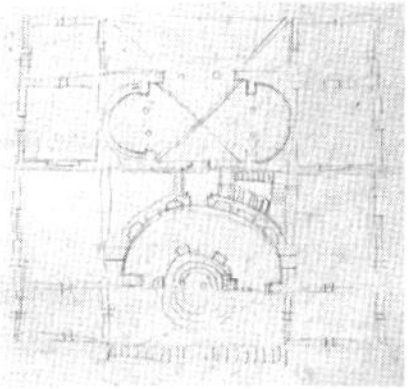
31

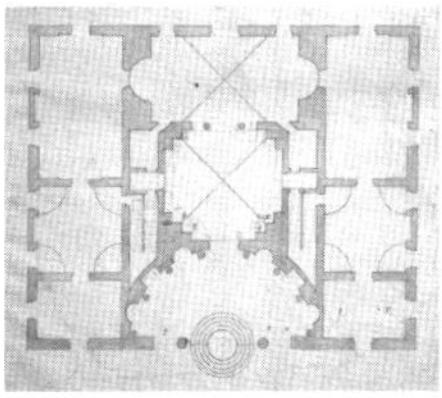
32

known as Villa Madama, under Raphael's supervision, would soon arrive (or had already arrived) in Vicenza. [33] [34]

This wonderful building standing on the slopes of Monte Mario, with its curved façade and gardens designed to form clearly defined geometric spaces, may have seemed to Marco Foscari and to Vettor Pisani a modern and brilliantly ordered translation of the Paduan building that both would otherwise have seen as an anachronistic, perhaps even an incomprehensible reference to the past. Namely, they would have been reminded of the large *fabbrica* built by the Scrovegni on the edge of the Roman Arena, a *casa* distinguished by its singularly concave façade, and fronted by a large and perfectly elliptical *corte* bounded by the ancient walls of the Roman Arena. [35] [36]

Certainly, if things did happen in the order ideally recreated here, it seems likely that the whole matter may have started to escape the grasp of a man like Marco Foscari who, over the course of his long life, had never been responsible for any building operation of architectural significance.

At this point, as a way out of an increasingly complex state of affairs, it is conceivable that he resumed the strength of mind, and above all the attitude of the politician whom Andrea Gritti had called to sit on the special commission responsible for a revision of Venetian law. It was in this frame of mind – as far as we can understand – that he heaped a series of prescriptions on the novice architect regarding the significance of a *casa* for a patrician built within the Venetian *Stato da Terra*.

It must take the form of an act of *delenda memoria,* wiping out any evidence of the previous feudal regime. Therefore, it should rise above the ruins of the old castle, burying them forever. Yet, on the other hand, it must be an explicit act of *instauratio Rei publicae:* it should not, therefore, follow the example set by the powerful Bishop of Padua, Cardinal Francesco Pisani, who, a short time earlier, had started to build a princely residence [37] in the centre of the bishopric's rural territories, nor should it follow the equally misguided example set by the adventurous

33

34

financier who was erecting an imposing *casa* to a design by Jacopo Sansovino at the heart of a large country estate (*villa*) he owned at Pontecasale, in the Polesine. [38]

This rejection of any form of "Romanism" was founded on quite explicit grounds. As an erudite individual, Foscari contrasted such displays of grandeur with the precepts outlined by Palladius Rutilius Taurus in *De Villa* (a classical treatise with which Palladio was undoubtedly familiar) [39] in which he asserted that no *casa dominicale* should be built on a property unless it could be constructed using the profits of a single year's farming. As a politician who had lived through the catastrophic events of the first four decades of the century, Foscari did not fail to resort to an argument he had expounded with particular vigour in his presentations to to the Senate at the end of his embassy to Florence: grand houses spread throughout the territory of a Republic are a cause of political weakness – "timidity" was the word he used on that occasion – because a Republic that allowed its ruling class to behave in this way lived in constant fear of being sacked by the enemy or destroyed during an invasion.

In a "well ordered" Republican regime, therefore, a *casa in villa,* or country estate house, must not be large. Nor should it have ornamental architectural elements – just as the houses built by the ancient Romans on their estates during the Republican era were devoid of ornamentation.

If we focus for a moment on this last aspect, the rejection of *ornamenti,* it is fascinating to see how the young stonecutter, who was prevented from practising his trade – specifically the production of *ornamenti* – discovered the possibility of evoking "antiquity" by exalting the *ars aedificatoria* that in many ways represented the essence more than the form of Roman architecture.

That the building works in Bagnolo ran into difficulties, were interrupted at some point and eventually ground to a halt is hardly surprising given the experimental approach that characterised their inception and the very concept on which the project was founded. Before the works even went on site, the project was a sort

35

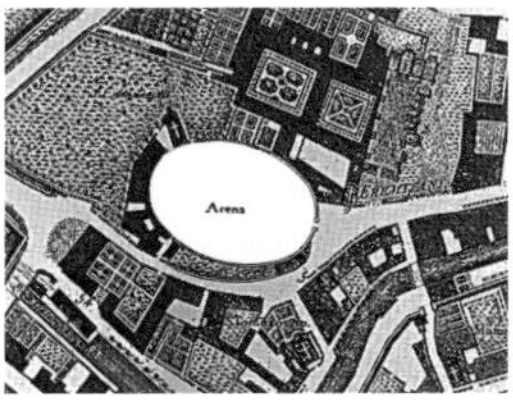

36

of intellectual adventure in which a mature member of the Venetian ruling class tried to define the conceptual nature of a *casa in villa* as an expression of a Republican regime.

In the light of what has been said so far, it seems almost natural that Palladio developed what was more than a passing interest in Polybius while travelling between Vicenza and Padua. It revealed – if we are not mistaken – his clear-headed and utterly pragmatic attempt to position himself, in ideological terms, between the approach advocated by Giangiorgio Trissino and that by Marco Foscari.

For Foscari, a leading political figure of the Signoria under a doge who had successfully led the Venetian reconquest of the Terraferma, Polybius – the Roman historian who, more than any other, had documented the expansion of the Roman Republic eastwards, beyond the Adriatic – was the classical intellectual who provided the most authoritative historical legitimation for Venice's policy of expansion into its hinterland.

For Trissino, on the other hand, Polybius – above and beyond his reputation as an intellectual – was the man who never lost pride in a cultural formation permeated with the traditional values of his homeland, Hellas, and who nurtured the sense of independence rooted in the collective psychology of each Greek city, just as it was in the city of Megalopolis, Arcadia, from which he was taken to Rome as a slave in 166 BC.

For Palladio, who had heard the arguments put forward by both these proudly erudite aristocrats, Polybius was the intellectual to whom a man from the Terraferma, aware of his own identity and cognisant of the cultural specificity of his native city, could and should look in order to understand and accept the course of history, irreversible as it might seem. [40]

Such were the ideas to which Palladio had been exposed by the time he was summoned by the brothers of Venetian patrician, Francesco Contarini, who.had been *Podestà* of Vicenza at a time when the works at Cricoli were in progress, and therefore certainly knew Giangiorgio Trissino. Moreover, Polo Contarini, like

37

38

Marco Foscari, was also a faithful supporter of the policy of *instauratio Rei publicae* launched by Doge Andrea Gritti in the Venetian Terraferma. And as proof of his loyalty to this ideology, he had married Vienna Gritti, the doge's only grand-daughter.

THE CASA FOR THE CONTARINI AT THEIR VILLA IN PIAZZOLA

Once again, this was a house that was to be built as a good augury for family continuity. It was to be sited on the foundations of a castle that had stood at the centre of the family's vast properties for over two centuries, in a place called Piazzola to the west of the Brenta. And again it was decided that this *fabbrica* should be built without ornamentation to emphasise the Republican nature of the message it had to convey in this relatively remote corner of the *Stato da Terra*.

Although the reasons for the project and the goals it aimed to achieve are clear, it is difficult – and will perhaps always be impossible – to know the procedure by which the building works were started and carried out.

One starting point for researching a question hampered by the lack of documentation, and above all by the alterations made to Palladio's original building over time, may be RIBA drawing XVII.15. [41] In it we can recognise choices that appear to derive from observations made in Bagnolo: the evocation of Roman bath-type structures to give a Roman connotation to a *fabbrica* otherwise devoid of ornamentation and the search for an architectural solution that would mark the centre of the façade in figurative terms, without resorting to that form – the loggia – which Giangiorgio Trissino incorporated at his *casa* at Cricoli.

Of no less significance, in this drawing, is the appearance of two separate entrances of equal architectural dignity on the façade: made using Serlian openings, their shape – as Guido Beltramini recently highlighted – conjures up those openings that can still be seen today on the façade of Contarini's house in Piazzola.

However, this valuable insight raises new questions. The choice of giving a *casa* two entrances, as documented in the RIBA drawing XVII 15, prompts us to turn attention to another of Palladio's

LA VILLA
DI PALLADIO
RVTILIO TAVRO
EMILIANO
TRADOTTA NVOVAMENTE
PER FRANCESCO SANSOVINO,
NELLA QVALE SI CONTIENE IL MODO
di coltiuar la terra di mese in mese, di inserir gli
arbori, di gouernar gli horti, & i giardini,
CON LA PROPRIETA DE FRVTTI,
delle herbe, & de gli animali, con molte altre
cose utili à prò del contado.
CON PRIVILEGIO

39

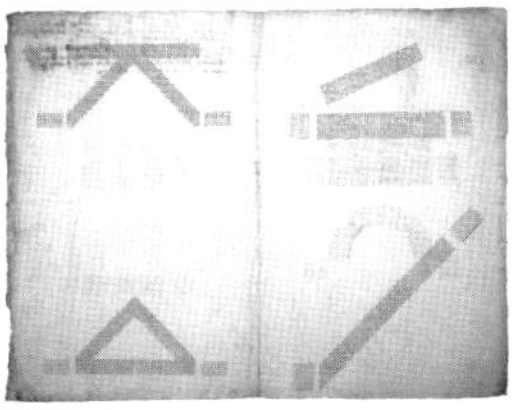

40

41

proposals that reveals the same distinctive feature: illustrated in RIBA drawing XVI, 16. To do so we must go back to RIBA drawing XVI, 18 [42] and to the sketch in the centre of RIBA XVI, 16. [43]

In an attempt to identify the assumptions that may (perhaps) link these drawings to a single commission, it is worth noting that all the plans shown on the drawings are based on a five-bay layout (following the model that Palladio had first experimented with in the *casa* he built on a hilltop in Lonedo for Gerolamo Godi). Moreover, RIBA drawings XVI, 18 and the central sketch on RIBA XVI, 16 show a *fabbrica* that is a virtual duplication of the building type shown in RIBA XVII, 27, [44] the latter being not dissimilar to the *fabbrica* built by Palladio at this time for Vincenzo Gazzotti. All this leads one to suppose that Palladio drew up these designs for a patron who planned to obtain four *appartamenti* in his *casa*.

Precisely this unusual suggestion might link this nucleus of early, and somewhat uniform, proposals to a preliminary phase of the *invenzione* of the *casa* in Piazzola.

Bearing in mind the family structure of Zaccaria Contarini's descendants, the request for four *appartamenti* would seem justifiable: one for Filippo's descendants – the only one to have married by then and who had predeceased him – and one for each of the other three brothers.

If one of these had renounced his rights (let us suppose that this might have been Pietro, who was a supporter of Ignatius Loyola in Venice and who would go on to become Archbishop of Zara and Bishop of Baffo), three of the four *appartamenti* would have been used as follows: one by Francesco (who had been *Podestà* of Vicenza and in 1536 had embarked on a *cursus honorum* that would take him to the highest offices of State), one by Polo (the brother who, by marrying, would have been expected to ensure the family's continuity) and one by Vienna Gritti, his wife. The fourth *appartamento* – in a situation of inheritance that did not allow any division of the assets – would have remained at Filippo's disposal.

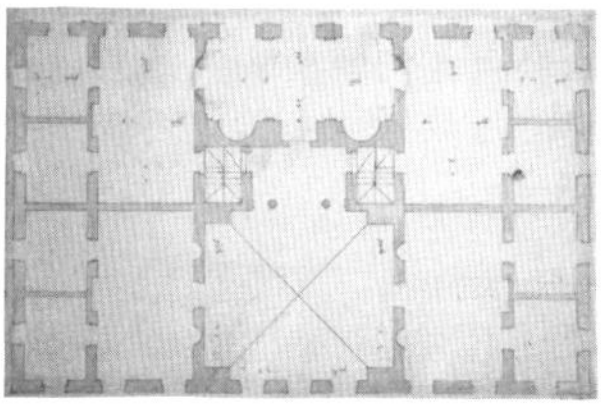

42

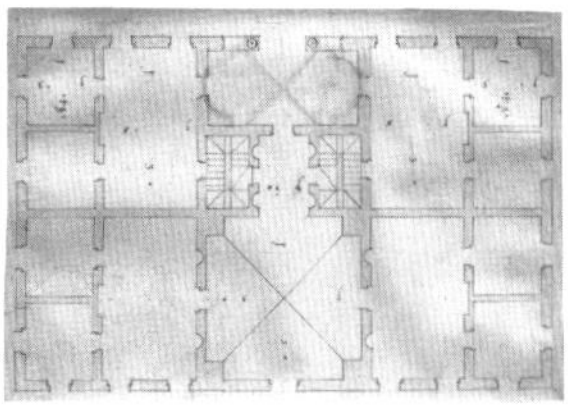

43

Only when the challenges of a logical scheme of this kind had been overcome, at least in part, was the solution apparently rendered in the upper part of RIBA drawing XVI 16 developed. By reducing the domestic area reserved for Francesco and Pietro to a single room, the central part of the house acquires a monumentality that is enhanced by the appearance of Roman bath-type structures similar to those in the proposal shown in RIBA XVII, 15. [45]

This bold digression, undertaken in an attempt to decipher these drawings, clearly makes no claim to resolve a problem that will remain an open topic of research for a new generation of scholars. However, it does suffice to show the arduous task facing a young architect who made every effort to impose some order on the expectations and requests that his patrons often expressed in vague terms.

THE CASA FOR VINCENZO POJANA IN POJANA

At the same time it also gives us a better understanding of the unrepeatable specificity of the experience Palladio was able to acquire when he was summoned by Vincenzo Pojana, a Vicentine nobleman who intended to build a *casa* on the country estate from which his family took their name, to a design by the architect who had worked for both the Pisani and the Contarini on their country estates.

Here, in Pojana, Palladio did not hesitate to adopt the type of *casa* developed by Trissino with such precision, making no inconsistent changes. This was all that was needed for this *fabbrica* to find the dimensions and volumetric autonomy that would make any further reflection or alteration unnecessary. [46]

He still showed some uncertainty about including a loggia. Once again he resorted to placing a *serliana* opening at the centre of the façade, while the form of the frontispiece with its broken pediment – like the ancient Roman baths – alludes to the vaulted structure inside the *fabbrica,* starting from the centre of the façade. Behind the façade is a cross-vaulted room running across the building. This space acts as a loggia but its functional purpose cannot be seen from the outside. The windows on either side of

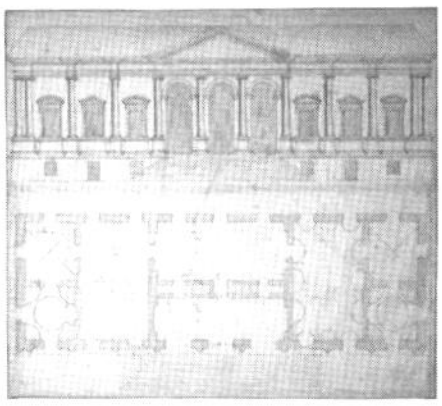

44

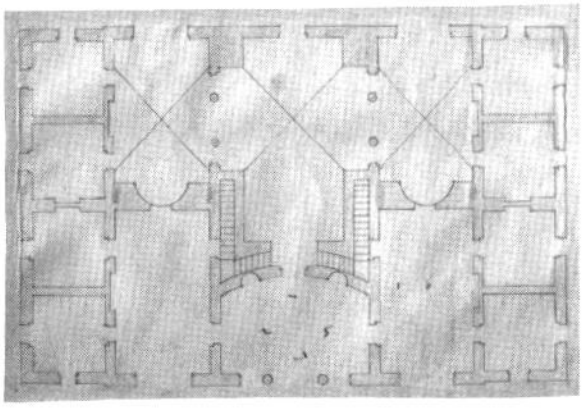

45

the *serliana* opening, which help to light the space behind, deceive the observer because they are the same shape as the windows of the adjoining rooms.

The "quandary of the loggia" is a subject that is worth dwelling on a little longer.

Palladio's Venetian patrons and those who followed their example (Pojana was a member of the pro-Venetian faction of the Vicentine nobility) had no difficulty in conceiving an "opening" in the centre of the façade; indeed, they explicitly suggested it in each *fabbrica* because, in turn, it represents a form that emphasises how the proprietor of the *casa* – far from claiming a right to the use of arms – relied on the defensive system for the mainland provided by the Republic and on their individual safety guaranteed by the Venetian magistracies. But they appeared to be biased against the form used by Trissino for the centre of the façade at his *casa.* They compared it to the loggia that Alvise Cornaro had built in the mid 1520s as the backdrop to his courtyard in Padua. In other words, they compared it to a theatrical structure.

Thus, the loggia form would not be freely adopted until its symbolic significance had been convincingly defined. This only happened once it was realised that it could be incorporated, like the loggias built in cities, into an architectural structure used to house a magistracy exercising its legislative functions. In this case, it became a *sign* that ideally permitted the *Signore,* whose house played an emblematic role in the area, to claim an institutional function, at least in abstract terms.

Once it acquired this accepted meaning, the loggia became a qualifying feature of the *casa:* a form that was further enhanced, also symbolically, when it was topped by a frontispiece that sanctioned its dignity and exalted its centrality in the composition of the façade.

The validity of this model – now perfect in its conceptual completeness – is confirmed by Palladio's use of it over the twenty years separating the construction of the *casa* for Biagio Saraceno (c. 1545) [47] and that for Marco Zeno (c. 1565), [48] regardless of

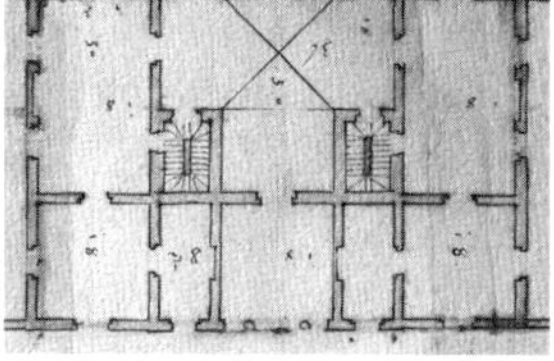

46

47

whether the *edificatore* was a Vicentine noble or a Venetian patrician. Moreover, it was a building model that – a few years on, when recollection of the events surrounding the War of the League of Cambrai had almost completely faded from collective memory – he would further exalt by the addition, at long last, of ornamentation. But we will return to that later.

Having identified the start of a reflection on the theme of the *casa di villa* at Bagnolo and having followed the evolution of this thought through to the formulation of a sort of canon that could be used ideally throughout the Republic's territories, we have – almost without noticing – strayed from Vicenza and the circumstances that led Cardinal Niccolò Ridolfi to visit the city in the autumn of 1543. For this reason, we have not mentioned the fact that Giulio Romano was also present in the city during the months when plans started to be laid for the ceremony that would accompany Bishop Ridolfi's triumphal entrance to finally take possession of his diocese.

GIULIO ROMANO IN VICENZA

It does not take much to see that no one was more qualified to advise on the organisation of Pope Leo X's nephew's solemn reception in the city than the architect who had worked with Raphael on Villa Madama, the suburban residence that was Leo X's most innovative and exciting architectural project, [49] and who a little earlier had planned the ceremonies and built the *apparati* for Charles V's triumphal entrance into Mantua.

It is likely that Trissino (who several years earlier had been summoned to Mantua with Baldassar Castiglione to assess the intellectual potential of the young Ercole, who later became a cardinal) and Marco Foscari (who had used his Venetian house for the celebrations in honour of Ercole's older brother before he became Gonfaloniere of the Church) prompted Cardinal Ercole Gonzaga, [50] regent of the Duchy of Mantua, to send the Gonzaga court architect to Vicenza. Marcantonio Thiene may also have played a role, mindful of the welcome given by the Mantuan court to his father Galeazzo during the years of exile inflicted by the Republic.

48

What is certain is that Ercole Gonzaga would not have authorised his architect's involvement in a project within the territory of the Venetian *Stato da Terra* without the consent of the Signoria, especially such a conspicuously high-profile project with certain diplomatic implications.

The vagueness with which Giulio Romano [51] replied to the *Provveditori della fabbrica* for the Palazzo della Ragione, when asked for his opinion regarding the restoration of the loggias (indeed, he only went as far as to confirm an opinion previously voiced by one of the Republic's representatives) is evidence that Giulio Romano was aware of the need for prudence during his time in Vicenza.

THE "APPARATI TRIONFALI" FOR CARDINAL RIDOLFI'S ENTRANCE

He obviously received no payment for orchestrating Niccolò Ridolfi's entrance or for his advice on the choice of ephemeral architecture to be prepared for the prelate, given that, as a cardinal, he was one of Gonzaga's "colleagues". He took on the responsibility of directing the works which, although temporary, raised technical problems that called for careful supervision at every stage. All practical matters were delegated – in return for a relatively small fee – to the man who, of all the craftsmen present in Vicenza, knew about the "antique" style and had given proof, at all levels, of exceptional reliability.

By accepting this office, Palladio was well aware that he was being offered an exceptional opportunity to learn from an architect who had been a leading figure in Italian cultural and artistic life for the past three decades. What's more, it would open the doors to research in a field that represented an alternative to his experiments *in villa*.

He was not restrained by any sense of pride or presumption: instead, he approached Giulio knowing that the latter had trained as an assistant in Raphael's workshop (just as naturally as Baldassarre Peruzzi had also trained in that same workshop and Sebastiano Serlio had grown up alongside Peruzzi). By working with Giulio, Palladio knew he was associating himself with that

4 Giovanni Bellini, *Barbarigo Altarpiece* (detail), 1488
5 Marco Basaiti, *Christ Praying in the Garden* (detail), 1515

6 Francesco Squarcione, *The territory between Padua and Venice. A landscape of towers* (detail), c. 1465

10 Michele Sanmicheli, *Porta Palio in Verona*, 1542–1557

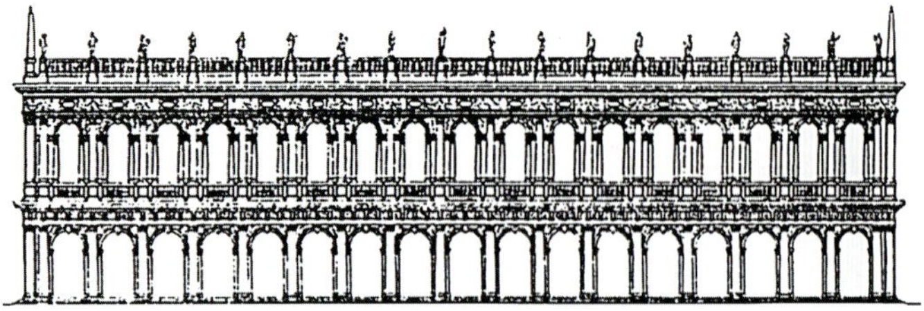

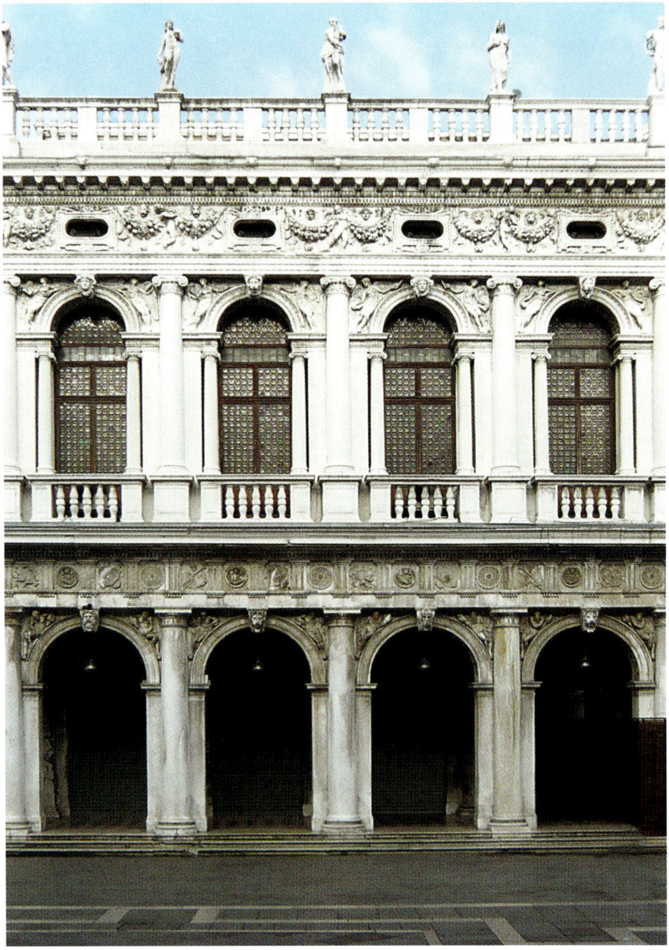

15 Demus Dalpozzo, *Elevation of Libreria Marciana* (detail), Venice
16 *Detail of the Libreria Marciana*, Venice

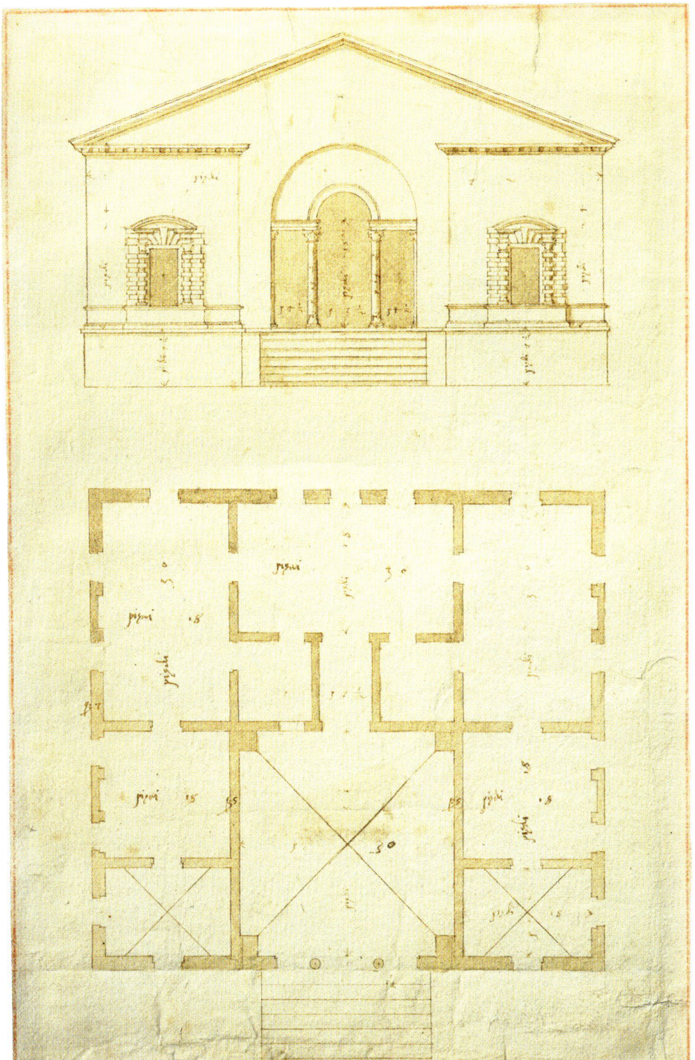

24 *Villini giovanili*

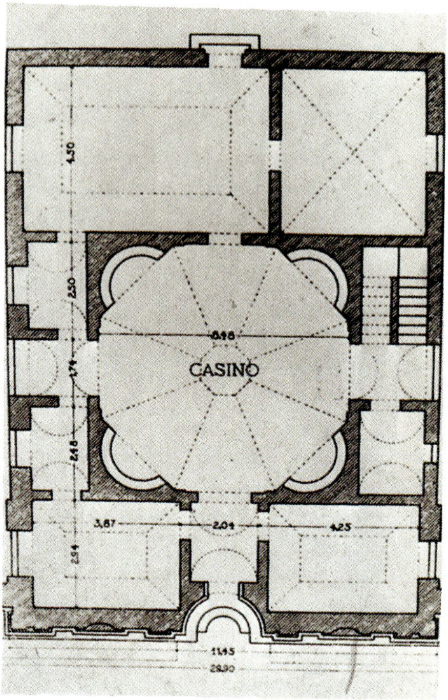

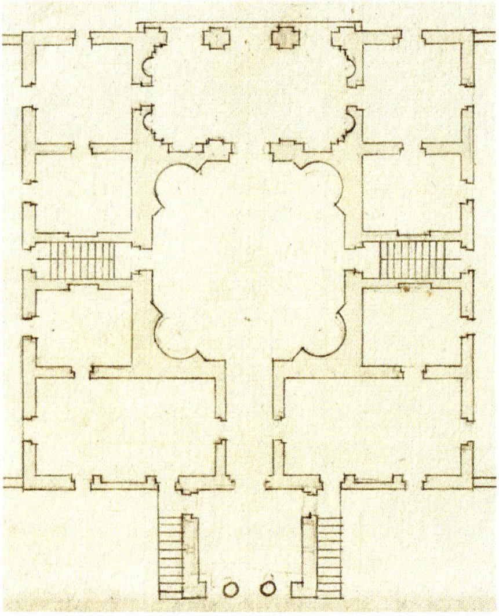

26 *Cornaro Odeon, ground floor plan,* Padua
27 *Preliminary study for Villa Pisani* (detail), Bagnolo (Vicenza)

28 *Preliminary study for Villa Pisani*, Bagnolo (Vicenza)

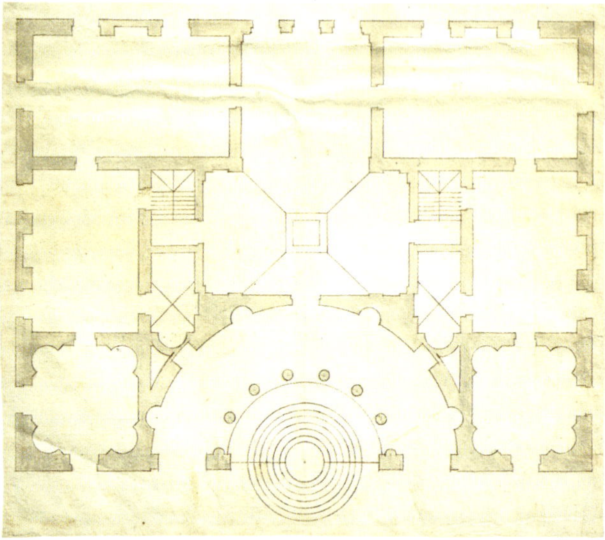

30 *Preliminary study for Villa Pisani* (detail), Bagnolo (Vicenza)
29 Sebastiano Serlio, *I Sette Libri dell'Architettura* (detail)

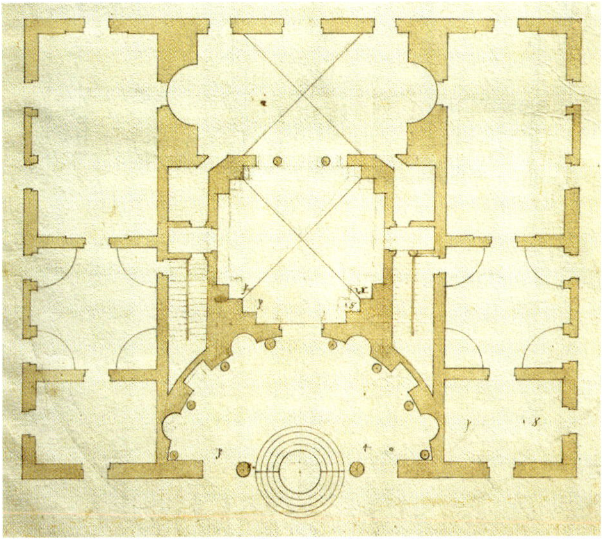

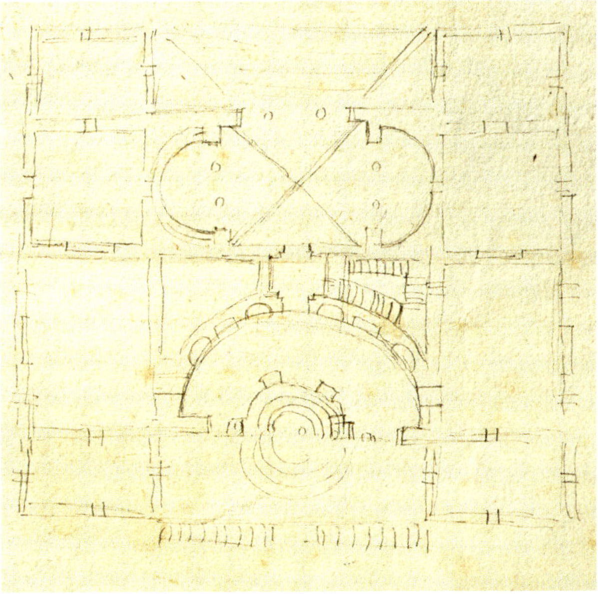

32 *Preliminary study for Villa Pisani*, Bagnolo (Vicenza)
31 *Preliminary study for Villa Pisani* (detail), Bagnolo (Vicenza)

33 Giulio Romano, *Battaglia di Ponte Milvio* (detail)
34 Giulio Romano (and Raffaellino del Colle?), *The Madonna and Child with Saint John the Baptist* (detail)

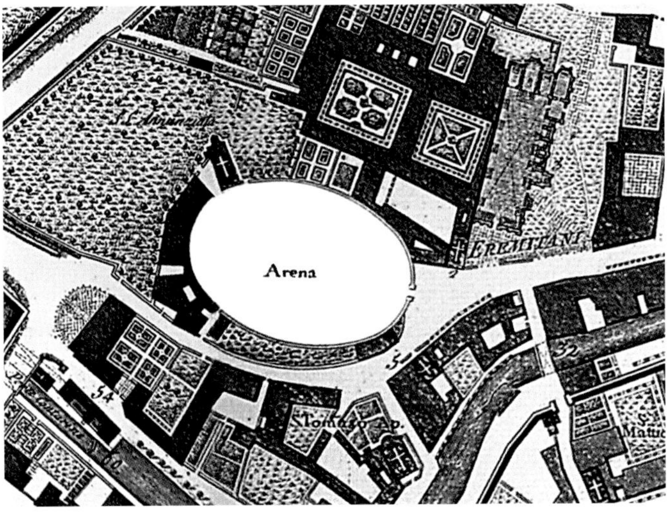

35 Alessandro Buzzaccarini draughtsman, Fioravanti Penuti engraver [from the watercolour by Marino Urbani], *Interior of the Arena at Padua* (detail)
36 Giovanni Valle, *Plan of the City of Padua* (edited), 1784

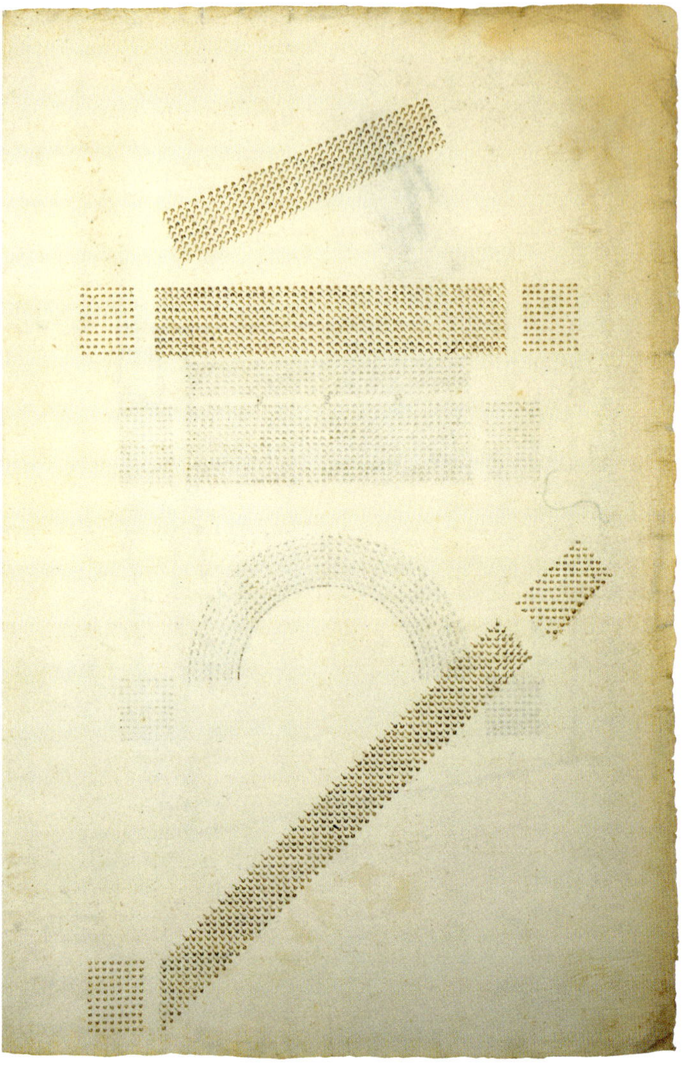

40 *Studies of Military Formations* (detail)

41 *Project for a casa di villa with two entrances,* presumably Villa Contarini, Piazzola sul Brenta (Padua) (identification proposed by Antonio Foscari)

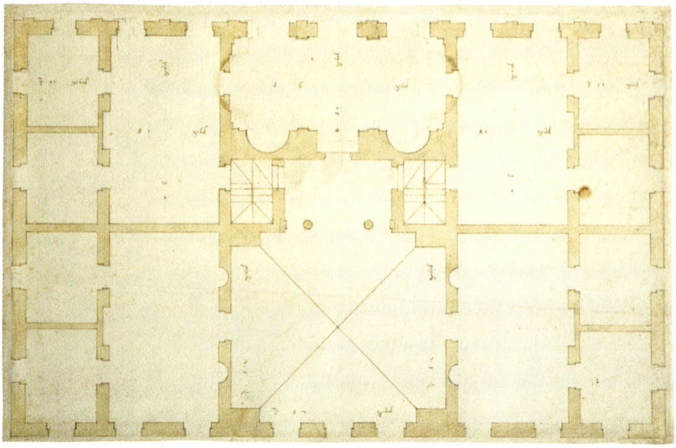

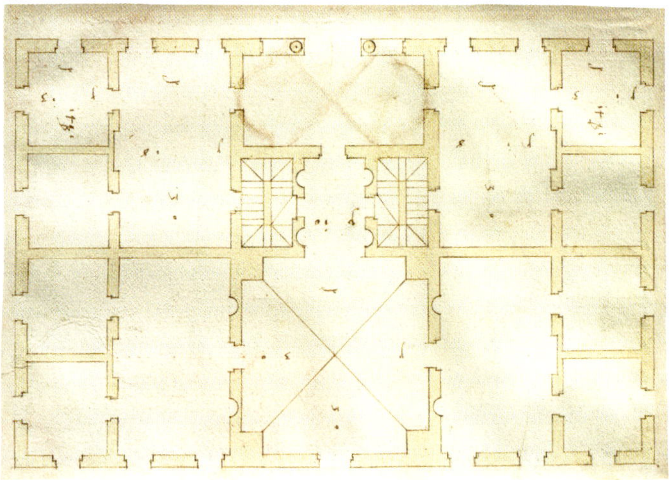

42, 43, 45, 44 *Project for a casa di villa with five bays,* presumably Villa Contarini, Piazzola sul Brenta (Padua) (identification proposed by Antonio Foscari)

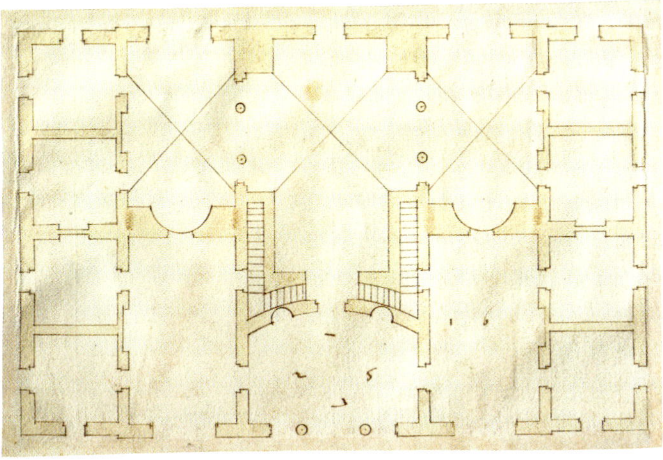

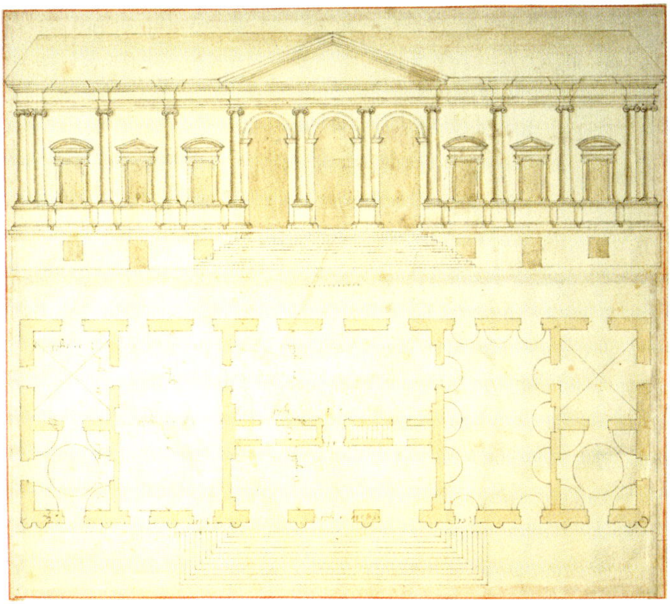

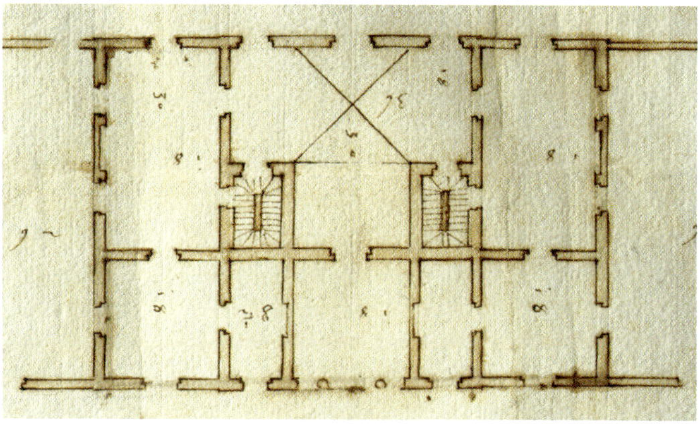

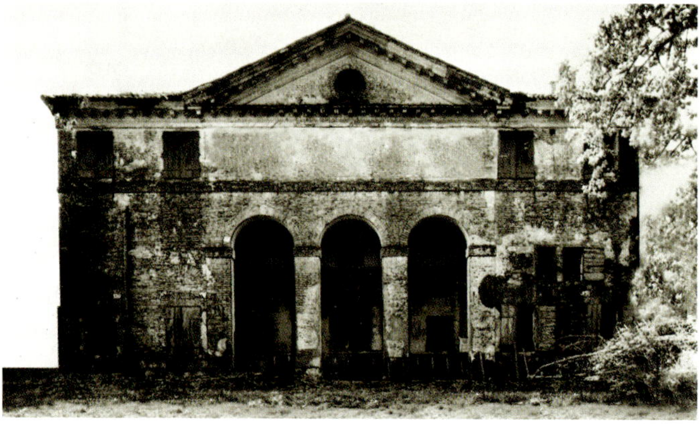

47 *Villa Saraceno* (edited), Finale (Vicenza)
46 *Villa Pojana, preliminary studies* (detail), Pojana (Vicenza)
48 *Villa Zeno* (edited), Cessalto (Treviso)

tradition of architectural culture that had developed over the past decades, which until then he been able to explore almost only indirectly or at one step removed.

THE PALAZZO IN VICENZA FOR THE THIENE

It was in this spirit – without losing sight of his own cultural identity or jeopardising his intellectual autonomy – that Palladio was with Giulio when, after Gian Galeazzo Thiene's death in 1542, his son Marcantonio Thiene asked the famous "Roman" architect to draw up a model for a palace through which he planned to assert his family's power and authority in the heart of Vicenza.

Clearly, inspired by such ambitious motives, Marcantonio Thiene would never have considered entrusting such a challenging task to a young man who had not completed a single work of similar importance, and who for years had been known in the city as the employee of a stonemasons' workshop.

Instead, based on the wealth of experience he had accumulated in Rome and Mantua, Giulio was commissioned. He was the one architect who would have had no problem interpreting Marcantonio Thiene's self-celebratory requests. Indeed, to satisfy the ambition of this Vicentine nobleman, Giulio Romano conceived such a disruptive design that, had it been completed, would have destroyed the late medieval framework of Vicenza's urban fabric, right at its centre.

This palace, with its square layout like Bramante's Palazzo dei Tribunali [52] or the Palazzo Te in Mantua, [53] was on a scale that dwarfed all other private buildings in the city and it would have stood in isolation (*in isola,* forming an entire block, as Palladio would say[2]), surrounded by four streets.

Its autonomy would have been emphasised by four virtual towers that added weight to its corners, also in visual terms; but this was not all. On two sides, it would also have been given perhaps even greater emphasis by setting its façades back from the existing street alignments. A volume jutting out from the main façade of the *fabbrica* would have confirmed – as if it were a tribunal (one might say an imperial tribunal) – the patron's desire for power.

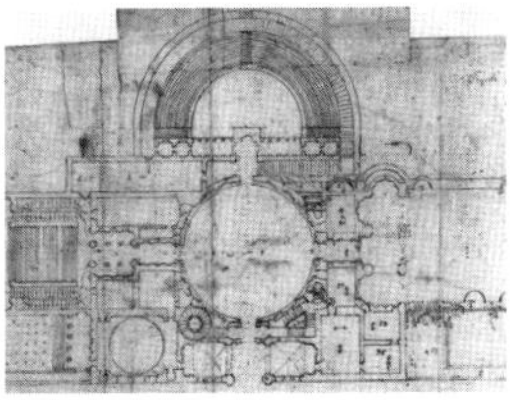

49

50

51

It was almost to be expected that the operation was never completed. (Moreover, the corresponding project that Marcantonio Thiene embarked on at his *villa* in Quinto was never finished either; it, too, was marked by the same heroic ambition and, once again, used a model that clearly bears the mark of Giulio Romano's live "intervention").

It was no coincidence, therefore, that Palladio – when he included the project for this urban palace in his *Second Book* [54] many years after Giulio's death – felt the need to redimension the explosive force of the programme embarked on by the Thiene family (reducing the size of the piazza created opposite it; minimising the perception of the corner towers rising above the main road; and opening shops on the façade facing the city centre, whose presence alone diminished the aristocratic lordliness of the *fabbrica*).

What's worth underlining, instead, is how shrewdly Palladio interpreted Giulio Romano's model; he knew how to mitigate the flights of extravagance, the infractions, those forms of *sprezzatura* or nonchalance that the Gonzaga court architect had grown accustomed to using in Mantua, as though seeking to demonstrate a sort of detachment between himself – Raphael's most gifted pupil and Pope Leo X's architect – and his new working environment in the Po Valley. [55]

The ebullient personality of the *maestro* did not constrain, indeed it hardly affected, Palladio's sense of proportion or that search for equilibrium (more conceptual than formal) that was an almost natural praxis of his mental approach. Working alongside him was therefore not a frustrating process for Palladio. On the contrary, it was a stimulus that – had he needed any incentive – prompted him to return to Rome and, this time, stay there for as long as was necessary to make an in-depth study of the ruins he had evoked so ephemerally – almost as if they were ghosts – when he was summoned to work on the arches and other decorations with which the city of Vicenza welcomed Cardinal Ridolfi.

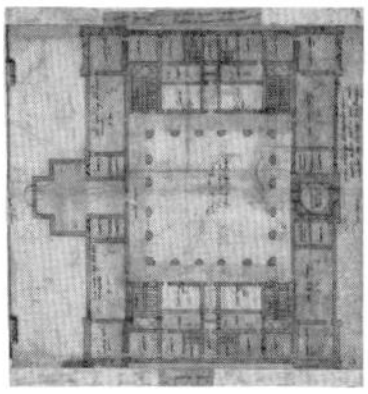

52

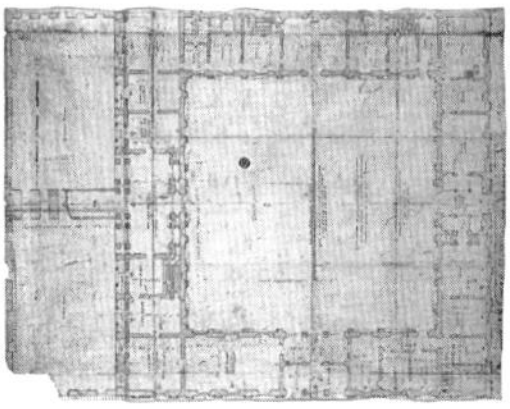

53

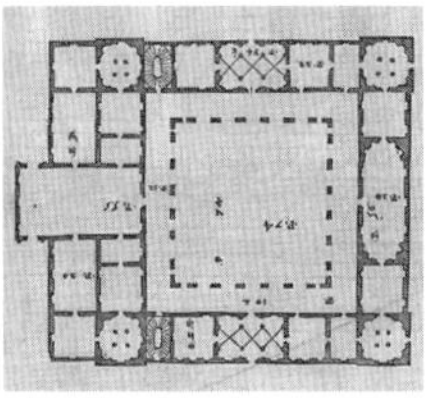

54

The idea of "going to Rome" was, in a way, a journey of the mind, above and beyond the physical journey down the peninsula. However, it was a journey that was essential for someone who had realised how the past – that unique blend of memory and customs – weighed heavily, and unproductively, on the minds and consciences of many of his patrons, even the most influential.

Once he was in Rome, Palladio – who did not miss the opportunity to mingle with the exclusive circles hosted by Trissino and the Thiene family – was not distracted by the papal court, by the theological debates, the network of power or the conflicting views on cultural questions and more besides that constantly flared up between the various *nazioni* or communities present in the city. Furthermore, he was not taken in by the notion of tradition as an expression of historical continuity, and so he had no trouble in setting aside the many centuries of Roman history that were interwoven with the period of Christian history.

Thus, Palladio was able to fuse the the classical *virtù* of Rome with the *grandezza* of Venice – the city in which he had learned to discard, with equal simplicity, the centuries of history linking it to Rome through the prism of Byzantium. He did so without indulging in the contradictions of a past that was, to some extent, imaginary, embracing instead the originary ideals that formed the abstract frame of reference for his research. In this way, Palladio succeeded in forging past and future in a continuous link, without being affected by – indeed in many ways escaping from – the ideologies that were agitating and ripping apart the world around him.

It is interesting to note how he stuck to this mental approach – which presupposes a surprising self-awareness in such a gentle man – even when he studied and surveyed the architectural ruins of ancient Rome using "a collection of implements", as Bramante had done before him.

He explored the source for every *ornamento* – before even looking at the form – because he knew that this was the only way to turn it into a new language. He researched the primitive origin of

55

each artefact, the very matrix of the compositional logic that had generated it. [56] [57]

We should look more closely at this point, taking up an insightful remark made by James Ackermann. In his research Palladio studied whole artefacts, without setting aside those that called for the unique skills of archaeological expertise to be understood. Then, once he was quietly sitting back at his drawing table, he started to reflect on the works he had surveyed in order to use these artefacts – even when they no were longer artefacts by definition – as *exempla* to be recovered for contemporary use (at least for contemporary use as he was beginning to understand it more clearly).

His reworkings of the architecture of the Pantheon and the ideal reconstructions he made to define the original structure of the great temple complexes at Praeneste and Tivoli bear eloquent witness to this intellectual process.

If, on the subject of the Pantheon, he wrote that "none is more famous"[3] among the Roman temples – avoiding an aesthetic judgement – it was because its formal perfection was, in his opinion, undermined by two aspects: the fact that the temple had sunk into the ground, and the unconventional manner in which a *portico* (albeit, a "most beautiful" one, as he hastened to add) had been joined to the body of an existing *fabbrica* (built "in the time of the Republic") that had already had its own, different façade. [58]

To raise this monument to the dignity of *exemplum,* Palladio drew inspiration from the ruins of a circular-plan building with a portico that he had found "near the church of San Sebastiano, on the Via Appia"[4] [59] and used this as the basis for a model rotunda in which the raised floor of the temple stood above the surrounding countryside and the portico was perfectly consistent with the main body of the building behind it, thus eliminating the contradictions that detracted from the Pantheon's architectural perfection.

No less determined – and executed with remarkable open-mindedness – is the way Palladio set out to define the structure of the

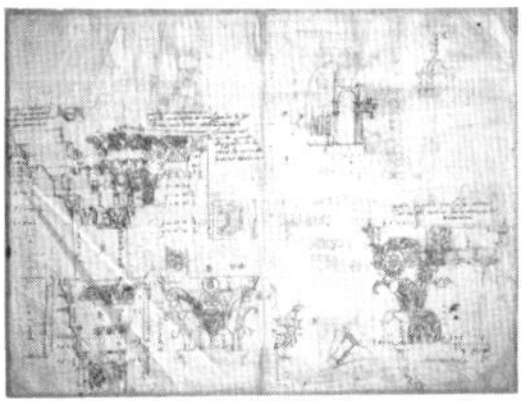

56

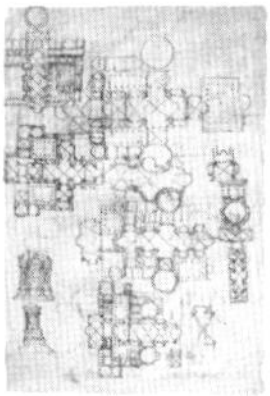

57

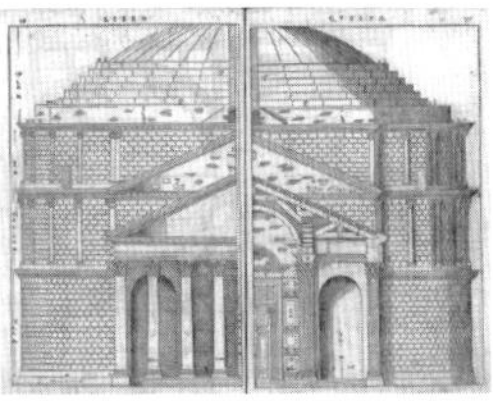

58

classical temples (like those at Praeneste and Tivoli) [60] given that there was no clear perception of these at the time (that only became possible after the air raids on Palestrina in 1944 which razed to the ground the buildings that accreted over the centuries on the ruins of the ancient structures).

Andrea's reconstruction of the system of buildings and terracing spread over the hillside on which these two imposing sanctuaries had been erected is a unique and extraordinarily important synthesis of field surveys and critical intuition. It can be summarised in his proposal that the classical temple that used to stand on the hilltop at Praeneste and Tivoli, forming the concluding apex of the sacred complexes in compositional terms, was circular and corresponded in form to the model Palladio had drawn up in his attempts to "reduce" the Pantheon to the status of *exemplum*. [61] [62]

Through exercises of this kind and by frequenting intellectuals and artists from the most varied cultural backgrounds – as was the norm in the city of the popes – Palladio returned to Vicenza "greatly moved and inflamed by such profound studies".[5]

At this stage, however, Vicentine society – even at its most emancipated – was not ready to use the cultural maturity, let alone the expertise, that Palladio had acquired during months of fervent research on the Roman ruins. There was still a persistent fear of making the wrong ideological choice in the eyes of the Venetian magistracies, and more generally, in the eyes of history. Each member of that social class had to have some kind of institutional approval before embarking on the new course that had opened, metaphorically speaking, in front of him.

Yet, the appearance of the triumphal *apparati* that – albeit for a short time – had offered a completely different vision of the city, the provocation that Marcantonio Thiene had embarked on with a building project that would profoundly change the very image of the city, and lastly the enigmatic *case* that some Venetian patricians had started to build not far from Vicenza; all these things taken together proved to be a turning point, To the most receptive minds, they generated an awareness of the change that was sweeping the European cultural panorama, not least of all Vicenza.

Given the long history of their construction and the ongoing debate surrounding their rebuilding, it seems almost logical – one might even say obvious – that, at this stage, Vicenza's ruling class resumed, and strongly reproposed, the project to rebuild the loggias surrounding the Palazzo della Ragione in the heart of the city.

THE PALAZZO DELLA RAGIONE AND THE LOGGIAS

However, in order to understand the significance of this event, we should perhaps focus our attention on an earlier period, just after the mid fifteenth century, when the Venetian Signoria started work on the imposing bulk of the building in a solemn gesture to celebrate Vicenza's surrender to the Republic half a century earlier (1404), and to demonstrate that the exercise of law – and the "reason" that would be administered within it – was the primary means of government by which the Republic ensured that this city, too, became part of its *Dominio.*

The massive building that appeared at the heart of the city, with its allusions to the image of the Venetian Ducal palace (its marble cladding and tracery), was therefore emblematic of a central power that did not need to conceal but rather flaunted its desire to use its magistracies also (indeed above all) to control the behaviour of the Vicentine nobility. It was not only a celebration, but also a warning. [63]

A generation passed before this somewhat intriguing message was absorbed by the city's ruling class. It was only in the sixth decade of the fifteenth century that the ruling class felt the need for a structure that would allow it to attend the palace, which had become the fulcrum and symbol of the city's political life, in accordance with a convention that had already been adopted in Padua: one that enabled them to remain above the piazza.

Due to the political and social implications of this theme, responsibility for its definition lay with the Venetian Signoria. In

59

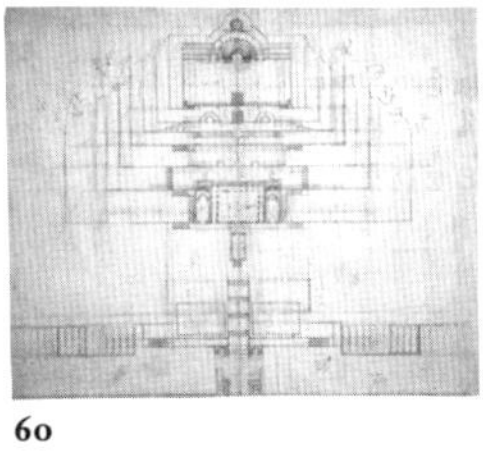

60

addition to the fact that the cost of this operation remained on the central government's books, this is confirmed by the involvement of the Republic's most highly qualified technicians (the *proti* of the Procuratia di San Marco) who promptly inspected the building as soon as the first signs of structural collapse were detected, at the end of the century, barely two decades after the loggias had been built by the architect Formenton without due diligence.

The loggias would have been rebuilt by the end of the century or, at the latest, by the early years of the sixteenth century if the war started by the League of Cambrai and orchestrated by Pope Julius II had not intervened, resulting in Vicenza's defection from the Republic. In this sense the continued presence in the heart of the city, around the Palazzo della Ragione, of loggias that had partly collapsed and were barely fit for use, can be seen almost as a sort of Venetian revenge against the Vicentine ruling class to keep alive the memory of its shameful betrayal.

It was therefore not coincidental that the need to proceed with the rebuilding had become a matter of urgency by 1535 (during the same period that prompted Giangiorgio Trissino to define the innovative form of the *casa* at Cricoli). It was a moment when it finally seemed possible to bridge the ideological divisions that had separated families and ripped Vicenza's civic society apart for too long.

The complex affair that resulted at this point can only be understood by bearing in mind the decisive role still played – as in the past – by the Signoria's most authoritative official in the field of architecture: Jacopo Sansovino, the *proto* of the Procuratia di San Marco.

However, by the mid 1530s, the Procuratia was not interested in making its *proto* available to a city within the *Dominio* because he was committed to designing an impressive programme for the *renovatio* of the Marcian *platea*, right in front of the Doge's Palace, in order to emphasise its political and ideological quest for power on the Venetian political stage.

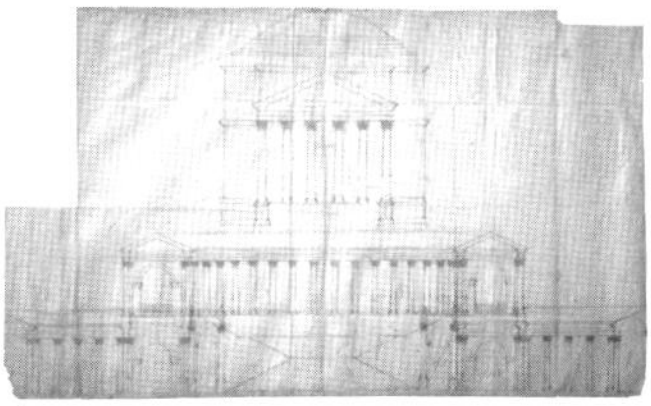
61

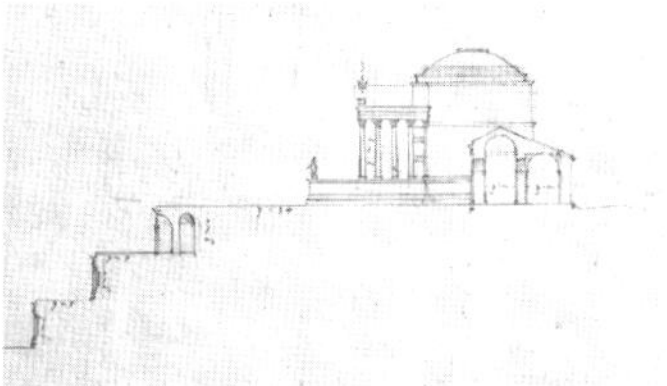
62

For his part, Jacopo Sansovino had no difficulty in complying with this request from the magistracy on which he depended: not only – or not merely – because of the obedience he owed them but also because he had been waiting for at least seven years (if not longer) for an opportunity to show off his ability as a specialist in *all'antica* architecture in Venice, a city in which, until then, he had not been allowed to build any public work that was an expression of the Signoria's political authority.

In 1535, therefore, Jacopo Sansovino did not even bother to come to Vicenza to look at the problem of the loggias. When he finally did arrive, three years later, in 1538, he limited himself to offering generic advice. It was not in his interest for building work to commence in a city within the *Dominio* that might be compared to the works that were by then underway in St Mark's Square under his supervision.

That this was a real risk is quite clear: there were too many analogies between the two initiatives. Both works, the *Libreria* and the loggias, were at the heart of a city – the former in Venice, the latter in Vicenza – and through their appearance, both aimed to change the city's image. Both, unusually, were stone buildings. Both proposed a modular succession of equal bays facing the urban setting. Both were inspired by Roman models. In both buildings it was the corner – the *canton,* as might have been said at the time – that offered the greatest challenge to the architect's specialist knowledge.

Everything that happened after 1538 was therefore influenced by the attitude taken by the Procuratia and the unwillingness of its *proto* to become involved: Sebastiano Serlio left Venice after having been accused of "lèse majesté" against Jacopo Sansovino for responding to the requests of the *Provveditori della fabbrica* for the Palazzo della Ragione and providing them with a model for the reconstruction of the loggias. Michele Sanmicheli, the Republic's influential military engineer (*Ingegnere alle Fortezze*), kept silent, having learnt from experience not to contradict the Florentine architect; and lastly Giulio Romano did not hesitate to assert

63

64

nonchalantly that the old loggias could be reinforced using the basic procedures suggested many years earlier by one of the leading *proti* sent by the Signoria to inspect the works. Therefore, only a crisis of Jacopo Sansovino's authority could break the impasse to solving this problem.

AN ACCIDENT DURING WORK ON THE LIBRERIA

That is precisely what happened when, on a very cold day in the winter of 1545, the first arcades of the *Libreria,* which had been under construction for almost ten years in front of the Doge's Palace, at enormous cost, suddenly collapsed. It was an event that instantly undermined the *proto*'s reputation (given that he also had to face the shame of spending a few days in prison).

All the criticisms that had been raised against the *renovatio* of St Mark's square from the very outset – criticisms that had been shelved on grounds of political opportunism in the late 1530s – re-emerged with almost explosive force in the wake of this incident.

Moreover, the head of the government at the time was a patrician who had never supported the idea, let alone the euphoria, of allying the Republic with the pope and the emperor with the view to launching an offensive against the Turks. Even in 1538 (when the magnificence of the *Libreria,* designed to celebrate this alliance, was starting to become apparent opposite the Doge's Palace) Francesco Donà (in line with other leading patricians, including Marco Foscari) had again intervened in the political debate with all the strength he could muster to support the case for peace with the Sultan. Furthermore, the following year he outlined the diplomatic steps that would have allowed this to be achieved. [64]

When Francesco Donà was elected doge, he certainly did not authorise Sansovino's appointment to oversee the construction site for the Zecca, given that the latter had recently completed the construction of the Loggetta. [65] [66] What's more, on the strength of his rights as doge, he assumed all responsibility for the rebuilding of that enormous welfare complex, the Ca' di Dio, on which work had recently started based on a project by the

65

66

proto of the Procuratia di San Marco and, once again, under his technical supervision.

Jacopo Sansovino's crisis of authority reached a peak in the early months of 1546 and this undermined the quasi-prohibition he had imposed – using the institutional power at his disposal – on rebuilding the Vicentine loggias.

A PALLADIAN DESIGN FOR THE RECONSTRUCTION OF THE LOGGIAS

It was at this point that Palladio returned from Rome where he had been occupied by his surveys. Clearly, he was kept informed of the sequence of events and, in particular, of the fact that the debate on the reconstruction of the loggias had been reopened. Fully aware of the wealth of knowledge he had now accumulated, he drew up a design for the reconstruction of the loggias and presented it to the *Provveditori della fabbrica* for the Palazzo della Ragione, with the encouragement – as seems likely – of Giangiorgio Trissino, prompted by a few of the *provveditori* themselves, and with the not entirely disinterested backing of his Pedemuro companions who were still the Vicentine contractors best suited to carrying out the rebuilding work. It seems that the broad nature of this consensus convinced the *provveditori* to take the decision to translate his proposal into an almost life-size wooden model that would allow them to make a better assessment. Having made his move both swiftly and effectively, Palladio left for Rome again almost immediately.

While Palladio carried out new explorations around Rome – in Tivoli, Albano and Palestrina – Giulio Romano also delivered a model for the reconstruction of the loggias to the *Provveditori della fabbrica* for the Palazzo della Ragione. This man – Raphael's pupil, the prestigious architect to the Mantua court, the disillusioned artist who had impressed the collective imagination of the Vicentines by coordinating the triumphal *apparati* that had created a different perception of the city, and author of the model of the *fabbrica* for the Thiene family that would have altered the appearance of the city, right in the centre – was the only person whom the *provveditori* could find in the Po Valley to replace Jacopo Sansovino, without the *proto* of the Procuratia di San Marco being able to object.

The decision to summon Giulio – who showed no embarrassment at contradicting the opinion he had expressed four years earlier – was an act of pure pragmatism. It did not exclude Palladio, in the sense that many (including Giulio himself) probably took it for granted that if the loggias were rebuilt using his model, their actual construction would be managed by the specialist who had worked alongside him in preparing the triumphal *apparati* and who was working competently on the building site for the Thiene family palace.

Perhaps it was to demonstrate his lack of interest in a solution of this kind that Palladio left Vicenza when the debate on rebuilding the loggias moved into its final phase. Instead, he preferred to remain on the property of the Vicentine aristocrat who had "discovered" him and backed his proposals with youthful enthusiasm.

A DEVELOPMENT AT THE VILLA IN ANGARANO

Palladio himself describes the venture in Angarano, which was primarily intellectual rather than architectural, working alongside Giacomo Angarano, in his *Second Book* in a passage that, on more than one occasion, has somewhat disconcerted experts. [67] Indeed, the tetrastyle form of the façade of the *casa dominicale,* or owner's house on an estate, the frontispiece above it completed with an impressive set of acroterial statues, the appearance of a system of double arcades in the centre of the rear façade, and the double staircase included in this *casa* to provide access to the upper floor were all formal and typological acquisitions whose inclusion in such an early work by Palladio hardly seems probable.

But this is not the point we wish to highlight now. We can be confident that the architect agreed with Angarano the choice of design to be published in the *Second Book,* given that it was Angarano (as Palladio states in the preface to his treatise) who had not only encouraged the architect to write *The Four Books,* but had also backed part of the cost of their publication. What

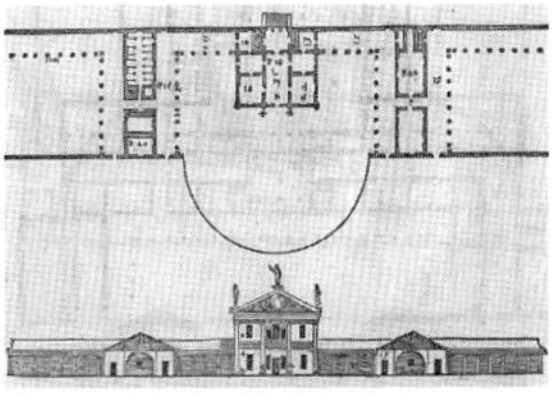

67

we need to understand is the message which the drawing and the few lines of text accompanying its presentation were meant to convey.

In this drawing, the *casa* – the actual residence of the *Signore* – broadly seems to conform to the model devised by Giangiorgio Trissino. It stands within a courtyard surrounded by porticoes, like an antique temple standing in its enclosure. Behind these porticoes, which open onto other courtyards, are rural outbuildings.

In short, this *casa* is no longer a symbol located in the territory while preserving its proud isolation, as if it were nothing more than a demonstration of the authority of the owner who visits occasionally to collect his tithes from the agricultural produce grown on his estates. Instead, it is a *fabbrica* which – ennobled by its form and ornaments – shows no hesitation or embarrassment in being associated with its surroundings: with the physical environment in which it stands and also with the human environment of the workers and the farming activities. In other words, it acts as the centre of the farm, a focus for the waters that flow down from the hills to the west and for the roads that serve the surrounding countryside.

This gives us an idea of the degree to which Angarano must have shared in the intellectual stimulus as he followed Palladio's elaboration of a typological model that would liberate – or, at least, start to liberate – the concept of a country house from the ideological schemes imposed by the Venetian patricians for whom Palladio had worked until then *in villa*.

IN VENICE TO TAKE LEAVE OF DANIELE BARBARO

Palladio may have left the countryside around Vicenza – perhaps precisely the Angarano estates – to travel to Venice in early September 1548, taking a boat along the Brenta together with Angarano. He was on his way to meet Daniele Barbaro, [68] an erudite Venetian patrician a little younger than him, who, the year before (as he himself tells us), had decided to start work on a definitive translation of Vitruvius's treatise; to do so, he had set up a workshop – following the example of his ancestor, Ermolao,

68

the great humanist – in which, together with mathematicians, astronomers, engineers and technicians from every field, he had enrolled Palladio as the architectural specialist.

Daniele Barbaro was due to leave as ambassador to London shortly afterwards (on 12 September), on a diplomatic mission to the English court that would keep him abroad for at least a year. Before he left, the management of the translation needed to be organised in view of the prolonged absence of its backer.

Palladio stayed in Venice for a few days after Barbaro had left. Since Trissino now resided here almost permanently, Palladio made a point of visiting him, perhaps for the last time. He also spent time with Tiziano Minio (an artist who had participated in the decoration of the Odeon built by Alvise Cornaro in his courtyard in Padua). On 28 September he helped Angarano to complete a sale. And perhaps – as Zorzi suggested some time ago – he was consulted about the construction of the tomb for Doge Gritti which, ten years after the latter's death, had still not been built.

Apart from all this, Palladio still found time to look into the continuing difficulties facing Sansovino's building works at the *Libreria*. This only confirmed his conviction that he was now the only architect in the Veneto who had the expertise to work on the rebuilding of the loggias, for so long the subject of debate in Vicenza.

FOUR DRAWINGS SHOWING THE REBUILDING OF THE LOGGIAS

The *provveditori* in Vicenza did not yet seem to have come to the same conclusion and, as a reflection of their continued lack of certainty, they asked Palladio to submit not one but four drawings. Clearly, they intended to play for time in order to choose the most convincing proposal among the various projects presented by Sebastiano Serlio, by Giulio Romano, the suggestions (perhaps) supplied by Jacopo Sansovino and others besides, which had accumulated in connection with this topic over the years.

By then it was October. It is worth noting – in the light of what happened next – that the *podestà* in Vicenza was Francesco Bernardo, a patrician who may well have heard about about the city's affairs from Marco Foscari given that, only a year earlier, at the end of 1547, the latter had agreed that Bernardo should marry his grand-daughter, the daughter of Agostino who had died at a young age.

Francesco Bernardo was a very enterprising man with extensive international experience and proven diplomatic skills, who – for whatever reason – showed a particular interest in Vicenza and succeeded in holding the role of *podestà* of the city until 1550, an exception to normal practice which set a maximum of one year for administrative offices of this status.

From this position of authority he followed the final phases of the debate on the rebuilding of the loggias, perhaps influenced their progress and certainly approved the conclusion that was reached on 1 May 1549 when Palladio was appointed *proto* of the *Fabbrica.* But we should not get ahead of events and must instead return to the moment when Palladio submitted the four drawings.

It took at least a year for the *provveditori* to tackle a subject that, from the start, also had symbolic implications that were not easy to define, let alone express.

By examining the drawings that document the early phases of Palladio's thoughts on the subject, it is clear that the architect explored various solutions before arriving at the one that he submitted to the *provveditori.*

The only constant feature in each of the drawings is the assumption that lay behind the decision to rebuild the loggias: the need to reduce the width of the arches of the *portico* at the level of the piazza in order to overcome the static instability that had so severely endangered the fifteenth-century loggias.

In order to achieve this result, instead of the succession of large diameter arches whose weight was supported by slender columns (a solution that would have evoked the pre-existing structure), Palladio designed a narrower arcade within the body of a massive stone wall. At the same time, he ensured that the wall separating the openings from each other was embellished with a pair of half-columns, also in stone. Therefore, to some extent he attempted

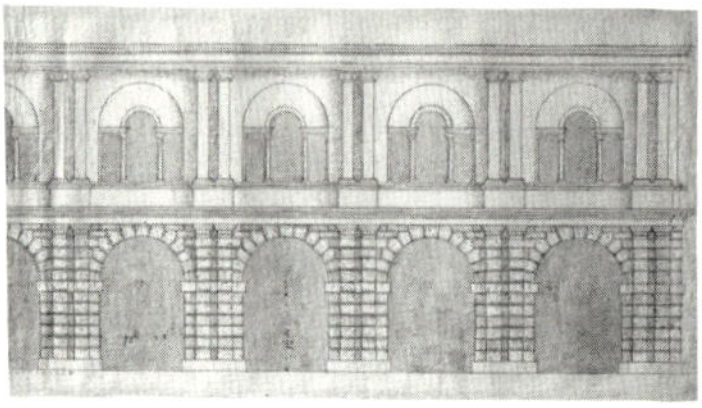

69

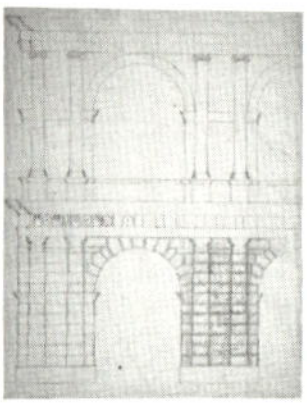

70

to evoke – not without elaborating it – the *exemplum* offered by the first storey of the Colosseum. [69] [70]

This evocation of the Colosseum was enough to prompt the compositional choice that automatically became an ineluctable feature of each future project: to eliminate the archaism implicit in halving the upper loggia module compared to the division of the *portico* on which it stands.

While working on these drawings Palladio followed a criterion that had also influenced Sebastiano Serlio some years earlier; namely the firm conviction that a conceptual distinction existed between *portico* and *loggia*, and that this differentiation had to be expressed in formal terms. He saw the *portico* as a structure that complemented the piazza: it was at ground level and open so that people could use it. Instead, the *loggia* over this *portico* was, in his opinion, a structure that complemented the palace given that it was destined for those using the areas reserved for the administration of justice: this meant, almost exclusively, the city's ruling class.

Even when Palladio decided at a later stage to unify the compositional layout of the upper *loggia* with that of the lower *portico* – using the paired columns mentioned earlier – he kept the idea that there should be a distinction between *portico* and *loggia*. He showed this through the rustic (*rustica*) appearance of the ground floor structures in the Doric order and a smooth (*polita*) surface for the upper level structures into which he also set *serliana* openings between the pairs of columns, the same shape that he had intended to use on the façades of the *case di villa* he was then designing.

REBUILDING THE LOGGIAS

The definitive design of the *portico* was therefore reached through clever refinements intended to maximise the amount of light inside the *portico* and also for the businesses installed on the ground floor of the palace. He therefore rejected the paired columns that would have needed to be set into a broad wall and, at the same time, made another no less important choice: the rustication of

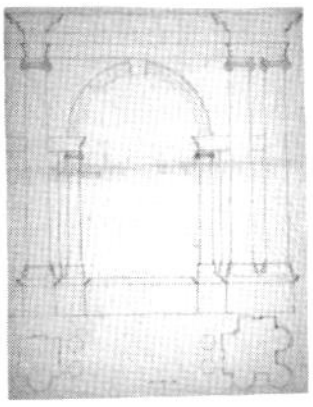

71

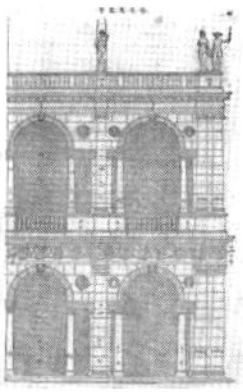

72

the lower storey. Between the columns that divide the façade into bays, he introduced a *serliana* opening whose form was reminiscent of the solution devised by Giulio Romano to create the side aisles in the large Gonzaga church of San Benedetto in Polirone. The paired columns used to support the central arch of this robust *serliana* opening are also reminiscent of the solution used by Jacopo Sansovino for the upper storey of his *Libreria.*

By means of this long and complex research process Palladio came to a masterly synthesis that also enabled him to refine the solution of the, corner of the building, turning it into a striking and distinctive architectural feature both structurally and compositionally: it was a solution that Palladio was rightly proud of and indeed he dedicated a page of his treatise to illustrating the design.

The corner revived the concept of the column device that Bramante had used on the upper storey of the house that Raphael bought from the Caprini as his Roman residence. The reduced width of the last bay of the building produced by means of this device, with a simplicity that offers one of clearest testimonies to the analogical method behind Palladio's creativity, is acknowledged as a feature that, by creating moderate formal excitement, announces and sanctions the end of the sequence of modules running along the entire length of the loggias. [71]

If it is true, as the documents appear to show, that the final decision on the form of the upper storey, namely the actual *loggia,* was not taken by the *provveditori,* in its definitive version, until 1564 – many years after the date when work first started – it would seem that the conceptual distinction between *portico* and *loggia* continued to pose an intractable problem. The fact that, in the end, no differentiation – whether functional or symbolical – was needed and the decision was taken to build superimposed structures that differed only in terms of the architectural orders used is proof of the mastery with which Palladio tackled complex operations without compromising the consistency of his work and without abandoning the virtue that enlightened his work as an architect: a sense of hope. [72]

It was on the strength of this hope – which was so intense that he thought of it as a form of certainty – that, when describing this work which he would not live to see finished, he wrote that it would one day be "included amongst the greatest and most beautiful buildings built since antiquity".[6] The greatness and *virtù* of this architecture are implicit in the process by which he developed this *invenzione*.

It was during the course of the long and impassioned debate leading to this outcome that some members of the Vicentine nobility took the same step that Giacomo Angarano had already made earlier with such remarkable resolve. Giovanni Alvise Valmarana and Girolamo Chiericati, two influential members of the Vicentine aristocracy, had come to appreciate Palladio's prudence, his breadth of knowledge and his unstinting willingness to listen. Moreover, they had started to show a clear understanding of the cultural and political message implicit in the architectural language that Palladio so masterfully deployed.

It was not just this recognition of his intellectual role that reaffirmed Palladio's self-worth at this stage; it was also the knowledge that, following Giulio Romano's death and as result of the latter's moral bequest, he was responsible for representing a discipline, architecture, in which there were no first-rate practitioners among his generation in the Veneto.

While it did not conflict with – if anything it exalted – the "natural inclination" for architecture that he had and was conscious of having, the weight of this mission prevented him from being seduced by the power or advantages that might ensue from his appointment to manage the building works that would be the largest public project in the city for many years, with a budget of 60,000 ducats.

THE CASA DI CITTÀ FOR ISEPPO DA PORTO

In order to obtain some idea of the faith and moral integrity with which Palladio took on this task (and to glimpse the sort of cultural metamorphosis that Vicentine society underwent during the years between the 1540s and 1550s) we need only compare the form of Palazzo Thiene and that of the palace that Palladio now designed for Iseppo da Porto, [73] a Vicentine nobleman who was linked to the Thiene through close family ties.

In order to define the solution that would finally be chosen, Palladio drew up a number of alternatives. In doing so, he followed a procedure that he would resort to quite frequently in his work, even in later years.

In practice, rather than a series of different projects, it involved alternative developments of one study that followed a perfectly linear thought process. A constant of all the solutions was the Bramantesque concept of a *fabbrica* with a basement, above which rose the *piano nobile.* What changed was the formal definition of the façade of the *piano nobile.*

Palladio first interpreted this *ornamento* as tall Corinthian pilasters supporting a continuous entablature. In a later phase, as a variation, he opened windows to let in more light and air to these rooms with incredibly high ceilings behind the façade. [74] Then – in an inventive change of direction, resulting from a compositional choice introduced for the internal layout of the *casa* – he abandoned the Corinthian order for the ornamentation of the façade, and instead used the Ionic. At the same time he opted to build columns, rather than pilasters, to provide structural details with a specific, material volume. [75]

These columns (which in fact were half-columns) were shorter than the pilasters had been. The volume of the rooms on the *piano nobile* therefore rose above the entablature supported by the half-columns, forming an attic. (It was at this stage that windows designed to ventilate the main rooms on the *piano nobile* were opened in surrounding wall of the attic.)

Through this consistent research process, therefore, the architect arrived at the solution expressed in the drawing catalogued as RIBA XVII, 3. [76] In this we see how the basement (for which Palladio had in the meantime drawn six different solutions) assumed a layout of exceptional figurative mastery, now merely evoking the concept – because its elaboration has no material

73

74

emphasis whatsoever – of the *exemplum* offered by Bramante in Palazzo Caprini, which Palladio had used as a source for the formal compositional definition of the solid basement at Palazzo Thiene.

In short, by patiently and painstakingly developing a model, the form of this *casa* was purified of any "Romanist" features. Gone were the virtual towers that had given Marcantonio Thiene's *casa* a sense of peremptory isolation from the urban fabric of the city, and gone too were the paired columns that had so emphatically enhanced the dignity of the *piano nobile.* Those linguistic elements used in the ornamentation of Palazzo Thiene had also disappeared: they had been explicit references to Giulio Romano's mastery (the type of windows, the rusticated *bugnato* achieved through a special working of the masonry walls, the virtual image of an *opus quadratum* produced on the façade of the *piano nobile* using a particular plaster finish).

These were not sacrifices but gains: gains whose significance is clarified if we focus attention on the solution that Palladio outlined in this superb drawing for the courtyard of this *casa:* a courtyard formed by a void of absolute geometric precision, perfectly square in plan and impressively rich in form because it is embellished on every side by gigantic columns.

The use of the Corinthian order as the *ornamento* of these large columns is sufficient to highlight the consistency with which this internal architecture complements the choices made for the façade: the reduced height of the columns on the façade acts as a sort of introduction to the explosion of measurements that would have occurred within the *casa* if Palladio had completed the works as intended. In the same way, the Ionic order used as the *ornamento* for the external columns introduces us to the Corinthian *ornamento* of the internal ones, in a giant order.

Leaving aside the compositional expertise behind this *invenzione,* there is also a conceptual component that should not be underestimated. The giant order that so explicitly interprets and exalts the self-celebratory inspiration underlying Iseppo da Porto's

75

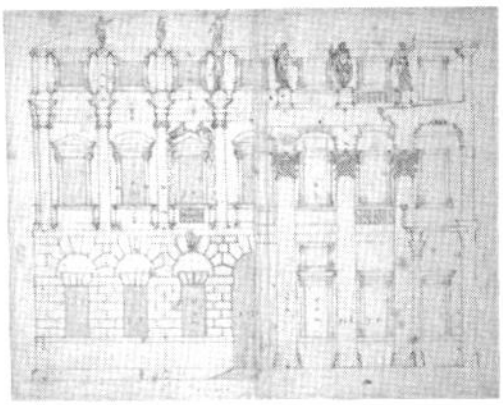

76

action is confined to the interior of the building. Towards the city, this *casa* – which conforms in height to the other houses overlooking the same street and eschews the figurative opulence of the Corinthian order – while not exactly being a true manifestation of *mediocritas* (because any learned person would have understood the triumphal nature of an entablature that projected above the columns), nonetheless represents a masterly exercise in moderation.

By introducing a clear distinction between the form of the façade of this *casa* and that of its *corte* (one "public", the other "private") Palladio showed that – in addition to managing a sophisticated theme of architectural composition – he could handle the distinction, which was clearly still appropriate in Vicenza, between civic conduct and individual pride.

This may not have sufficed to allay the Venetian magistracies' wariness of any operation that appeared to glorify a member of the city's ruling class (indeed Iseppo da Porto would be the first to renounce having a giant order of columns). Nevertheless, it prompted many other Vicentine noblemen to follow his example. In many cases – on an impulse prompted more by ideological grounds rather than practical reasons – they limited themselves to renewing the façade of the house facing the city and displaying, as if it were a manifesto, the political faction with which they identified.

This started a process that led to a transformation of Vicenza's image and identity that would have been inconceivable just a decade earlier. Throughout this process the architect – seen by the inhabitants of Vicenza as expressing the spirit of municipal autonomy they still held so dear – almost naturally acted as a magnet to those *gentil'huomini* of "deep erudition", those *Signori*, and the numerous intellectuals and artists in this city "of no great extent". Palladio did not forget to mention them in the preface to the *Four Books* that were printed in 1570, demonstrating the friendship that still bound him, many years later, to this group of individuals who had understood the meaning of his work and appreciated his *virtù*.[7]

THE CASA DI CITTÀ FOR GIROLAMO CHIERICATI

In the turbulent atmosphere that marked the start of the 1550s, a very special role was played by a Vicentine noble who had vigorously supported Palladio with his particular gift for eloquence at the meetings of the city's Great Council.

That he did so with the approval of the *podestà* – the same Francesco Bernardo who was mentioned earlier – seems likely. Girolamo Chiericati was so closely linked to Venetian political circles that he was awarded the title of count as a reward for his services to the Republic. But everything points to the fact that he was also moved by a sincere sense of fervour and intellectual curiosity. It was this, more than anything else, that prompted him to follow Palladio when he embarked on a project that, in the light of the facts, it would be reductive to call experimental.

The proof – almost the demonstration of the understanding, also the human involvement, that built up between the architect and patron in this venture – is the unique, problematic, almost disconcerting beauty of the *fabbrica* they prepared to build together.

The form of this *fabbrica* contradicts every solution that Palladio had explored until then for a *casa di città*. It was not an *invenzione* (an expression he often used) in the sense of the rediscovery of an *exemplum* offered by, or at least implicit in ancient architecture. It was the outcome of an unending research process that did not falter in the face of material or bureaucratic difficulties that might otherwise have appeared insurmountable, because it was driven by the awareness (and the need to demonstrate) that no constraint or limit can curb or prevent the attainment of a particular quality (*qualità*) in the field of architecture, if the architect knows how to respect the internal coherency of this discipline.

In an attempt to understand the "research process" that culminated with the appearance of an almost ethereal building, raised on a double storey of strong columns, we can only undertake a provisional, and purely instrumental, simulation.

It is easy to imagine that, at the outset, having been offered a site that was particularly long and narrow, Palladio must have thought back to the solution he had applied to the *casa* for the

Civena brothers a decade earlier (when he was still absorbing the teachings of Giulio Romano with lively intellectual curiosity). In other words, he conceived a *casa* whose *piano nobile* – whose façade was embellished with columns – rested on a *portico* extending along the façade, or *a longo la fazada* (to use Girolamo Chiericati's expression when he asked the City Council for permission to occupy the public space necessary to build a portico in front of his *casa*). [77]

The Council's unwillingness to grant this request may have prompted Palladio to resort to a solution not unlike the one conceived earlier for the façade of Palazzo Thiene (which was longer – but not by much – than the Chiericati site): in other words, a volume projecting from the centre of the façade which would enable him to create a large central *sala* in this *casa* too. [78]

It must have been the Council's continuing resistance to any form of privatisation of public land that led to the decision to use columns – rather than dividing walls as in the design for Palazzo Thiene – to support the part of the *sala* that projected into the public square. [79] Only an external factor such as this could have prompted a decision that would lead to a compositional approach he had never before explored. The model of a *casa* on a basement was therefore replaced by the innovative form of a *casa* whose façade revealed an order of columns on the ground floor as well, so that it rose up in two storeys. The consequences of this were truly unexpected. Since the ground floor had to be high enough to ensure that the columns ornamenting its façade were proportionally correct, this meant that it, too, assumed the status of *piano nobile* (with the result that the *casa* had to be raised off the ground sufficiently to create a basement floor in which to house the *commodità* – or domestic service functions – that a residence of this nature undoubtedly needed).

The combined effect of these circumstances meant that the *fabbrica*, this *fabbrica*, was unusually high compared to the surrounding buildings and acquired a dominant role within the public space it occupied.

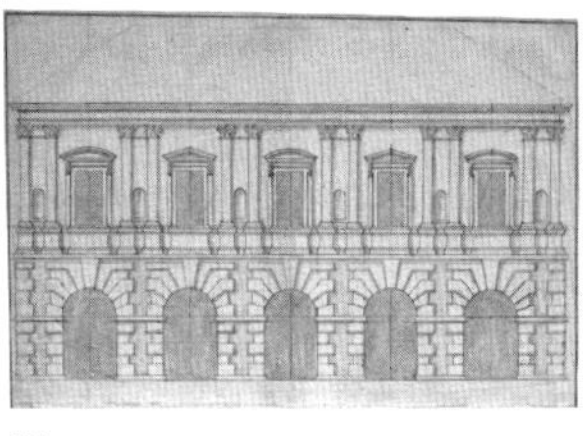

77

Therefore when the City Council – persuaded by Chiericati's insistence or convinced of the wisdom of the choice of the columns – granted the use of a strip of land along the entire façade, instead of altering the ground plan of the *fabbrica,* which by then had been finalised, Palladio brought forward the row of columns he had planned to build, on two storeys, on the façades of the two wings of the *casa,* aligning them with the projecting central façade. [80]

This simulation obviously does not claim to be a reconstruction of the actual events. It only serves to point out that only an unusual and anomalous event might have produced such a surprising architectural result – one that Palladio never tried to replicate, in any other edifice. It offers another opportunity to verify how capable Palladio was of taking a building operation to a form of absolute quality, absorbing, as it were, into the compositional process, all the accidents and setbacks that occurred.

Palladio's creative process is analogical; it only obeys the canons of the language that Palladio used with unwavering discipline and rigour, and responds to the need – which was urgent in his eyes – to achieve a formal balance in his works that could translate in practice into the "true beauty and elegance of the ancients".[8]

The drawings attesting to the final part of this research process are proof of his mastery of this procedure. The limpidity of these drawings and the clarity that illuminates them recall the clarity of some of Raphael's architectural drawings, almost making us think that Palladio did succeed during his studies (or was simply guided by instinct) in tracing the very source of Giulio Romano's development, where what was "ancient", as Raphael conceived it, was an abstraction that did not allow manipulations. [81]

The sense of liberation, or perhaps it would be more correct at this point to call it "freedom", that this *fabbrica* expresses so perfectly, is a sort of testimony that Palladio was ready to take up new challenges with the confidence of knowing that he could use a language that set no limit, or impediments, on the exercise of *invenzione.*

78

79

This experience therefore stimulated his ambition. If he had limited his activities to Vicenza, he would have been able to build numerous *fabbriche* in that city, which would have been superb *latinorum rerum fragmenta* (as we might perhaps call them by borrowing, and inverting, the phrase *vulgarium rerum fragmenta* that Petrarch used to describe the wonderful sonnets in his *Canzoniere*) – and this is what he certainly did. But he would not have been able to show the universal value of the language that he now felt he had fully mastered. He was also conscious (as Petrarch was) that a language has no status if it is not officially acknowledged by a power that makes it a central element of its state identity, and indeed recognises it at the hub of its political power.

For this reason, from Vicenza, Palladio looked, and continued to look, to the East, to Venice, to that political entity which transformed the geography of its *Stato da Terra,* diverting rivers and launching an "agricultural revolution" that was unprecedented in modern history; which, after the Sack perpetrated on the papal city, claimed to be the only representative on Italian soil of the "freedom" enjoyed by ancient Rome; which engaged Sanmicheli and Falconetto to give an ideological eloquence to the defensive works that it erected in Verona and in Padua; which chose to present to the world an image of La Serenissima as the fulcrum of an international balance of power, displaying in the Marcian *platea* a series of works that were intended to give its Roman nature a contemporary presence in the European political arena.

Venice, the political entity that "is the only example of the grandeur and magnificence of the Romans" (as he himself wrote)[9], was therefore the arena that Palladio was compelled to enter. He knew that it was the obligatory passage through which the cultural message he bore would become part of history.

It was in response to this call – a call that was moral even more than intellectual – that he prepared to submit his resignation to the *Provveditori della fabbrica* of the Palazzo della Ragione and left the site of the loggias in Vicenza so that he could work more assiduously for "Venetian gentlemen".

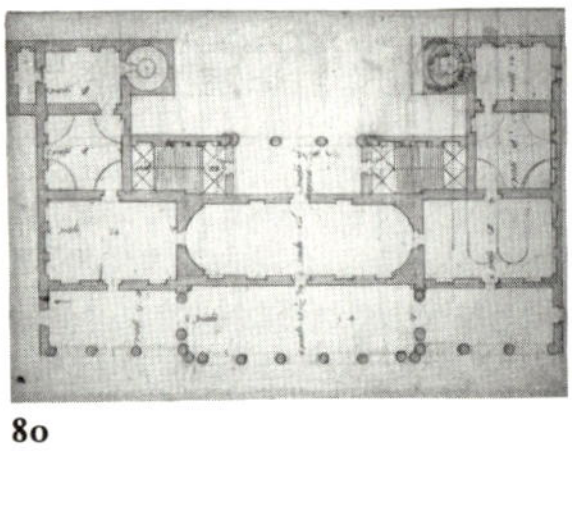

80

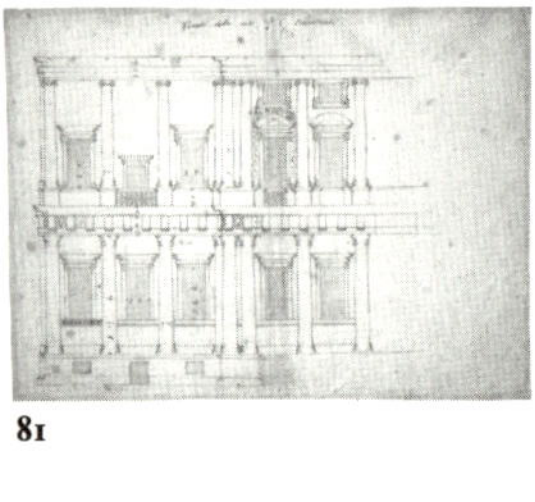

81

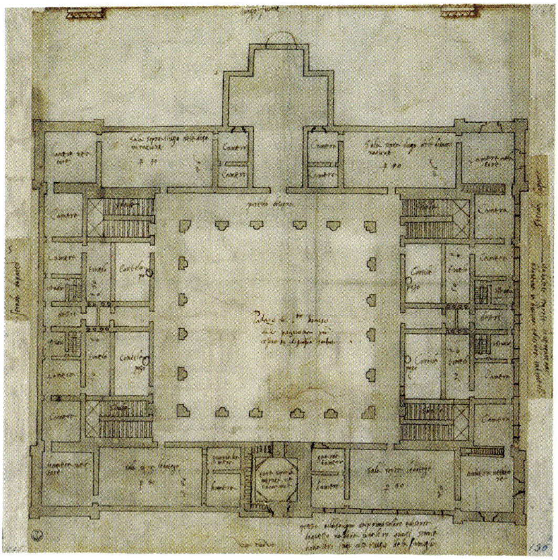

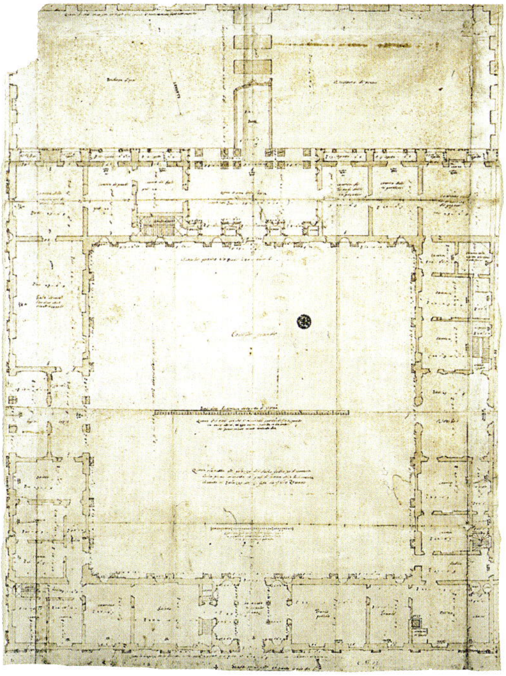

52 Antonio del Pellegrino, for Donato Bramante, *Ground floor plan of Palazzo dei Tribunali*, Rome
53 Giulio Romano, *Ground floor plan of Palazzo Te,* Mantua

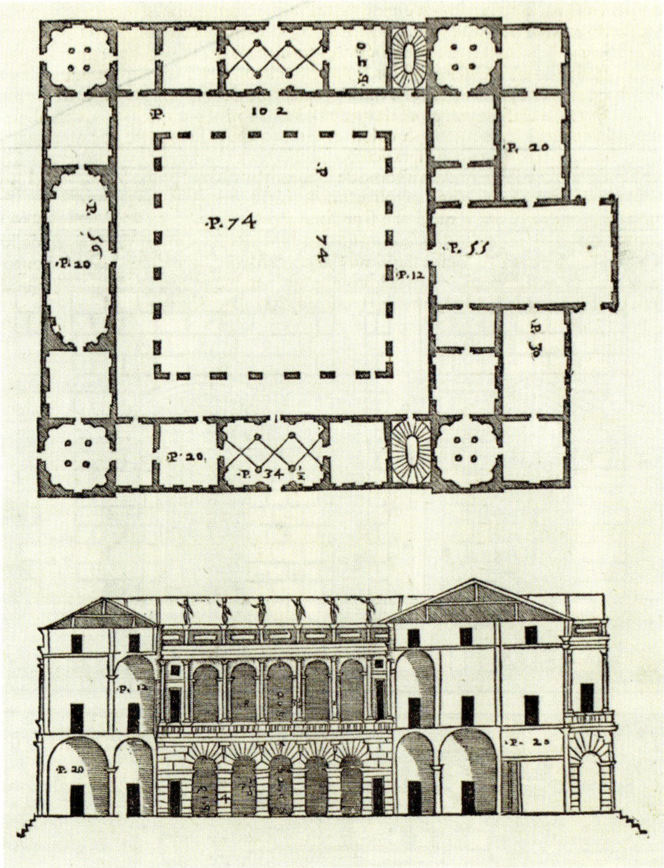

54 *Villa Thiene* (detail), Quinto (Vicenza)

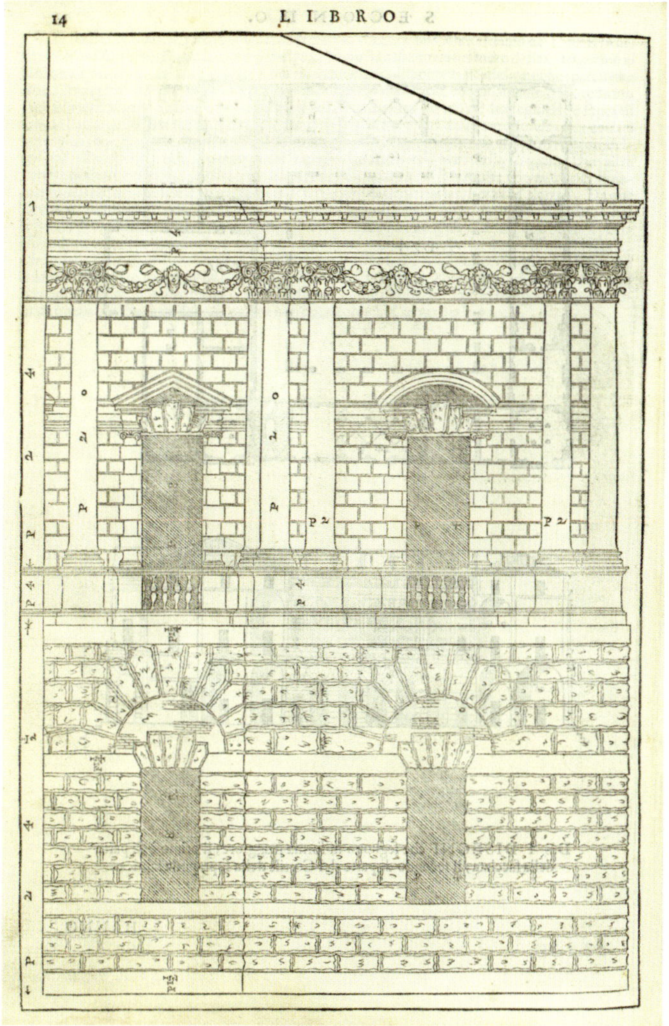

55 *Villa Thiene,* Quinto (Vicenza)

56 *Baths of Caracalla* (detail), Rome

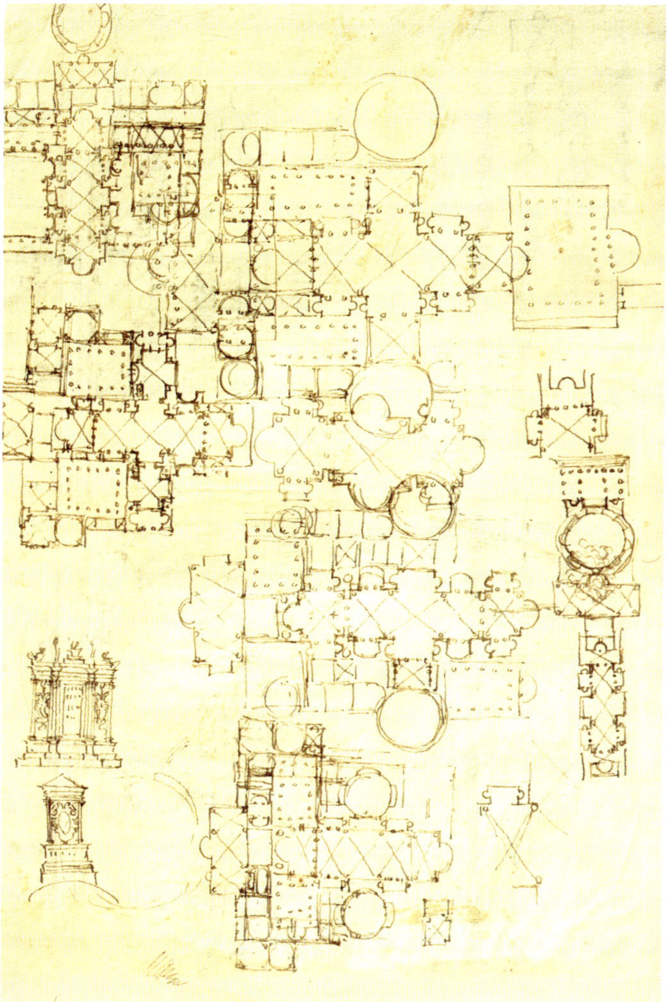

57 *Baths of Agrippa,* Rome

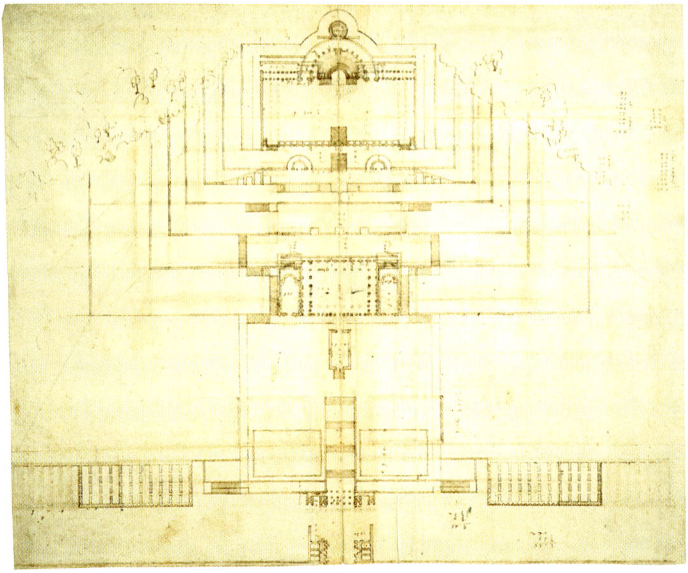

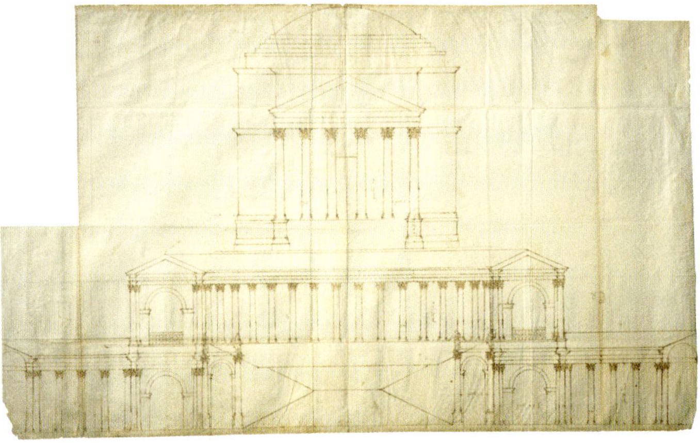

60 *Temple of Fortuna, plan,* Palestrina (Rome)
61 *Temple of Fortuna,* Palestrina (Rome)

62 *Roman theatre,* Verona

63 *Monumental structure of the Palazzo della Ragione,* aerial photo (detail), Vicenza

S E C O N D O. 63

LA SEGVENTE fabrica è del Conte Giacomo Angarano da lui fabricata nella ſua Villa di Angarano nel Vicentino. Ne i fianchi del Cortile vi ſono Cantine, Granari, luoghi da fare i uini, luoghi da Gaſtaldo: ſtalle, colombara, e più oltre da una parte il cortile per le coſe di Villa, e dall'altra vn giardino: La caſa del padrone poſta nel mezo è nella parte di ſotto in uolto, & in quella di ſopra in ſolaro: i camerini coſi di ſotto come di ſopra ſono amezati: corre appreſſo queſta fabrica la Brenta fiume copioſo di buoniſsimi peſci. E' queſto luogo celebre per i precioſi uini, che ui ſi fanno, e per li frutti che ui vengono, e molto più per la corteſia del padrone.

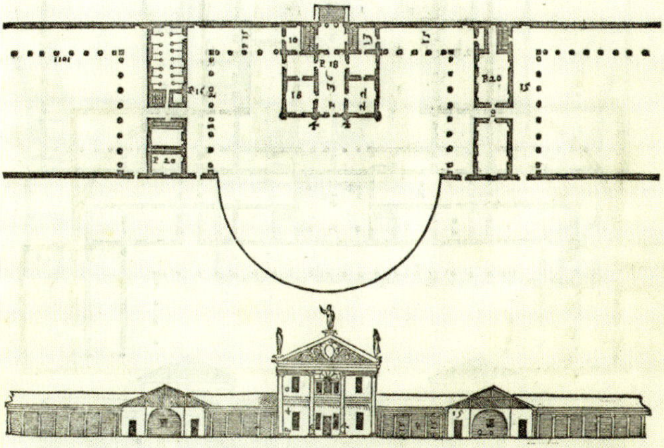

I DISEGNI

67 *Villa Angarano,* Angarano, Bassano del Grappa (Vicenza)

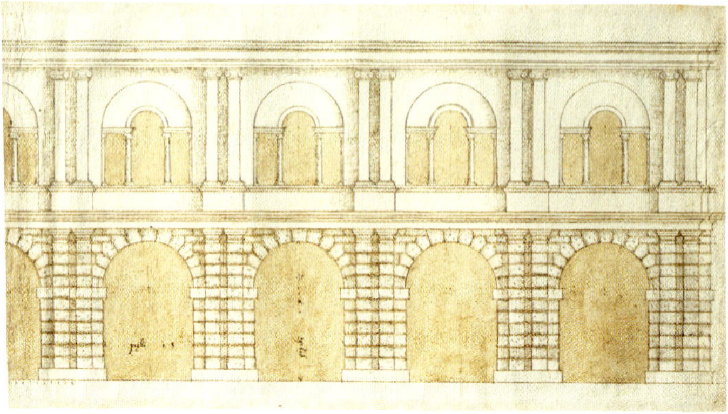

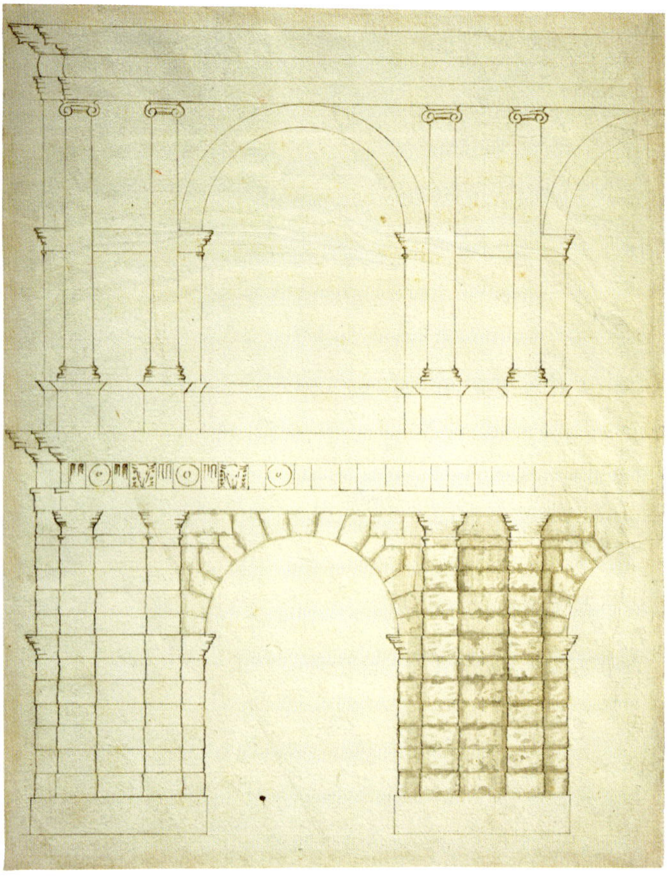

69, 70, 71 *Project for the loggias of the Palazzo della Ragione,* Vicenza

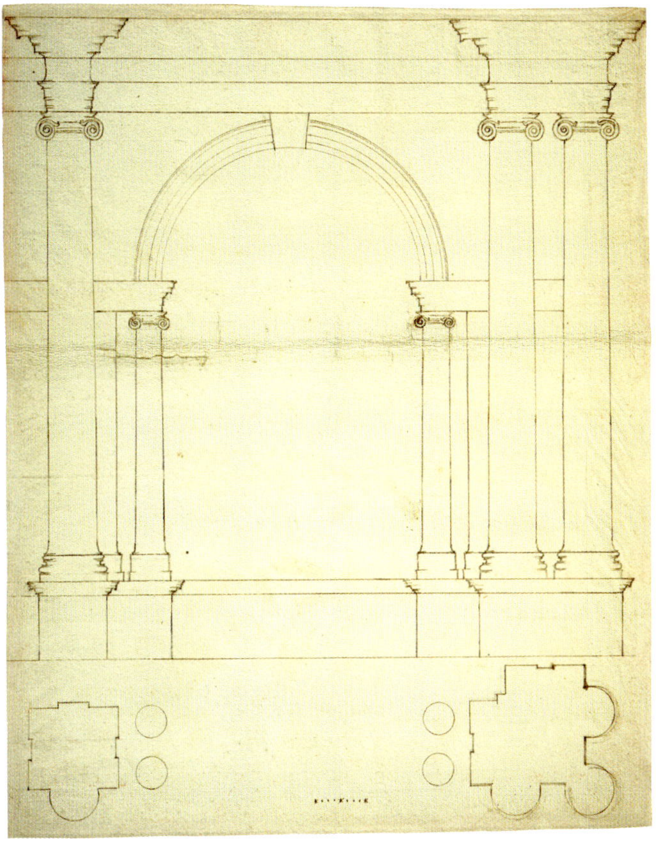

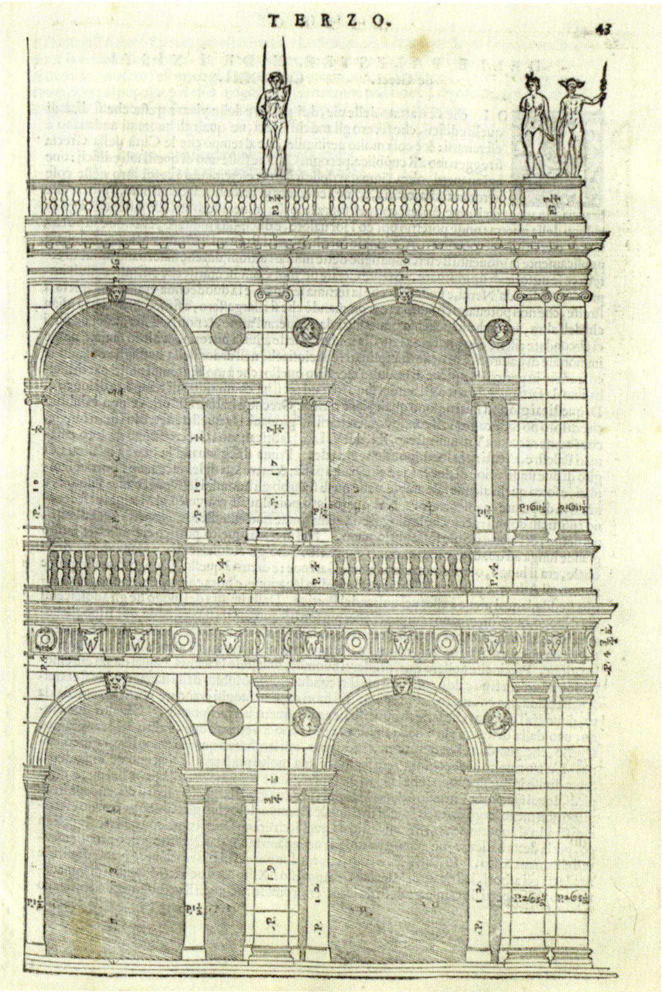

72 *Palazzo della Ragione,* (detail of the corner), Vicenza

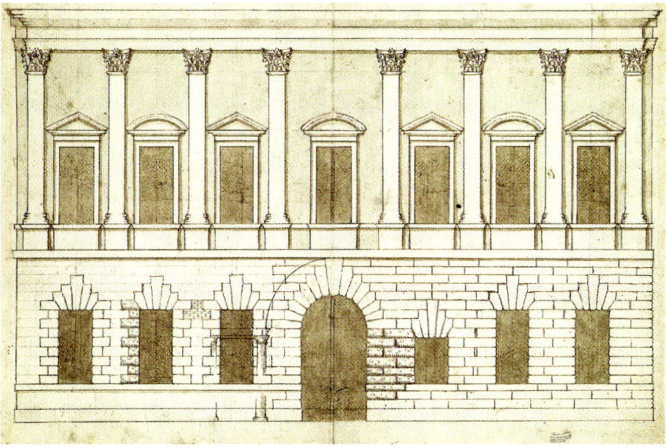

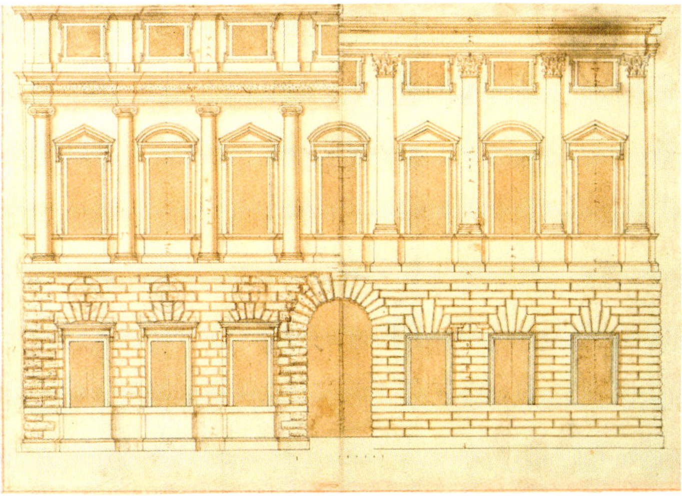

74, 75 *Project for Palazzo Porto*, Vicenza

76 *Project for Palazzo Porto,* Vicenza

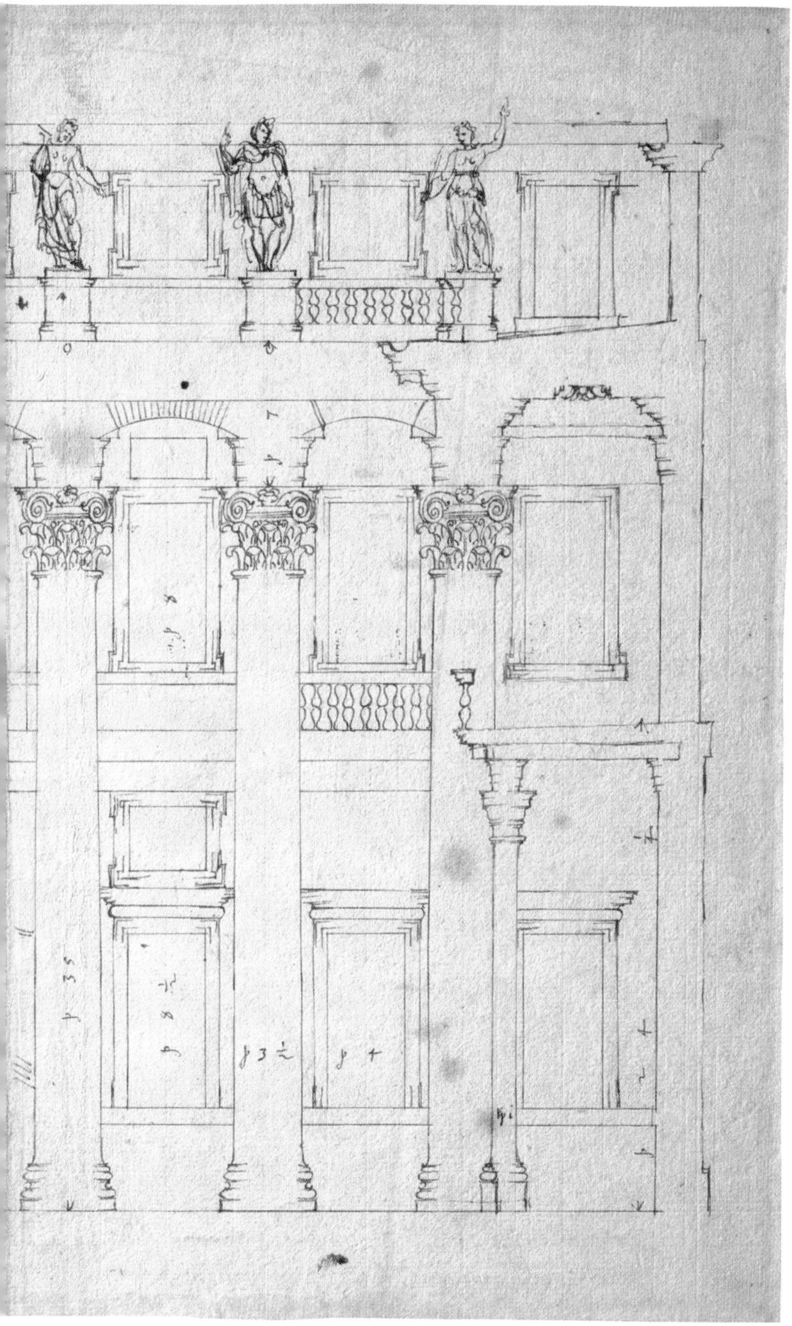

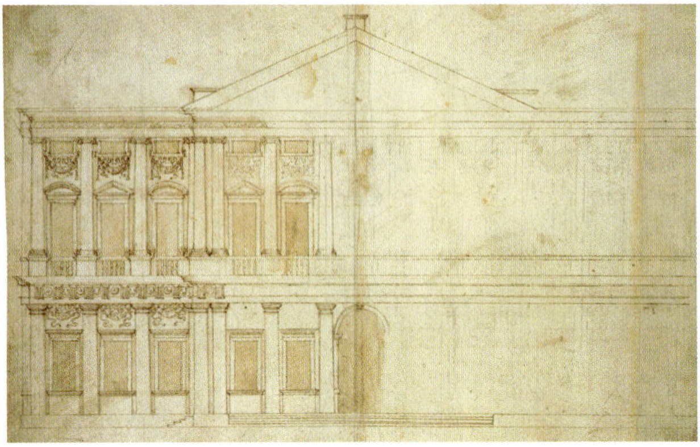

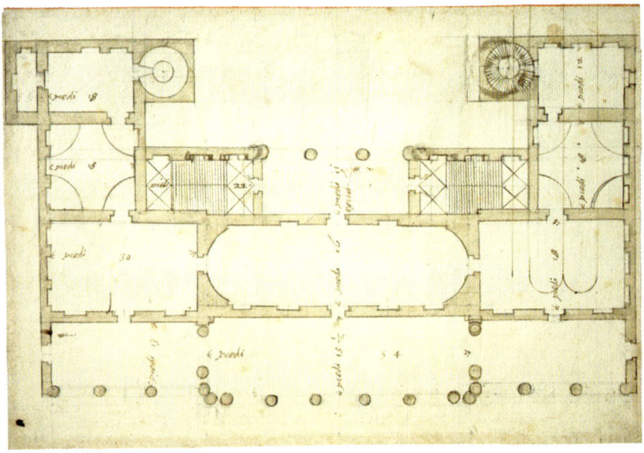

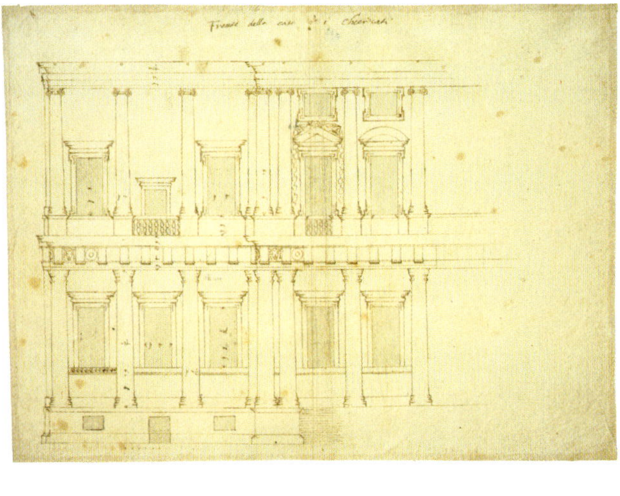

79, 80, 81 *Project for Palazzo Chiericati,* Vicenza

DANIELE BARBARO AND THE TRANSLATION OF VITRUVIUS

Daniele Barbaro [82] had returned from London, where – in application of the Aristotelian scientific methods he had learned at the University of Padua – he had set up a workshop in which he painstakingly catalogued all the fish in the Atlantic. [83] As soon as he reached Venice, he was rewarded for his service to the Republic by being appointed Patriarch of Aquileia, a post he took up following the death of the Patriarch in office.

Barbaro took advantage of the authority, albeit largely symbolic, that this office conferred on him, in order to give renewed impetus to the translation of the Vitruvian treatise and the compilation of the *Commentaries* he felt should accompany it. Palladio's role in this was crucial: his knowledge of Roman architecture enabled him to help interpret obscure passages in the treatise, while the experience of building sites he had acquired since boyhood meant that he could link Vitruvius's theoretical proposals to actual building practice, as also discussed in the *Commentaries.*

The area in which Palladio made a less incisive contribution than he might have done was the "graphic translation" of the ancient treatise, where his expertise would have been none less useful. [84] The problem is not the quality of the drawings he provided, which indeed possess a clarity of line and balanced proportions that illuminate, one might say, the drawings he made to finalise the definitive project for Palazzo Chiericati.

Rather it is their limited number and, more so, the fact that some offer an interpretation of controversial themes in the treatise that Palladio did not share in his own projects: one therefore gets the impression that on these aspects he was obliged to concord with the Patriarch's opinions.

This suggests that Barbaro and Palladio had quite significantly different views in their understanding of architecture. As a committed Aristotelian, Barbaro's understanding is in many ways dogmatic, backed by the conviction that it can be mastered using logical procedures, while Palladio rejected any form of dogma, as the development of his project for Girolamo Chiericati's *casa di città* alone can show.

82

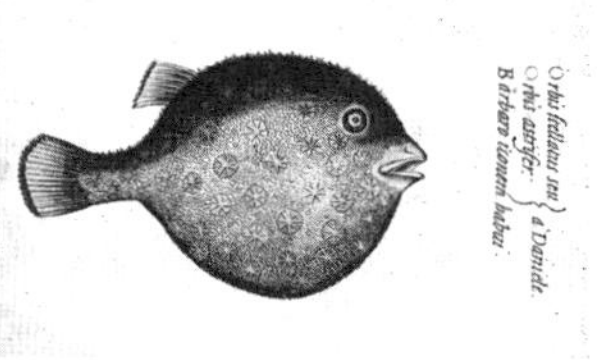

83

For Palladio, this collaboration with Daniele Barbaro was invaluable because it offered him a chance to acquire new knowledge, but at the same time did not prevent him from supervising the building sites now in progress on the Terraferma. By working alongside the other specialists engaged by the patrician, Palladio was able to develop further the "universal" concept of architecture that informs his cultural approach so specifically. From his patron he was able to learn, almost by osmosis, about the political dimension of "making architecture" which was, in the end, the real reason why he came to work in the heart of the financial and maritime empire that had loomed on the horizon since childhood, as the main driver of events in his lifetime.

It is not known where Barbaro held the meetings with the specialists he had convened: perhaps in his ancestral *casa*, the house with Gothic features that stands near San Vidal, or perhaps in the residence at the far eastern end of the Giudecca. Indeed, this island slightly set apart from the rest of the city was an area where, for at least a century, those members of the Venetian patriciate who cultivated intellectual interests to a greater extent than others lived and met.

However, Daniele Barbaro's intellectual excitement at discovering, thanks to Palladio, the possibility of putting Vitruvius's theories into practice in contemporary life also extended beyond this working group or *officina*. Through this collaboration with his "architectural specialist" he grew increasingly aware, perhaps more so than he might have imagined when he summoned Palladio, of the extent to which Venetian political life was conditioned by its attachment to tradition and the need for continuity with its past, both of which had, over the centuries, become key components of its citizens' *forma mentis*.

The erudite Patriarch Elect conveyed these convictions and sentiments, as might naturally be expected, to those members of the patriciate with whom he thought he could develop a cultural affinity that might translate into political action. With his characteristic strength of purpose, he recommended that they

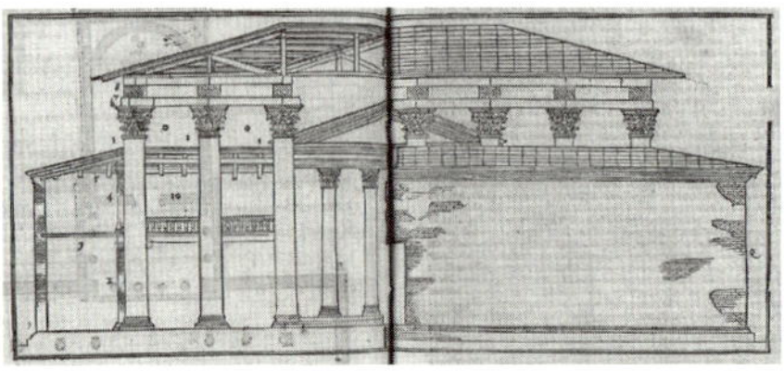

84

should take advantage of Palladio's wealth of experience and his incomparable expertise in architecture.

It was on the strength of such prompting that some patricians approached Palladio, during the years while he was working on the *Commentaries*, asking him to build houses outside Venice.

A CASA BUILT FOR TWO FOSCARI BROTHERS

The *casa* he built on a site "not far from the Gambarare"[10] overlooking the Brenta, the extremely busy waterway linking Padua and Venice, was not the first of these. But for a number of reasons that constitute something of an *unicum* in Palladio's vast output, it is worth considering as an emblematic chapter in this period of the architect's life. [85] [86] [87]

One of these reasons is that its volume – as it would be built towards the mid 1550s – and a few details of its form correspond so surprisingly to the volume and some details of the *fabbrica* depicted in RIBA drawing XVII, 6, that it is difficult to avoid the suggestion of a link between this edifice and that drawing, which scholars generally date to the early 1540s, in view of the clear influence it reveals of the "lesson" imparted by Giulio Romano. [88]

Continuing to reflect on this aspect, it is worth noting that it would have been reasonable, given the social customs of the time, that, on the death of the last member of the *fraterna* set up by their father Federico, one of the two brothers, Nicolò and Alvise Foscari, should marry to ensure the continuity of the branch of the family that they alone now represented. This meant that, if the wedding had been concluded, custom would have required (as demonstrated by the Pisani family in Bagnolo and the Contarini family in Piazzola) the construction of a *casa* on this estate, which lay close to the lagoon and had been purchased a few years earlier, almost certainly with this purpose in mind.

The very absence of an interlocutor of their father's generation would have prompted the most authoritative member of the secondary branch of the family to enter the fray: Marco Foscari, whom we have already seen in action in similar circumstances. The hypothesis that he may have asked the young architect to

85

86

87

produce an *invenzione* to celebrate the marriage of one of Federico's sons by building a *casa* is therefore not unlikely. For Palladio to let himself be guided in this case too by the teachings of Giulio Romano, who was his most authoritative mentor in those years, would also be logical. And that this isolated *casa* (whose rear façade is shown in RIBA drawing XVII, 6) should in some way take the form of a *casa di città* rather than of a *casa di villa* also seems comprehensible, in view of the site's proximity to Venice.

But curiously, neither of the brothers married then. Nicolò, the elder of the two, married over a decade later, in 1555, because – it seems – he could not escape the family and social pressure that was put on him after his mother's brother, Francesco Venier, was elected to the highest position in the government of the Republic.

It is perhaps worth noting that, as he prepared to take this step, Nicolò Foscari – together with his brother, under the unbreakable rules of the *fraterna* – ordered the construction of a huge altar (Palladio's first Venetian work) dedicated to the miracle-working saint, San Pantalon (Pantaleone), the patron saint of the parish in which his *casa grande di città* was located. [89] But this is not the point on which we should focus our attention. Instead, we should turn to the figure of Nicolò's bride, not only because she was the widow of a nephew of the powerful Cardinal Francesco Pisani (and therefore a first cousin of Daniele Barbaro), but also – no less importantly – because she was the daughter of Zuan Pisani, the patrician who (on his return from the mission he and Marco Foscari made in 1535 to congratulate the young Emperor Charles V on the victorious outcome of his African expedition) had begun building the imposing *fabbrica* at the foot of the Rialto Bridge that was the first palazzo built in Venice by Jacopo Sansovino. These were circumstances whose implications were quite clear to Palladio.

It was with this in mind that he started work on the *invenzione* of this *casa*, counting on the fact that, because it stood on a very visible site, it would offer him an opportunity to show the

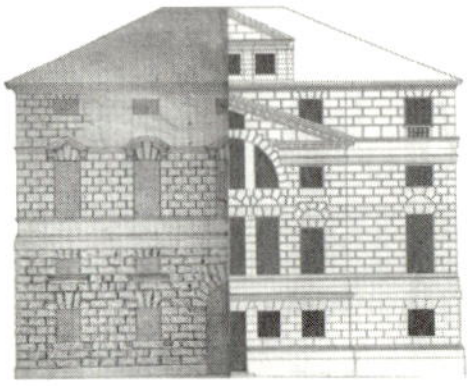

88

89

Venetians (or perhaps we should say to demonstrate to them) the extent of his *ars aedificatoria.*

He therefore (according to our interpretation) took up a drawing he had prepared for this same site in 1542 and he adapted it to meet the requirements of his patrons (in this case, also Daniele Barbaro) and to reflect the convictions that he had matured in the meantime. Not only did he conceive a structural design inspired by Roman architectural logic such as had never been seen before in the lagoon, but he also followed a compositional process that bore surprising fruits: the appearance on the front of this *casa,* atop a very high basement, of a *portico* that unequivocally recalled the *exemplum* of a Roman temple. [90] [91] [92]

It was a very striking choice and one that might have seemed scandalous to many. But thanks to their humanist education, Palladio's two clients also knew full well that a *portico* resembling that of a temple had been erected in front of only one *casa* in Rome: that of Julius Caesar. Nor could they forget that their forebear, Francesco, had been deposed from the position of doge a few days before his death with a procedure whose only justification – given the doge's venerable age – had been to evoke the tyrannicide that had taken place in the Roman Senate on the Ides of March. Indeed many had been convinced that during the thirty-four long years for which Francesco Foscari had ruled the Signoria in an authoritarian manner, the republican foundations of the State had been all but vilified and the premises had been established for the transformation of the Republic into a Signoria.

The thought comes to mind that the reference to Caesar implicit in this proposal of the form of an ancient *portico* in front of the new *casa* could not even have been conceived, let alone carried out, if the individuals behind this enterprise had not been able to rely, or believe they could rely, on the political backing of Francesco Venier [93] who, for many years before he was elected doge, had belonged to an Academy, the Accademia degli Uniti, of which Alvise Foscari, the younger of the two brothers, was *conservatore.*

90

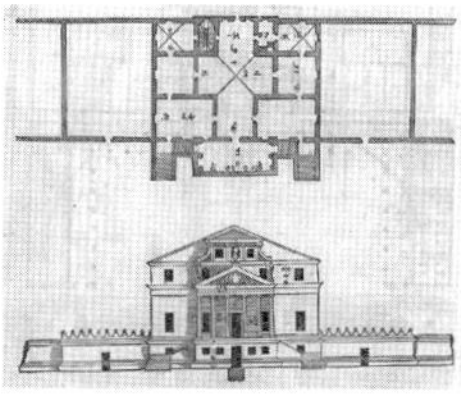
91

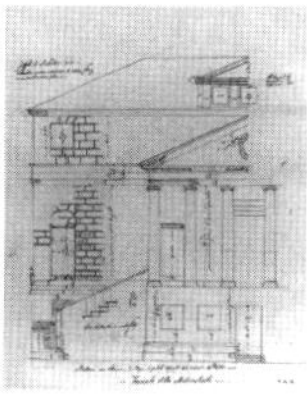
92

For all these reasons, when working on the design for the *casa* to be built at Malcontenta, Palladio certainly marshalled all the arguments – no matter how abstract – that might help to rebut, at least in dialectal terms, the accusation that he had created a building, within sight of Venice, whose form most would interpret as a reference to an "imperial" architectural style. The decision to reveal the poor material – brick – used for the *ornamenti* of this *fabbrica* on the banks of the Brenta was intended to demonstrate that this *casa* was an expression of the virtues of the Republican age in Rome. The same intent lay behind the choice of *exempla* used to compose this form: according to Palladio, the *body* of the Pantheon was built "at the time of the Republic", and he borrowed it to define the *exemplum* of a central plan temple, which he explicitly evoked here, transposing its form into a quadrangular plan; the temple of Fortuna Virilis, which he took as an *exemplum* for the *ornamenti* of this remarkable *portico* and the stucco finish of the façades, is configured in such a way as to simulate an *opus quadratum* and also dates back to the days of the Republic. [94] [95]

Owing to this set of singular circumstances, this *fabbrica* remains unparalleled in Palladio's oeuvre, as noted earlier. Palladio would never again build a *portico* flanked by columns as he did here at Malcontenta, giving proof, as a result, of his exceptional building skills. (In the future he would normally use the solution of a *portico* with closed flanks that he conceived for Girolamo Chiericati's *casa* in Vicenza and reiterated almost simultaneously in a no longer extant *casa* in the grounds of a *villa* owned by one of Girolamo's brothers). By doing this, he prudently evoked not the *form* of a temple – a *fabbrica* which, at least conceptually, has a certain religious connotation – but that of a secular edifice (like the so-called Portico d'Ottavia, to cite the best-known example). [96]

Quite apart from its *quality*, the story of this *casa* on the banks of the Brenta is yet another demonstration of Palladio's ability to grasp his clients' requests, whether ideological or individual,

93

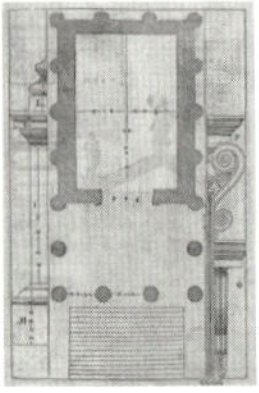
94

95

never failing to exploit them as opportunities, or simply as pretexts, to take his research into the specific disciplinary field of architecture to an even higher level.

We can find evidence of this very unusual aptitude of his if we turn our attention to the projects that he drew up for two Venetian patricians who, at Barbaro's prompting, decided to settle on the Terraferma: one in Piombino Dese, a village on the mainland not far from Padua, and the other in the residential area that was growing up outside the gate of Montagnana, on either side of the road to Padua.

GIORGIO CORNARO'S CASA IN THE BORGO OF PIOMBINO DESE

To the population who lived in the surrounding area, a patrician had no option but to outwardly express and represent the Republic of whose government he was, institutionally, a member. This is all the more true if we remember that "the magnificent Signor Giorgio Cornaro",[11] who decided to build himself a *casa* in the borgo of Piombino Dese, was a descendant of Caterina Cornaro, who presented to the Republic the kingdom inherited from her husband, the last Lusignano king of Cyprus.

With the immediacy that is a distinguishing feature of his intellectual approach, Palladio understood the *quality* (in other words, the specific meaning) that a *fabbrica* designed under these particular circumstances should possess: a patrician's residence should in many ways act as an institutional reference.

Yet, even when tackling a new challenge such as this, Palladio never interrupted the thread of his meditations and research in the discipline on which he concentrated his creative energy. This becomes clear when we recognise the continuous thread that is established between the *invenzione* he intended to formulate for Montagnana and for Piombino, and the solutions that he had tried out, entirely experimentally, in the *fabbrica* he had begun to build in Vicenza for Girolamo Chiericati.

When he designed these *case,* he discarded the solution he had previously adopted for other *case in villa,* which involved arranging the domestic functions on three separate levels, with the *commodità* or services on the ground floor, reception rooms on the first floor, and storage areas on the *piano di sopra.* He also abandoned the decision not to use *ornamenti.* After all, if a *fabbrica* in a residential area was to perform a function that could to some extent be considered public – welcoming the citizens who wished to meet the patrician to plead causes brought before the Venetian magistrates, or to sign contracts, taking advantage of the notary public who nearly always accompanied him – then the ground floor, where these visits took place, was no longer a purely private space.

This ground floor had to have a dignity – and with that, a ceiling height – that was not inferior to that of a *piano nobile.* But (and this was the important innovation compared to the ground floor of the Chiericati *casa*) it had to have a large central room: in this case a square space divided by four columns, that recalled the *exemplum* of a classical tetrastyle *sala* here on the ground floor. [97] [98] [99] [100]

This *invenzione* was not only dictated by the adoption of a model of *casa* with two *piani nobili,* it also called for innovation in the internal connections of the *casa* (a feature which was reduced to a minimum in houses with only one *piano nobile*). In the composition of the *fabbrica* Palladio therefore introduced two stairs that were "well-lit, spacious and comfortable to walk up".[12] Far from being mere connections, because of their symmetry and shape, these are architectural innovations that transform the very nature of an aristocratic residence.

The use of exterior *ornamenti* on these *fabbriche* – no matter how "poor" the material, namely brick – is sufficient to demonstrate that, with these *case,* the Venetians themselves were ready to seek a less austere way of conceiving an extraurban residence, a decade after the early experiments in Bagnolo and Piazzola.

Palladio did not miss the opportunity offered to him by the "regal" rank of the family to return to the idea of advancing the central body of the *fabbrica* that had so strikingly characterised both the façade of Palazzo Thiene and the first proposal for the façade of *casa* Chiericati in Vicenza.

96

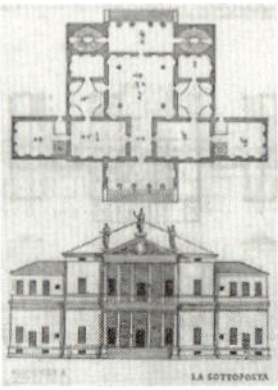

97

98

In Piombino Dese, this advancement of the central body of the *fabbrica* takes the form of a superimposed double loggia embellished with a frontispiece, but the flanks are still closed by a wall on both levels. This *invenzione* therefore opened a line of research that substantially innovated, in conceptual rather than formal terms, the type of loggia that had been developed somewhat laboriously in the first *case di villa* "ordinate" or designed by Palladio.

The extension that Palladio stamped on Cornaro's *casa* was evidently a device that allowed more *commodità* to be positioned on a ground floor that otherwise – because it was given over to official functions – would not have been able to contain the domestic activities essential for such an important family. But it also gives the façade a breadth – which recalls the front of Palazzo Thiene and of Chiericati's *casa* – that would offer valid support to sustain, in compositional terms, the peremptory *novitas* of the projecting central body of the *fabbrica* (even if this body with all its columns has an almost ethereal quality).

It is interesting to note that Palladio certainly discussed with Francesco Pisani – the friendly and dynamic patrician who had been the first to ask Palladio to build him an extraurban *fabbrica* – the compositional decisions that he himself had elaborated for the construction of Cornaro's *casa* in Piombino. [101]

In Montagnana, Palladio had not envisaged advancing the central body with superimposed loggias, or extending the body of the building sideways, because this *casa* for Pisani was bordered by roads on two sides. A reiteration of the proposals formulated in Piombino could only be conceived virtually in Montagnana, which is what Palladio did when he published the design for it in his *Second Book*.

He uses shading so that the system of loggias on the main façade appears to protrude (while the columns and frontispiece above the virtual upper loggia actually adhere to the wall of the façade); and he invents a brilliant, and unconventional, solution to provide service structures for the *casa*.

99

100

Because he could not attach any structure to the *casa* on its western side, due to the public road that borders it there, he envisaged the construction of a building on the other side of the road, connected to the *casa* by a bridge, at the level of the upper *piano nobile.* (In practice, the kitchen for Francesco Pisani's *casa* would have been on the other side of a public road, and meals would have been brought to the patrician's table via an elevated passage supported by a triumphal arch). This solution, which can legitimately be described as extravagant, would obviously have been replicated on the other side of the *casa* to the east, in keeping with the principle of repetition, based on the axis of symmetry, that is such a persistent feature of Palladio's compositional process.

These comments are sufficient to show how firmly established relations between the architect and his patrician clients had already become by the early 1550s. It also increases the significance of the fact that none of them – neither Barbaro, nor Foscari, nor the Cornaro family, nor Francesco Pisani – thought of starting to build a *casa* for himself in Venice, drawing on Palladio's proven expertise. They were all held back, it seems, by a sort of sacrosanct notion of their Venetian home, which they evidently regarded as the bedrock and symbol of their family identity – each for their own reasons.

Daniele Barbaro because his *casa* in San Vitale, owned *in fraterna* with Marcantonio, had been the home of the great Ermolao in the previous century, and had been modernised by Francesco Barbaro, one of the most distinguished intellectuals and politicians to grace Venetian public life in the first half of the fifteenth century.

The Foscari brothers because their *casa* – that *fabbrica* that stood *in volta de Canal,* at the curve of the Grand Canal, and surpassed "all the others in the city for its site and its size" (to quote Francesco Sansovino) – had been built a century earlier by Doge Francesco as a "monument" to himself (as one contemporary intellectual had highlighted in a pompous ode).

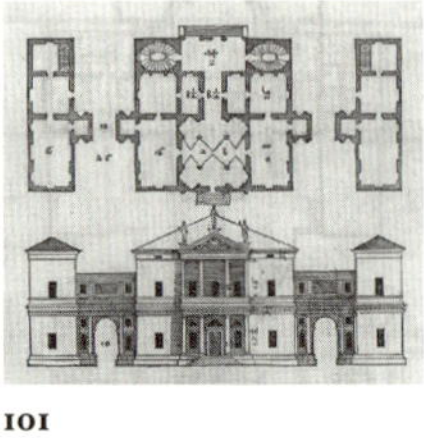

101

102

103

Lastly, Giorgio Cornaro because, when the inheritance was divided, he had been nominated as the family member, one of the sons of the great Zorzi, who was bequeathed the *casa* in which Caterina, Queen of Cyprus, was born.

But, even if Palladio's patrons had no intention of building themselves a new *casa* in Venice, they still pondered the question of the appropriate architectural language to be used when building a *casa* in Venice for an influential patrician family. All of them – taught by the "lesson" that Andrea Gritti had given them when he energetically expressed his indignation at the ostentatious display of wealth by some patricians in their building projects – could only criticise that form of "Romanism" that Jacopo Sansovino, on one hand, and Michele Sanmicheli, on the other, demonstrated when they built the *case* for Giorgio Cornaro's two brothers, one in San Maurizio and one in San Polo, and which Michele Sanmicheli had also displayed when he was commissioned by the Grimani family to build a large *casa* in San Luca. [102] [103]

The form of these *fabbriche*, which were conceived by drawing on the repertoire of architectural syntax that had been developed in Rome at the Court of the della Rovere pope and the two Medici popes who followed, was not acceptable to Palladio or to his patrician patrons for related, but different, reasons. These can be summed up briefly as follows: for the members of the Venetian oligarchy, they were unacceptable because those popes had proved in many ways and on many occasions hostile to Venice, to its republican government and to the fact that it professed to be a secular State. While for Palladio, this manipulation of the Latin sources undertaken in Rome, in the melting pot of different interests that had converged and amalgamated there, had moulded the "ancient world" to the cultural and political demands of the Church, undermining the *virtue* and *greatness* that were, in his opinion, the true essence of ancient Romanism.

It is probably in the context of his meditations on these questions that Palladio developed two *invenzioni* [104] [105] which helped

104

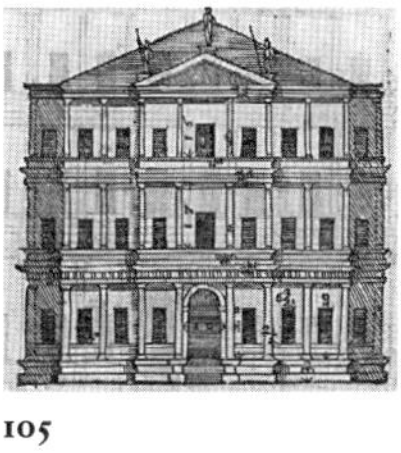

105

to outline, above all in his own mind, how the construction of the two projects in San Maurizio and San Luca could be approached.

In these projects – which he published in his *Second Book,* as if to highlight their theoretical significance – Palladio showed how the layout of a *casa* could be freely conceived even if it occupied irregularly shaped plots (which were almost inevitable in the urban fabric of Venice), and that, within such a *fabbrica,* it was possible to design spaces that were remarkably "Renaissance" in character. But this was the corollary of a more general assumption. With these two designs he intended to underline that any *case* to be built in Venice, even the most grandiose, must maintain on the outside a *facies* that was as uniform as possible (in this case a conventional superimposition of architectural orders), so as to respect the ancient laws that obliged members of the Venetian ruling class not to jeopardise, by introducing individual approaches, the unity of the patrician class that was an essential prerequisite for the very survival of the republican regime.

THE MAGISTRATO DEI BENI INCULTI

While these considerations were maturing, a debate begun some time earlier was being conducted strenuously in the austere rooms of the Doge's Palace and finally reached its conclusion. It regarded the most opportune steps to take, under the supervision of the public magistracies, in order to start reclaiming the large areas of land on the Terraferma that the Republic's daring operation to regulate the rivers had now freed from the floods or wetlands that had prevented their efficient exploitation as farmland in the past.

It was a topic with which Palladio was all too familiar. Not only because he had worked with the Pisani and Contarini families who had – presciently, it might be said – tackled the problem of reclamation in Bagnolo and Piazzola. But also because he knew Alvise Cornaro (the enterprising character whom Cardinal Pisani – Daniele Barbaro's uncle, as was mentioned earlier – had unexpectedly hired as "governor" of the Bishop of Padua's vast estates, only to dismiss him summarily when he finally concluded that Cornaro had been administering them in his own interest *dentibus et unguibus*).

Similar experience induced the Venetian Signoria – which had a vested interest in increasing the agricultural yield of the land within the boundaries of the Republic – to create a new magistracy with the specific task of promoting, or imposing, a general reclamation of any land not yet under cultivation, or *inculti* (uncultivated), as would have been said at the time. This meant that the Venetian patricians could no longer limit themselves to asserting their presence at the heart of their estates: they had to take on their management, in other words they had to become entrepreneurs themselves.

THE PROJECT FOR LEONARDO EMO ON HIS VILLA AT FANZOLO

Leonardo Emo was the patrician who understood, more fully and more rapidly than any other, the significance of what was in many ways an epoch-making debate in the Doge's Palace and, anticipating its conclusion, decided to embark on an intensive plan to reorganise the lands he owned in the Trevigiano, not far from Fanzolo.

The expertise that Palladio brought to this programme (which might be described, without overstatement, as heroic, echoing an expression that Daniele Barbaro would later use) was extraordinarily important; not merely for his elaboration of the ideological aspects of the debate (an area where Palladio was always cautious), but for his remarkable capacity to understand the ambition that motivated his patron and then translate this goal so explicitly and eloquently into architecture.

He confronted the theme with the tone and determination of a Roman general embarking on a centuriation process. As the reference point for his plan of action, he took a Roman consular road, running in a straight line to the south of the Emo estates (a road that "goes to Hungary" he explains, referring to the Via Postumia).[13] At right angles to this axis, he built a new road that ran north in a perfectly straight line for a few kilometres. [106]

It is Palladio who draws our attention to the reasons for making the roads absolutely straight: this would afford greater safety,

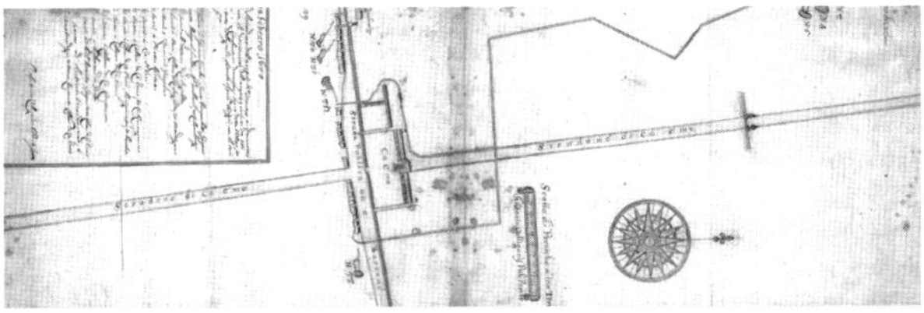

106

he writes, to anyone travelling on them but would also allow them "to see a great distance … and observe much of the country", an activity that "relieves one greatly from tiredness" and generates a mood of "great satisfaction and delight". The importance of the road was further highlighted, also in compositional terms, as a component of the physical layout of the land, which it traversed "slightly above the surrounding fields", by the fact that it was flanked on both sides by trees which, he writes, "cheer us up with their greenness" and provide "extremely comfortable shade".[14]

After running in a straight line for a few hundred metres, the road leads to a virtual tetrastyle pronaos – an architectural feature that can be seen from a great distance because of the simplicity of its design. This pronaos stands at the compositional centre of the façade of a *fabbrica,* the owner's house, lying on an axis of symmetry that coincides with the axis of the road. The road leads up to the level of the pronaos – which is higher than the surrounding countryside and the level of the road – by a ramp that is as wide as the road. [107]

The road continues beyond the house – still on the same axis – across an extensive garden area (measuring some twenty-five hectares), before resuming its function as a means of access to the reclaimed fields and running for another few hundred metres to the northern boundary of the Emo property.

Turning to the *casa,* we find that its internal layout complies with the precepts approved by Trissino in his extraurban residence at Cricoli. On either side – orthogonal to the axis of the road (and also to the house) – lie two building wings used for storage and shelter, both of which are functions that enhance the efficient running of the estate and at the same time emphasise the role of the house as the management centre, as it were. Whoever lives in the house, namely the patrician, assumes the role of entrepreneur: the manager to whom every business decision must be referred.

It is no coincidence that there is something schematic about the architecture of the house, as is evident from the repeated

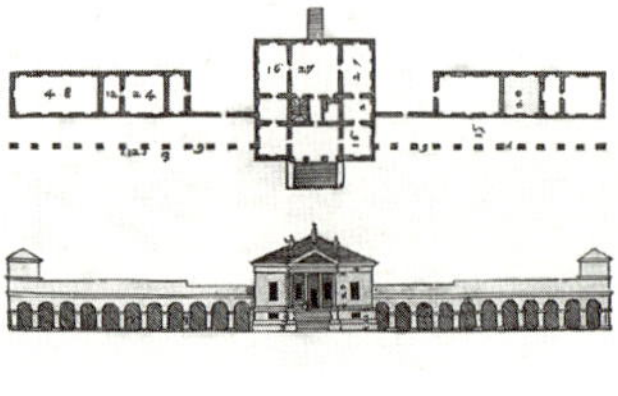

107

sequences of arcades forming the porticoes of the farm outbuildings. It wants to be assertive and does not deny its didactic tone. No display of *ornamenti* should detract from the purely conceptual substance of the Emo family's choice. That a *Signore* – rather than merely certifying his presence at the heart of his property – should deliberately place himself, his person as well as his image, among the *villani* and paid workers, among the cows and chickens, the dung-hills and the tuns of bubbling must, is not particularly surprising for Venetians who, for centuries, had sailed the seas on vessels crowded with sailors, ship-boys and galley slaves; but in the city-dwelling civilisation of the Po valley, it was regarded as nothing short of revolutionary.

To gain a clearer idea of the programme Palladio devised for Leonardo Emo, we must take a step backward to the time when such an innovative proposal first germinated, and one forward to the moment when it would be developed to such an intellectually radical formula that it encountered the limits of its practicability in the context of Venetian culture in the mid sixteenth century.

SETTING A PRECEDENT AT ANGARANO

It was for Giacomo Angarano, as we saw earlier, that Palladio traced a straight, wide road across his estate, from the hills to the south of the *casa* to the large bend formed by the river Brenta ("a river full of excellent fish") to the north.[15] Here, for the first time, Palladio placed "cellars, granaries ... stables and dovecotes", namely farming activities, beside the owner's *casa*. It is worth looking in closer detail at the structure of this proposal.

"Le cose di villa", in other words the equipment and buildings used for farming, were relegated to two dedicated courtyards on either side of a large court surrounded by porticoes, inside which the *casa* stood austerely, like a temple within its enclosure. In short, at Angarano there were still traces of the classification of functions based on traditional hierarchical principles, which did not explicitly, almost ostentatiously, reveal the novelty of this new way of managing rural estates.

THE PROJECT FOR MARIO REPETA AT THE VILLA OF CAMPIGLIA

Palladio's decision to move in this direction differed in every respect when he built a house at Campiglia for Mario Repeta, an intellectual willing to challenge the conformism of his day and who accommodated visiting intellectuals in whichever room – depending on the theme of its decoration – was dedicated to "the *virtù* to which their dispositions appear to him most inclined".[16] [108]

Here, too, Palladio built a courtyard.

In the centre of the courtyard, along the axis of symmetry of the composition, where one might expect to find the house, there was nothing, or, to be more precise, there was a void. Instead, on the two sides of the courtyard, acquiring harmony through symmetry, were the farming activities on one side and the *Signore*'s residence on the other. Moreover, "the part lived in by the owner and that for farm use are on the same level." In this way, as Palladio adds in order to ensure that he is fully understood, "what [the owner's] house loses in grandeur by not being more imposing than the farm, the farm gains in requisite ornament and dignity by being equal to the owner's house."[17]

The conceptual experiment is carried to its farthest limit, a fact that is emphasised by the appearance of loggias (even on two levels) at the corners of the *fabbrica* (a feature never again used by Palladio): loggias that clearly served to add lightness – one might almost say to disguise – the mediaeval looking towers built at the corners of the building in order to emphasise the feudal rights pertaining to Repeta's property.

If Venetian patricians looked askance at the conduct of this brilliant Vicentine aristocrat, there was no similar bias against the proposals first made by Angarano and then elaborated in exemplary fashion by Leonardo Emo (or, more specifically, by his sons given that Leonardo also died prematurely). This becomes clear if we consider the affair involving Palladio's most proven Venetian contact: Daniele Barbaro, together with his brother Marcantonio.

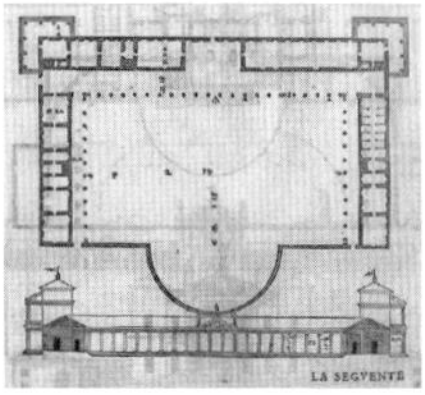

108

82 Paolo Caliari, known as Veronese, *Daniele Barbaro*, c. 1566

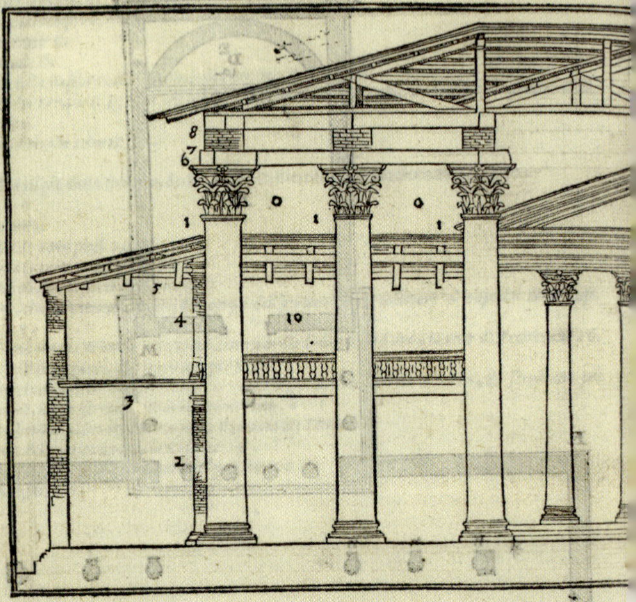

220 LIBRO

Dello Erario, Carcere, & della Curia come si deono ordinare. Cap. 11.

L'Erario, il Carcere, & la Curia deono esser congiunti al Foro, ma in modo, che la grandezza del compartimento di quelle risponda al Foro, & specialmente la Curia si deue fare secondo la dignità de gli habitanti, ouero della città. se ella sarà quadrata, quanto hauerà di larghezza, aggiugnendoui la metà si farà l'altezza. ma se la forma sarà piu lunga, che larga, egli si porrà insieme la lunghezza & la larghezza, & di tutta la somma si piglierà la metà, & si darà all'altezza sotto la trauatura. Oltra di questo si deono circondare intorno i pareti nel mezo di cornicioni, o di legname, o di stucco. ilche quando non fusse fatto, ne uenirebbe, che la uoce de disputanti troppo alzata, non sarebbe udita da quelli, che odeno le cause. ma quando d'intorno i pareti ci saranno i cornicioni, la uoce ritardata da quelli prima, che sia nello aere disipata, perueniràà alle orecchie de gli auditori.

Erario

84 Facade and cross section of the Basilica and the Temple of Fano, *I Dieci Libri dell'Architettura, tradotti e commentati da Daniele Barbaro,* 1567

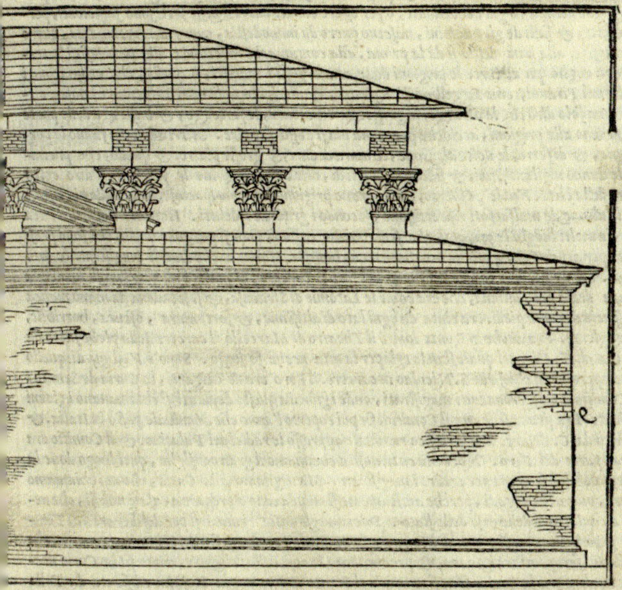

Erario è luogo doue si ripone il Tesoro, & il dinaro publico. i Romani nello Erario conseruauano tutti gli atti publici, & decreti del Senato. i libri elefantini, ne i quali erano descritte le trentacinque tribu di Iuda. Dice Suetonio, che Cesare abbruciò tutti i libri delle obliganze, che egli ritrouò nello Erario, per leuare ogni occasione di odio. Come esser debbia lo Erario, & il carcere non dice Vitru. perche sono parte del Foro, che hanno seco le loro necessità, che si rimetteno al giudicio dello Architetto, & però de i Granai publici, dello Erario, delle armerie, del nauale, del Fondaco, & della Cecca, non dice altro. Deono queste cose esser collocate in luoghi sicurissimi, & prontissimi, circondate d'alte mura, & guardate dalle forze, & dall'insidie de i seditiosi cittadini. Noi hauemo in Venetia i Granari, & la Cecca congiunte alla piazza. le armerie nel palazzo istesso, l'Arzana sicura guardata, & fornita, se altra ue n'è o sia stata al mondo. La Cecca sopra la piazza, opera del Sansouino. iui si batte, & cimenta l'oro, & l'argento: & si conseruano i depositi, & si riduceno alcuni magistrati deputati alla Cecca, sì per la cura delle monete, come per li depositi, & per l'uno, & l'altro conto c'è una marauigliosa somma di scudi. Le prigioni similmente sono sotto il pallazzo, alquale è congiunta la piu ricca che bene intesa chiesa nella testa della spaciosa piazza. Anticamente erano tre sorti di prigioni, l'una di quelli, che erano suiati, & immodesti, che si teneuano, accioche fussero ammaestrati. hora questa si dà

ai pazzi

88 Antonio Foscari, Collage of Elevation of an unbuilt *fabbrica,* presumably Villa Foscari (identification proposed by Antonio Foscari) and survey by Erik Forssman of Villa Foscari La Malcontenta

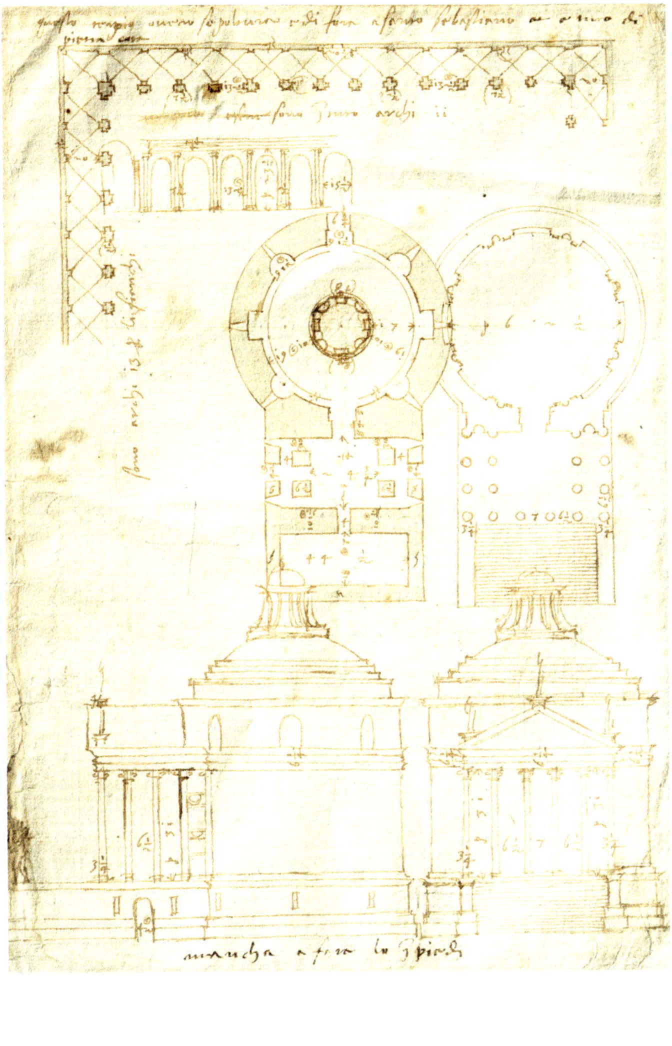

90 *Mausoleum of Romulus on the Via Appia,* Rome

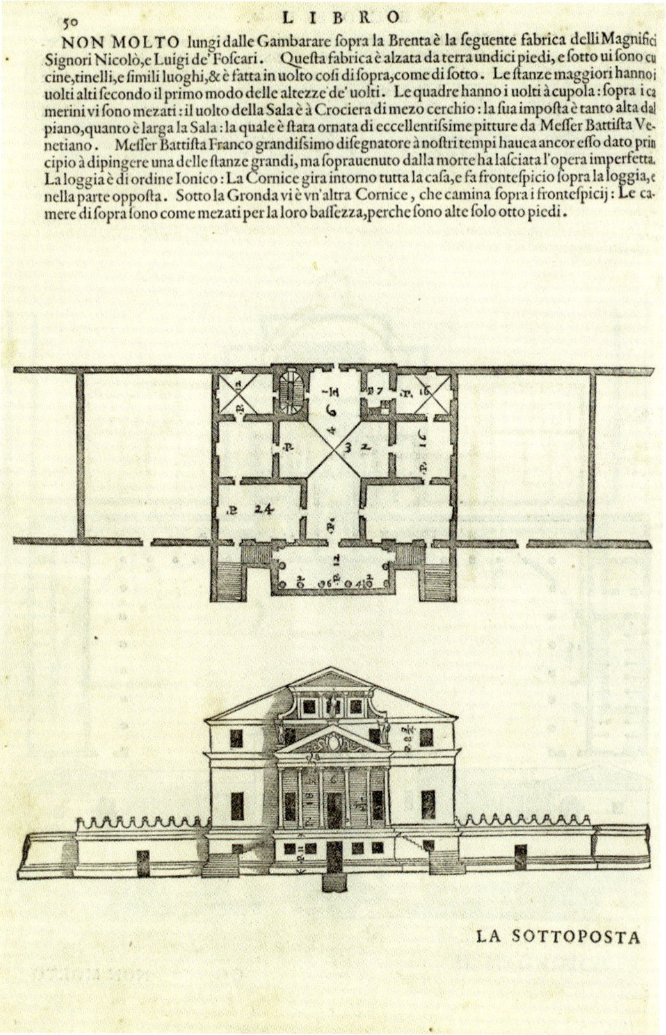

50 LIBRO

NON MOLTO lungi dalle Gambarare ſopra la Brenta è la ſeguente fabrica delli Magnifici Signori Nicolò, e Luigi de' Foſcari. Queſta fabrica è alzata da terra undici piedi, e ſotto ui ſono cu cine, tinelli, e ſimili luoghi, & è fatta in uolto coſi di ſopra, come di ſotto. Le ſtanze maggiori hanno i uolti alti ſecondo il primo modo delle altezze de' uolti. Le quadre hanno i uolti à cupola: ſopra i ca merini vi ſono mezati: il uolto della Sala è à Crociera di mezo cerchio: la ſua impoſta è tanto alta dal piano, quanto è larga la Sala: la quale è ſtata ornata di eccellentiſsime pitture da Meſſer Battiſta Ve- netiano. Meſſer Battiſta Franco grandiſsimo diſegnatore à noſtri tempi hauea ancor eſſo dato prin cipio à dipingere una delle ſtanze grandi, ma ſoprauenuto dalla morte ha laſciata l'opera imperfetta. La loggia è di ordine Ionico: La Cornice gira intorno tutta la caſa, e fa fronteſpicio ſopra la loggia, e nella parte oppoſta. Sotto la Gronda vi è vn'altra Cornice, che camina ſopra i fronteſpicij: Le ca- mere di ſopra ſono come mezati per la loro baſſezza, perche ſono alte ſolo otto piedi.

LA SOTTOPOSTA

91 *Villa Foscari*, Malcontenta di Mira (Venice)

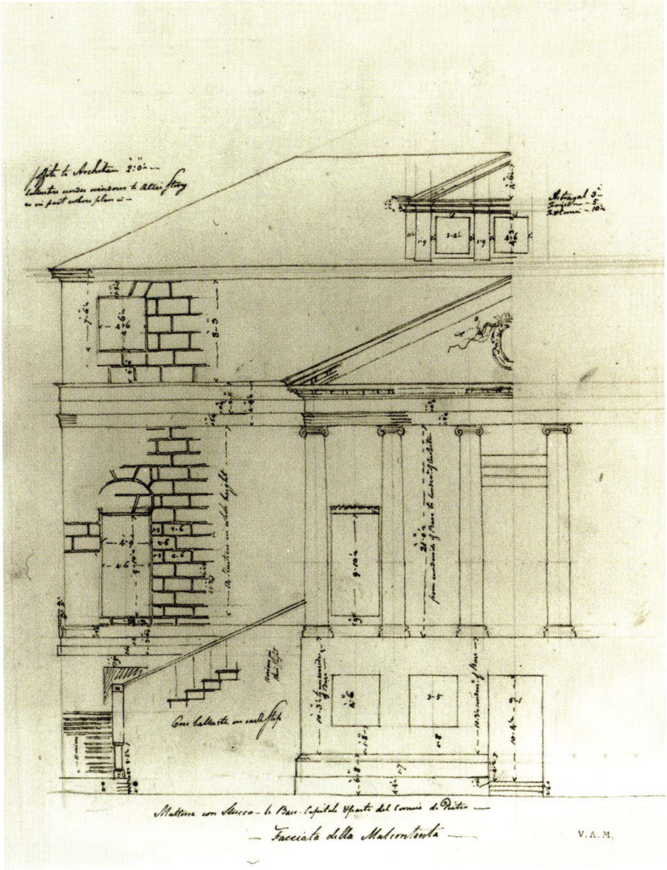

92 Richard Norris, *Facade of the Malcontenta,* 19th century

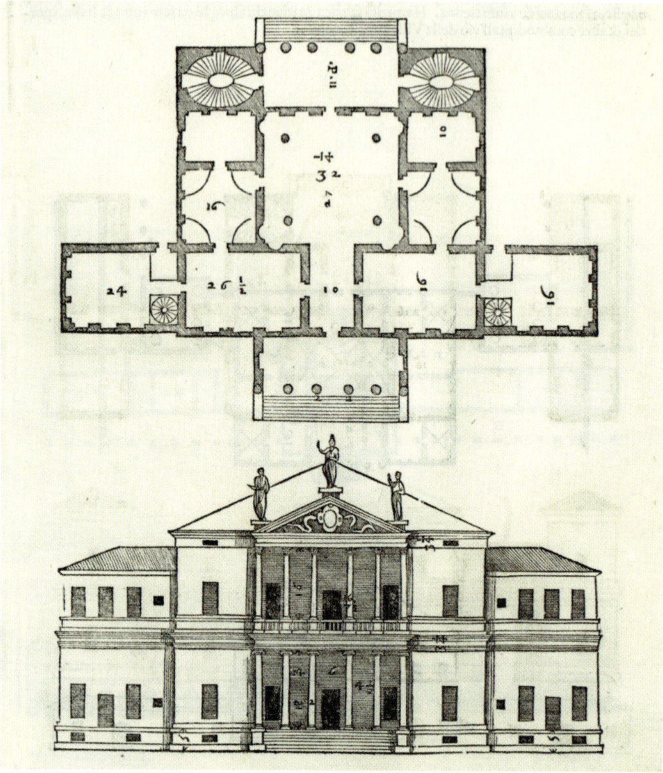

97 *Villa Cornaro* (detail), Piombino Dese (Padua)
101 *Villa Pisani* (detail), Montagnana (Padua)

The characteristics of the site chosen to build a *casa* on the *villa* of Maser are in themselves enough to convince us that the two Barbaro brothers – spurred on, one might imagine, by Palladio's enthusiasm – immediately considered the idea of evoking the physical setting of the great Roman temples in Tivoli and Praeneste by creating a series of terracing and ramps.

Nothing would have been more suitable for an operation of this kind – in the immense flatness of the Veneto plains – than the gently sloping hills rising to the north of the vast country estates owned by the two Venetian patricians.

If he had been able to embark on a study of this specific theme, Palladio would have transferred to the present, to the practical reality of the building site, the intuitions that had been sparked by his explorations of the Roman ruins only a few months earlier. He would have used every argument to convince Daniele Barbaro and his brother Marcantonio to follow this approach: among others, that the temples of Tivoli and Praeneste had both been built during the Republican era of Roman history and that evoking them – provided this was done with the theoretical precision he was able to guarantee – was therefore not ideologically incompatible with the Republican identity that Venice sought to confer upon its Terraferma possessions.

However, Daniele and Marcantonio Barbaro lacked the courage to embrace such an intriguing proposal, the former because any reference to pagan worship would have been incompatible with his ecclesiastical rank, and the latter because he did not want to jeopardise the *cursus honorum* he had embarked on with such determination and which would soon lead him to the highest state office.

As a result the two brothers focused on the models offered by Giacomo Angarano (the Vicentine nobleman whom Daniele had had the opportunity of meeting – according to our interpretation – before leaving for London) and by the Emo at Fanzolo.

Following their example, Daniele and Marcantonio Barbaro also marked out a long, straight, tree-lined road, running right through the estate they owned in Maser. The last stretch of the road runs up a slight slope and ends in front of the house.

Following the logic that inspired the definition of the building project, it is not surprising that the form of this house should correspond to that built for the Angarano family, which Palladio outlined in the drawing published in the *Second Book*.

It was small, with a distinctive façade featuring a portico with four Ionic columns (in the drawings published by Palladio it appears to jut out, thanks to the use of clever hatching, whereas in reality the columns adhere to the façade). This portico has a majestic frontispiece, with the family coat of arms in the centre; it also boasts a display of large acroterial statues. Inside, too, the typology of the house broadly corresponded to that designed for Angarano; it differed only in the decision not to include two square rooms and instead to create a single cross-vaulted room in the centre. The placement of the two symmetrical stairwells also corresponds to the same criterion of distribution. [109]

On the other hand, it is illuminating to note that the model for this country house, which was also equipped with extensive farm buildings, differs from those for the Angarano and Emo families for reasons that could be described as "representational".

The house for the Barbaro brothers does not stand in a courtyard. It emerges from a long alignment – like the one designed for the Emo – projecting towards the plain that stretches out before it. But the straight body of the building – which is also marked by a series of arcades and a block at either end (like at Fanzolo) – does not really qualify as an outbuilding. Instead of facing south on an axis running parallel to the house (as in Angarano), the farm buildings lie to the north, nestling into the hillside so that they disappear from sight.

In this way some of the functional and ideological aspects of the two models used at Angarano and Fanzolo were acknowledged but were weakened, so to speak, by the perception of the overlapping functions inherent in a house on a *villa* to be considered as the centre of a working farm.

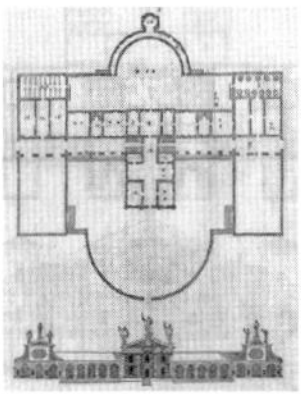

109

Clearly under pressure from his clients' requests that he could not refuse, the astuteness with which Palladio also resolved the problem of the size of the house is illuminating. If it was "small" for Angarano (as Giorgio Vasari did not hesitate to note), it would have been even more so for two such influential figures (in particular after two rooms on the *piano nobile* had been sacrificed to make way for the cruciform-vaulted room that becomes the spatial fulcrum inside the house).

On the upper floor of the house, Palladio included a series of rooms, not visible from the south (namely to anyone looking at the main façade of the house) because they open onto a terrace created on the north side of the house to take advantage of the sloping site. Morever, at the centre of this terrace he placed an attractive nymphaeum. [110]

Using a particularly brilliant – and in some ways ambiguous – procedure, this created the least Palladian of all Palladio's villas, to use Manfredo Tafuri's words. The result was that Palladio felt somewhat embarrassed by an outcome that did not comply with the conceptual rigour that was the primary goal of his every project. This embarrassment can be clearly sensed by the fact that – when describing the work in his *Second Book* – he says little if anything about its architecture. He restricts himself to describing the evocative presence of the hill and how the land gently slopes down to the valley following the rushing water that gushes from a spring above the house. Lastly, and as though to distract his reader, he describes the conceptual metamorphosis of the water which is transformed from being a natural element when it springs from earth into a mythological element when it flows into the nymphaeum behind the house, a human element when it is used in domestic activities, then a productive one when used to fill the fishponds and the drinking troughs, before finally being used to irrigate the orchard in front of the house where the slope runs gently down to the plain.

It may perhaps have been a sense of regret at this failed opportunity that prompted Palladio to accept the insistent request of

110

a patrician who wanted to build himself a house in Polesine, thus giving him an excuse to return, in abstract terms, to the subject of Rome's ancient temples sited on a hillside.

FEDERICO BADOER'S HOUSE AT FRATTA POLESINE

Federico Badoer did not want his house to be an institutional landmark for the inhabitants of Fratta Polesine, the village it faces on the other side of a watercourse, nor the centre of a farm. In short, perhaps out of self-respect, he did not want to replicate the model developed by the Cornaro and the Pisani, on the one hand, nor that suggested by Leonardo Emo, a close relative, on the other. [111]

To Badoer the *casa di villa* was a structure devoted to leisure purposes (a setting where thanks to "the exercise that one usually takes on foot or on horseback, the body will more readily maintain its healthiness and strength"), a place where one could be "visited by brilliant friends".[18] To give an example, if there had to be an outbuilding for animals beside the owner's house, then it should not be a proper stable but a provisional one used for short periods by horses led there from the larger outbuildings to await the pleasure of the Signore, or for his guests' horses during their short stay at the house. This is evident from the fact that there is no hayloft in the drawing published by Palladio in the *Second Book*. If a symmetrical annexe were added to the stable, its doorway should not be large enough for a cart or a barrel to pass through, thereby precluding any rural function.

It was in a building of this kind that Palladio used curved porticoes, embellished with the Tuscan order (as at Angarano), which Vasari described as "most beautiful", but also – and not by chance – "whimsical": it is particularly strange that, against a landscape as unremittingly flat as the Polesine, and in such a delightful setting, Palladio used forms that were ideally taken from an example like the Temple of Fortune at Praeneste, or the temple dedicated to Hercules Victor in Tivoli. [112]

(It is interesting to note how Palladio, who was always careful to note criticisms of his works, replied to Vasari's comment when he published the project in 1570. On the one hand, he wrote that

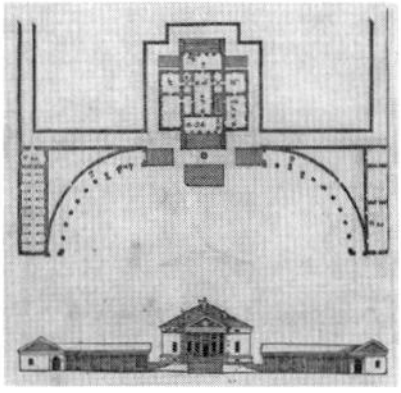

111

112

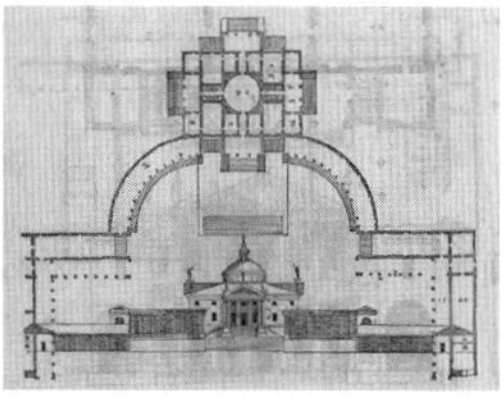

113

the site for the building would be "quite high" – something that was clearly untrue – and on the other he showed Federico Badoer's house with a higher base course, alluding to the physical configuration of the sites for which those curved porticoes had been designed in antique times. What was more, he tried to characterise his work as an expression of the *pax veneziana* because it stood – in his opinion – on the foundations of a castle that had been razed to the ground as an affirmation of the Republican regime.)

A PROJECT IN MELEDO FOR FRANCESCO AND LUDOVICO TRISSINO

Palladio returned to a subject that he considered particularly fascinating when he found a patron who owned "a hill … in the middle of a great plain": this "stunning" site,[19] whose physical setting made it particularly suitable for an evocation of the *exemplum* provided by ancient sanctuaries, culminating in a circular temple on the summit that was reached in stages through a succession of spectacular architectural events, including the same line of curved porticoes that Palladio had used as a pretext at Fratta Polesine. [113]

It is not surprising that the visionary architecture which Palladio designed on this occasion was never actually realised. However, it is particularly moving to visit the only room that was built (the one that forms the base of the "tower" that would have formed the southern end of this huge architectural complex). It is a square room with a vault decorated with grotesque frescoes; on entering through a smaller opening, one can still see the hinged leaves of a wooden door which was perfectly Palladian. It was here, beside a large fireplace that can only be described as *licentioso,* that Francesco and Ludovico Trissino listened, with a growing desire for lasting fame, as the architect expounded a project they would never have the courage to build. [114]

A CASA WITH FOUR LOGGIAS FOR A "MAN OF THE CHURCH"

Having realised the impossibility of recreating the *exemplum* of the antique temples starting from the bottom, namely from the hillside, as he had tried to do at Meledo when another opportunity arose to project a house on a "small hill that is easy to ascend"[20], Palladio started to build directly on the hilltop. It is possible to recognise in this central-plan edifice, cleverly reduced to a quadrangular form, the four-fronted typology of the temple that he supposed stood on the summit of the sanctuary dedicated to Hercules Victor at Tivoli. [115]

La Rotonda is so famous that it is unnecessary to describe its architecture, even merely in outline. We need only observe that Palladio, being well aware that a work of this kind was foreign to the set of political considerations he himself had often used as grounds for his choices, also abandoned any idea of describing the extraordinary *novitas* of the building, and the short passage dedicated to the project in his *Second Book* is deliberately vague. [116]

In order to legitimise such an anomalous but at the same time disruptive architectural outcome, he focused on the standing and authority of the patron, something that he generally did not do with such precision. Then, as if to distract attention from the edifice, he described the site on which it stands and the panorama it enjoys. This small hill "is surrounded," he writes, "by other attractive hills, which give the appearance of a large Theatre, and all are cultivated and abound with excellent fruits and very good vines." However, "because [the site] enjoys the most beautiful vistas on every side, some of which are restricted, others more extensive, and yet others which end at the horizon", an edifice would be built here with loggias "on all four sides".[21] [117] [118]

The "discovery" of the hillsides, the hills and this small hill, rising "a quarter of a mile" from the centre of Vicenza, have carried us forward in time and far from the flat stretches of brackish water in the lagoon. This digression can hardly be said to have interrupted the flow of the argument given that all these options were already present in the mind of an architect like Palladio, "inflamed by profound studies".[22] But the time has come to return to Venice, to the political arena in which Palladio chose to work, at the cost of giving up supervising the works to rebuild the loggias of the Palazzo della Ragione in Vicenza.

The reason why Palladio did not stand out against the Barbaro brothers at Maser (merely noting in his *Second Book* that "the

114

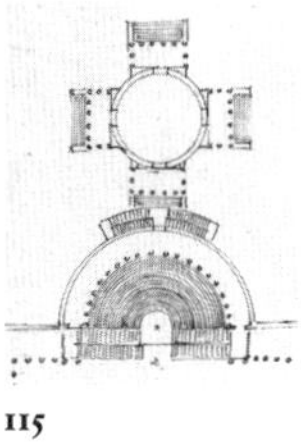

115

architect is frequently obliged to accommodate himself to the wishes of those who are paying rather than attending to what he should"[23]) was because he needed their support in order to obtain, as he hoped he would, an official role as architect within the institutional regime of the Republic.

REBUFFED BY THE SALT MAGISTRACY

However, the support of all the patricians for whom he had already worked was not enough, in terms of accreditation, to persuade the Salt Magistracy – the leading financial magistracy that had announced a competition to engage a *proto* who would manage the numerous operations that came within its administrative remit – to take him on as its director.

It is not hard to understand the perplexity felt by this body when considering his candidature: Palladio had criticised the type of "Romanism" practised by Jacopo Sansovino (who still held the powerful office of *proto* of the Procuratia di San Marco) and Michele Sanmicheli (military engineer in the service of the Republic). But it was not only this that made some see his appearance in Venice as a cause for concern. The disciplinary rigour that he constantly imposed and the way he applied a fully structured architectural language seemed to challenge the limits of a tradition, like that in Venice, which had evolved empirically over centuries, practically exhausting any innovative impulse.

In order to gain a clearer understanding of the significance of this step, it is worth noting that the Salt Magistracy was an extremely important institution in the Republic's administrative system, not only for the prominent role it played in the State's financial policy, but also because it was responsible for the building and management of the Doge's Palace, as well as for the bridge and marketplace at the Rialto that linked the trading centre to the Marcian forum, the hub of political power. In other words, it was responsible for managing parts of the city that were in many ways complementary – both symbolically and functionally – to those within the remit of the Procuratia di San Marco, whose responsibilities covered the Piazza di San Marco, the Doge's

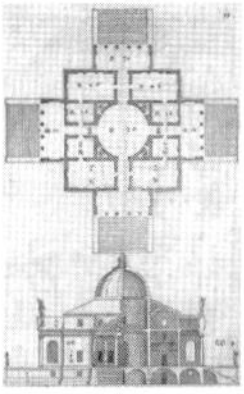

116

117

118

Chapel, and the important pedestrian artery leading from the Piazza to the Rialto.

The significance of this candidature was not lost even on the Procuratori di San Marco: the appearance of an *all'antica* language in the public sphere, inspired by scientific criteria (and backed by the imminent publication of the *Commentaries*), threatened to upset the established balance of the political, intellectual and entrepreneurial scene. What was more, an architectural redefinition of such symbolic structures as the Doge's Palace and the Rialto might be construed as a criticism of, or even a challenge to the criteria that had inspired the *renovatio* of the *platea marciana* which had been underway, not without problems, for the past twenty years or so.

It was almost inevitable that a candidate with these ambitions, who applied for a post announced by such an important magistracy with the backing of a group of patricians that was starting to show signs of a uniform cultural approach, should be overlooked in favour of a technician lacking any specific intellectual accreditation (who would clearly remain subordinate to the established powers).

THE RIALTO BRIDGE PROJECT

It should be added that the project Palladio drew up for the competition announced by the Salt Magistracy a few years earlier (1551) to build a new stone bridge at Rialto had certainly not helped to further his candidature. [119]

When drawing up his proposal Palladio was not concerned whether it would be regarded as provocative given that its construction – had it ever been realised – might have blocked part of the traffic that had navigated the Grand Canal for centuries, including perhaps the Bucintoro, the doge's magnificent vessel that was the emblem of Venice's sovereignty over the waters of the Adriatic.

Palladio had proposed to build a structure based on the model of a bridge he had surveyed on one of his trips to Rome: the bridge built by Augustus at Rimini. He copied it to the letter: with

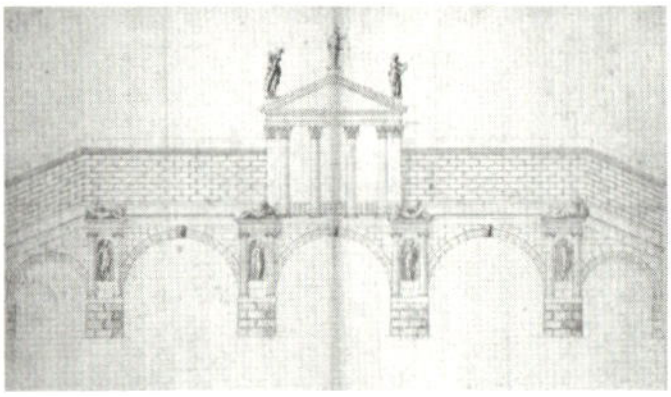

119

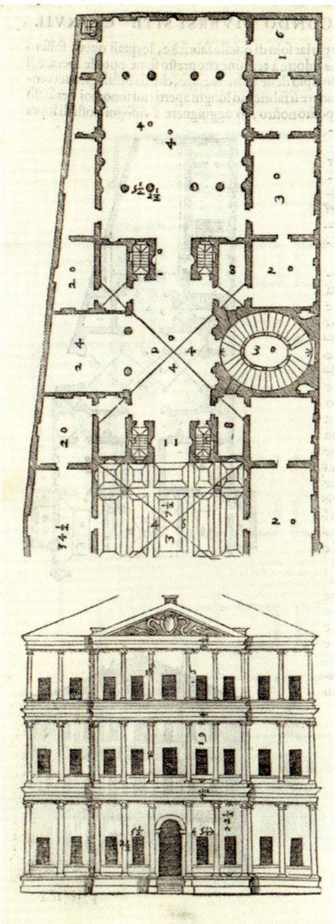

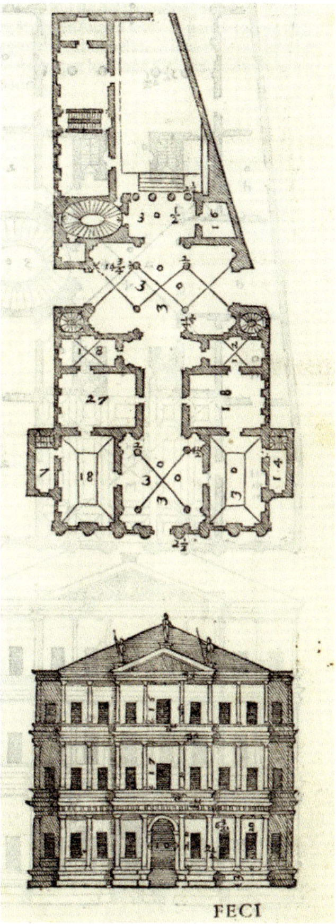

104 *Invenzione for a palazzo* (detail), Venice
105 *Invenzione for a palazzo* (detail), Venice

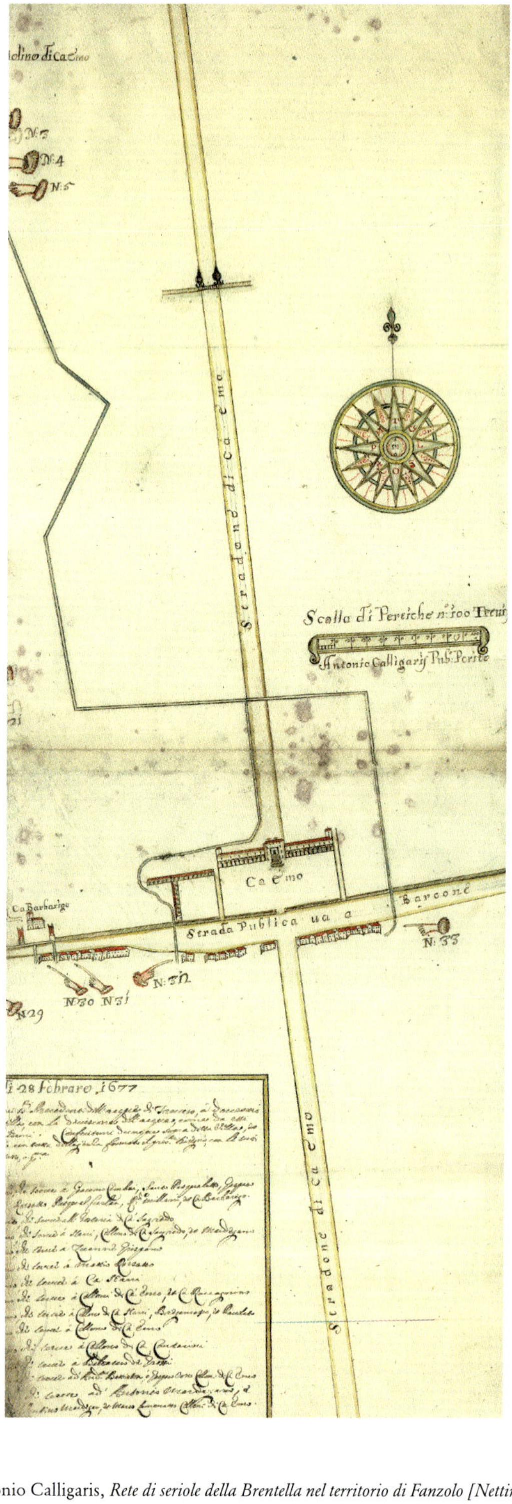

106 Antonio Calligaris, *Rete di seriole della Brentella nel territorio di Fanzolo [Netting Fish in the Brentella Canal near Fanzolo]* (detail)

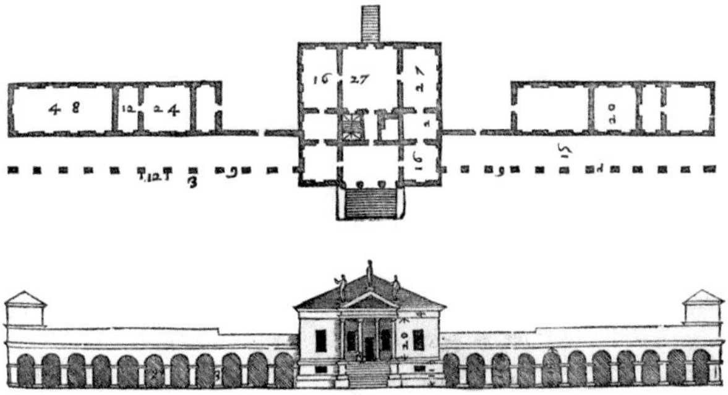

107 *Villa Emo* (edited), Fanzolo (Treviso)

S E C O N D O. 51

LA SOTTOPOSTA fabrica è à Maſera Villa vicina ad Aſolo Caſtello del Triuigiano, di Monſignor Reuerendiſsimo Eletto di Aquileia, e del Magnifico Signor Marc'Antonio fratelli de' Barbari. Quella parte della fabrica, che eſce alquanto in fuori; ha due ordini di ſtanze, il piano di quelle di ſopra è à pari del piano del cortile di dietro, oue è tagliata nel monte rincontro alla caſa vna fontana con infiniti ornamenti di ſtucco, e di pittura. Fa queſta fonte vn laghetto, che ſerue per peſchiera: da queſto luogo partitaſi l'acqua ſcorre nella cucina, & dapoi irrigati i giardini, che ſono dalla deſtra, e ſiniſtra parte della ſtrada, la quale pian piano aſcendendo conduce alla fabrica; fa due peſchiere co i loro beueratori ſopra la ſtrada commune: d'onde partitaſi; adacqua il Bruolo, ilquale è grandiſsimo, e pieno di frutti eccellentiſsimi, e di diuerſe ſeluaticine. La facciata della caſa del padrone hà quattro colonne di ordine Ionico: il capitello di quelle de gli angoli fa fronte da due parti: i quai capitelli come ſi facciano; porrò nel libro de i Tempij. Dall'vna, e l'altra parte ui ſono loggie, le quali nell'eſtremità hanno due colombare, e ſotto quelle ui ſono luoghi da fare i uini, e le ſtalle, e gli altri luoghi per l'vſo di Villa.

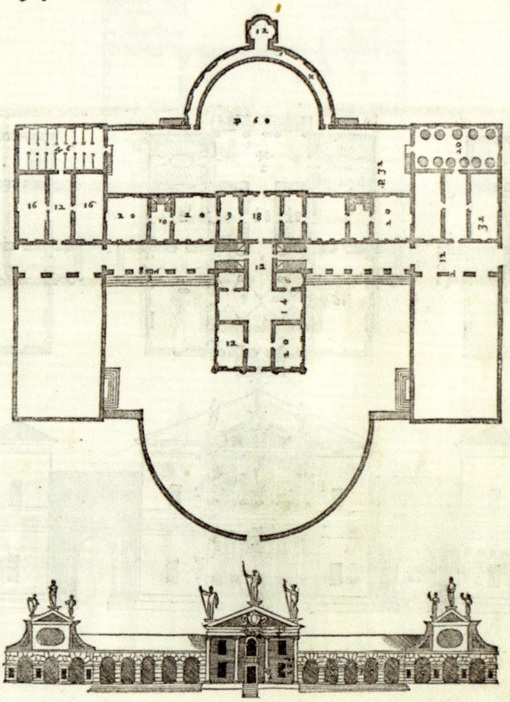

GG 2 LA SEGVENTE

109 *Villa Barbaro,* Maser (Treviso)

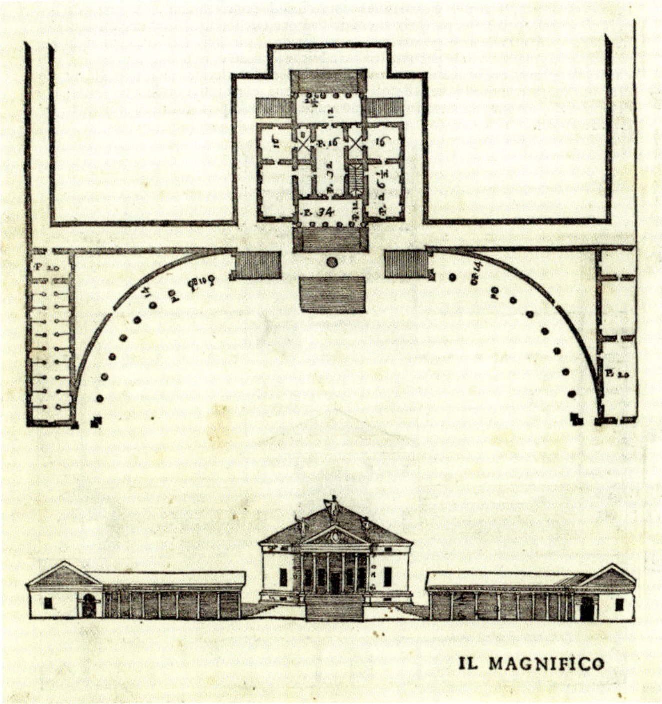

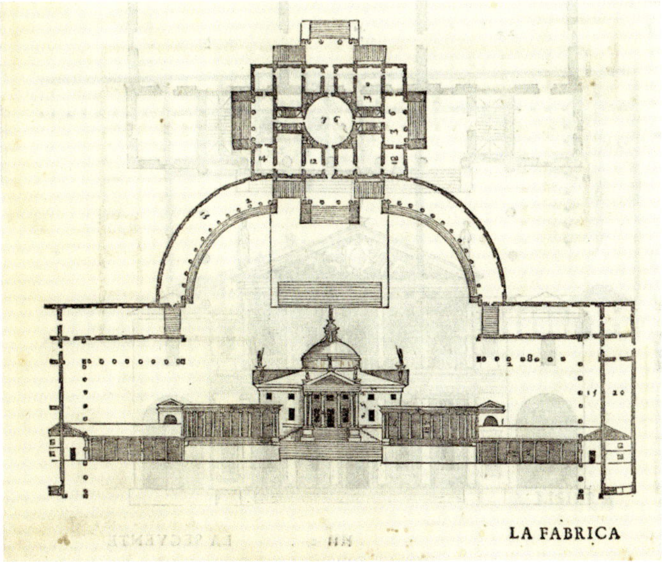

111 *Villa Badoer* (detail), Fratta Polesine (Rovigo)
113 *Villa Trissino* (detail), Meledo (Vicenza)

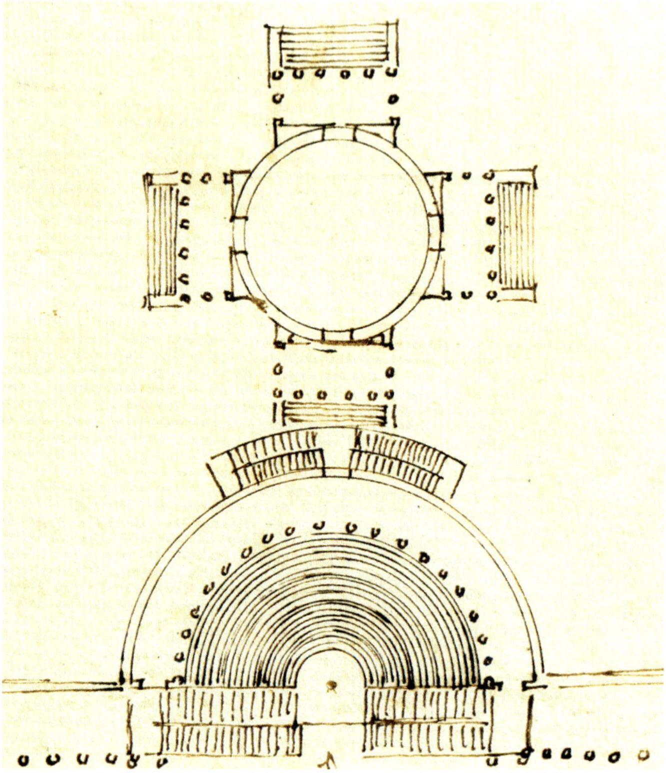

115 *Temple of Hercules Victor* (detail), Tivoli

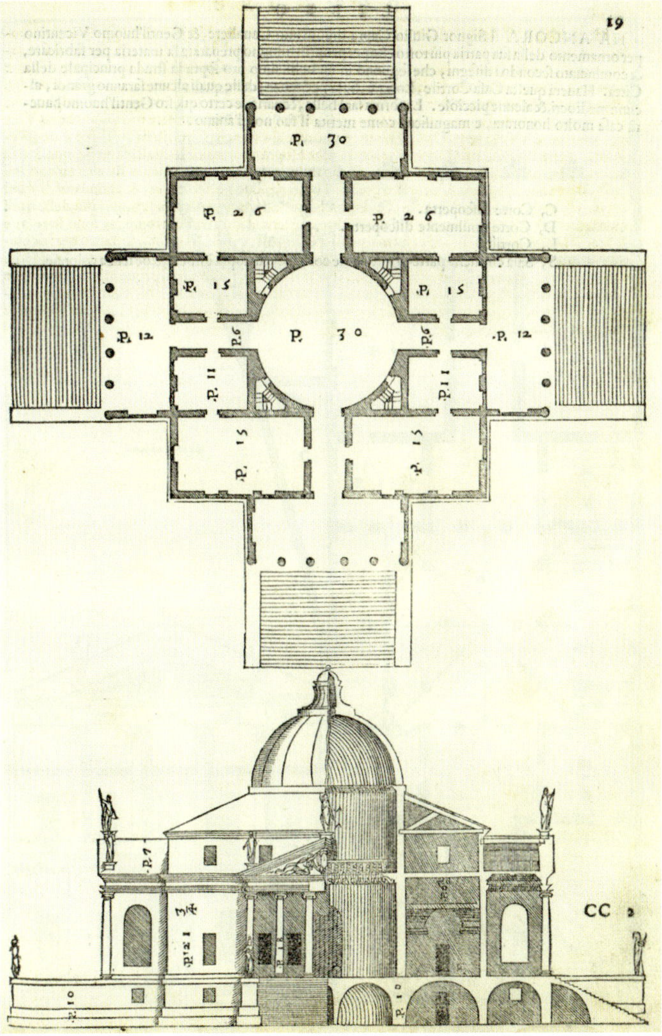

116 *Villa Almerigo Capra,* known as *La Rotonda,* Vicenza

117 *La Rotonda*, photolithograph 1880, Vicenza
118 *La Rotonda*, Vicenza

the varying size of its five arches supported on solid piers, and also (an aspect worth noting in relation to something that will be seen later) with the specially shaped piers designed in antiquity to withstand the turbulent currents of the Marecchia river; not to mention the *tabernacoli* that rise above the Rimini bridge on the breakwater buttresses of the piers.

The only concession that Palladio had made to the specifically Venetian setting was the inclusion of booths along either side of the bridge and the presence of a central "void" reminiscent of the opening in the centre of the fifteenth-century bridge used to house the drawbridge structures that could be raised to allow a masted vessel to pass below. [120]

THE COMPETITION TO BUILD A STAIRCASE INSIDE THE DOGE'S PALACE

This precedent did not dissuade Palladio from taking part in a new competition that was announced shortly afterwards by the Salt Magistracy: this time to build a staircase in the Doge's Palace.

To understand the importance of a project of this kind, it is worth remembering that, when it was announced in 1554, the construction of a direct link between the loggias and the upper levels was regarded as an innovative scheme, given that, according to Venetian tradition, connections between one floor and another had always been seen as external structures, to be built in the courtyards.

We do not know what solution Palladio submitted for this competition, but over the course of his long career he never showed any appreciation for the idea that buildings could include other structures to promote a more dynamic use of their spaces, since this disturbed the static equilibrium he thought they should have. It should not come as a surprise, therefore, that the competition was won by Jacopo Sansovino who certainly showed no uncertainty in knowing how to interpret this project. A staircase that led to the floor of the palace where the highest state magistracies were housed was, for Jacopo Sansovino, part of a triumphal passage that introduced that classical concept, which he himself had used to such magnificent effect on the Marcian *platea*, into the heart of the city's political power. [121]

120

121

It does not really seem plausible that the decision to leave for Rome again – together with a group of Venetian Signori – was merely Daniele Barbaro's reaction to these failures. The erudite patrician and Palladio, who once more accompanied him, clearly planned to meet architectural experts with whom they could carefully go over, yet again, any aspects that would guarantee the utmost philological accuracy of the Vitruvian translation, which was now almost ready to be delivered to the printer.

ANOTHER JOURNEY TO ROME

This second visit to Rome only served to confirm opinions that were already fully formed in Palladio's mind. This is borne out by Palladio's critical detachment towards the city's more recent architecture, however innovative. This behaviour serves to emphasise, once more, the distinction that was already clear in his mind between "Roman traditions" and "Romanism". Moreover, he wanted to prevent any external contamination with this conceptual universe, which was now in the process of being organised into a complete and logical system.

Evidence of this can be found simply by leafing through the guidebook to Rome that Palladio wrote during these weeks, in which he does not mention works by Michelangelo or Vignola, whose novelty and scale could not have failed to attract his full attention.

No document has been found that reveals the impact on the Venetian cultural scene in 1556 of the translation of the Vitruvian treatise accompanied by such extensive *Commentaries,* [122] published precisely at the time when – in a effervescent climate – many of the city's most eminent intellectuals were engaged in setting up an Academy, which would become known as the Accademia della Fama, whose aim was to discuss cultural and religious themes using an encyclopaedic, and hence reforming, approach.

From a few indirect clues – for example, the fact that Giannantonio Rusconi was so disturbed by the event that he could not complete the rival enterprise he had planned to carry out a few

122

years earlier – we can deduce how devastating it may have been for some.

However, it was a direct attack on the presumption of the man who, until then, had succeeded in convincing the political world in Venice that he was the sole fount of *all'antica* knowledge and who, because of this, had claimed almost exclusive responsibility for its interpretation. In short, what was now open to question was Sansovino's own authority, and, being fearful of just such an outcome, Sansovino had probably been among those who had most forcefully opposed Palladio's appointment within the Salt Magistracy.

Events of this kind could not fail to affect Daniele Barbaro who, having published his *Commentaries,* prepared to take up the cause in person and to give concrete support to his convictions by also involving his brother Marcantonio.

A PROJECT FOR THE PATRIARCHAL CHURCH IN VENICE

The fact that Barbaro decided to intervene on the Venetian patriarchal church when a decision on the construction of the façade of St Peter's could no longer be postponed and in Trent the Ecumenical Council was in full swing reveals the ambitious plans Palladio's promoter had in mind. This intention becomes even more explicit in view of the fact that a *renovatio* of the patriarchal church, if completed in time for the centenary of the death of Venice's first Patriarch – as Barbaro probably planned – would exalt Venetian religiosity in memory of a patrician, Lorenzo Giustinian, who had been regarded as a saint even in his own lifetime. At the same time it would have laid a new foundation – at least in conceptual terms – for the relationship between Church and State, here at the very heart of the Republic: the one represented by the codified *imago* of the Doge's Palace, and the other by the new form of the patriarchal church.

A few quick sketches in the margin of a letter he had copied support the notion that, immediately after Daniele Barbaro first conceived the idea, Palladio initially suggested that the existing patriarchal church should be completely rebuilt. [123] In its place there would have been a new church with a "circular or quadrangular" plan because, as Palladio writes in the *Fourth Book*, "these are the two Vitruvius mentions".[24]

A number of facts help to back this conjecture. All the rapidly sketched drawings on this sheet recall Venetian events. Only a religious building representing the State would be able to assume such a strongly rhetorical form (any "triumphal" representation of the Church in structures managed by the clergy was essentially forbidden according to the Republic's political tenets). No open area, without buildings, could be found in front of an existing church in any other partof the city except for San Pietro di Castello, and it was here that, in this sketch, Palladio suggested building two twin churches in front of a large "four-cornered" church, based on the model of the twin churches in Pola, not coincidentally a city within the Venetian *Dominio*.

Having ascertained that it was impossible to demolish the existing church (perhaps also because the Patriarch showed excessive zeal in collecting money for the project and, as a result, attracted harsh criticism in the Senate), the two Barbaro brothers decided to limit its scope to the addition of a new façade for the existing church while at the same time offering to provide personal surety to their friend Vincenzo Diedo, the patrician whom the Venetian Senate had recently elected as Patriarch of Venice, to give the building work adequate financial backing.

This fact alone would be enough to convince us that Barbaro – filled with pride from the success of his recently completed editorial project, bolstered by the ecclesiastical authority vested in him, and in the knowledge that he held the purse strings for the work – exerted too much pressure on the architect's creative process. One need only read the contract to be convinced that Palladio's *invenzione* for the form of this façade was not governed by the rules of composition he would apply to church façades in the years to come.

Whoever drew up the contract (on instructions clearly supplied by Palladio himself) specified that doors and windows would be

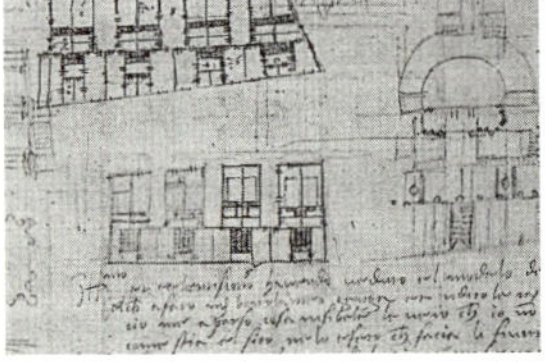

123

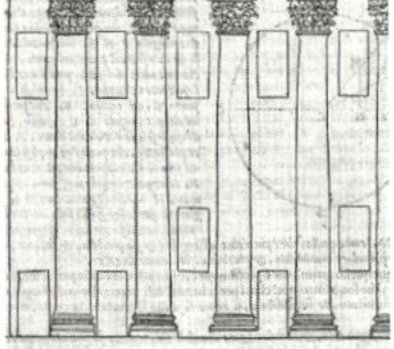

124

let into the façade, an operation requiring the removal of all the arches and tombs on the counterfaçade and producing spolia whose disposal was carefully set out in the terms of the contract. [124]

Based on these two observations – and on the agreement that the façade would include six large-diameter columns (the external kind that would envelop the corner of the *fabbrica* with part of their shaft) – it is almost self-evident to conclude that Palladio adopted an architectural division for the central portion of the church façade that evoked a hexastyle temple, embellished with giant Corinthian columns. (We can surmise that this design was conceived as a blend of two classical *exempla* which appear in relief in the same Palladian drawing: the Temple of Saturn, which is hexastyle, and the Corinthian temple dedicated to Venus Genitrix, a goddess in keeping with the myth of Venice.) [125]

However, a façade from a hexastyle temple designed with canonical proportions would never have fully covered the width of the existing church with a nave and two aisles, so beside the external columns – the ones whose shafts were "more than half" visible – Palladio planned to build two short "wings" in order to cover the projecting side aisles of the church behind. He embellished these "wings" with pilasters. [126]

Buoyed up by the hope that always provided such remarkable inspiration for his actions, Palladio worked in the conviction that, in this case too, his project would be built. With this in mind, he took another step forward by suggesting that the internal structure of the existing church would also have to be redefined sooner or later to give it an appearance in keeping with "his" façade. On impulse, he prepared two drawings: one showing the counterfaçade of this church characterised by the double row of windows opening between each of the gigantic columns that embellished the façade; and the other showing the side opposite the counterfaçade with the door to the presbytery where the Patriarch would have celebrated mass. [127] [128] [129]

Vincenzo Diedo died shortly after the works had started and the building site, which inevitably had invited criticism from those who regarded any dialectic between the Venetian church and the Roman curia as inappropriate, was forced to close almost immediately. The entire operation was suspended and the workers paid off.

A PROJECT TO REBUILD THE CHURCH OF SANTA LUCIA

There is no definite evidence that this crisis prompted Leonardo Mocenigo to think about rebuilding the church of Santa Lucia which stood at the opposite end of Venice compared to San Pietro di Castello, almost facing the Grand Canal. But several grounds can be put forward for taking this possibility into consideration: Mocenigo was related to Barbaro (they were cousins, since Mocenigo had also married one of the nieces of Cardinal Grimani, Bishop of Padua); moreover, Mocenigo's acquaintance with the architect dated back several years and Palladio had already convinced him to renovate a *casa* that the latter owned in Padua and also to build a *fabbrica* – an atypical *casa,* in some ways – in the Trevigiano where he owned a *villa.* [130]

Further support also comes from the fact that a little earlier, in 1556, Mocenigo's father, a Procuratore di San Marco, had been buried in the old church (in a tomb that the family did not yet own but which they used thanks to an ancestor who had married Michele Foscari's illegitimate daughter in 1493). The renovation of the church might therefore have seemed an act of self-celebration of his family (and, above all, an exaltation of his grandfather, an enterprising and influential figure who provided a role model for Leonardo when he became head of this particular branch of the family after his father's death).

Palladio clearly had no difficulty in interpreting this ambition, indeed he enhanced it by outlining an audacious plan to his client. [131] [132]

His project rotates by 180 degrees the lie of the old *fabbrica,* which was entered from the north with its apse in the south. This was the necessary premise to designing a façade along the line-defined by the polygonal vertex of the old church.

Moreover, based on the argument that a north-south orientation is not canonical according to Christian liturgical custom (nor,

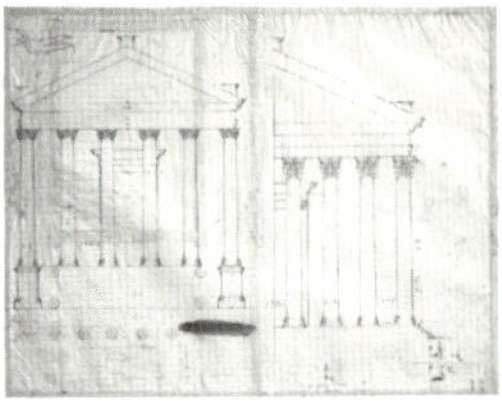

125

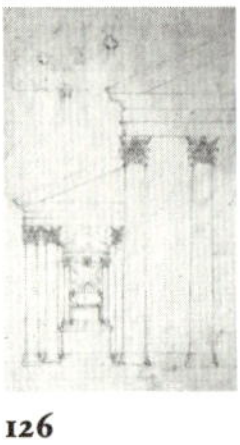

126

127

strangely, was the south-north orientation of the existing church), he introduced the east-west compositional axis in his *invenzione,* heedless of the fact that, as a result of this choice, the door of the new church, positioned according to liturgical practice, would open onto a narrow *calle.* At the eastern end of this axis he placed a chapel which – thanks to the robust architectural features based on a Roman bath model – became the *de facto* "main chapel" of the church.

The whole operation helped to give the *fabbrica* a central plan, at the point where the two axes intersected, forming a space with a square plan covered by cross vaults. But there was also another tangible purpose: to keep the counter-façade of the old church (on which the Mocenigo family probably already claimed rights) unencumbered so that they could build a monument that would become the visual endpoint for anyone entering the new church.

It seems likely that this would have been a monument not unlike that shown in the drawing now housed in the Fine Art Museum in Budapest, which Palladio gave to Vasari in 1565, specifically indicating the measurements in Florentine feet for the occasion. (The two side doors indicated in this drawing correspond to those leading into the nunnery adjoining the façade of the old church of Santa Lucia.) [133]

There is no doubt that this was an ambitious operation: this is confirmed by the fact that in order to carry out the entire project not only would it be necessary to demolish the old church's *campanile* and a number of buildings overlooking the Grand Canal, but it also required the consent of the nunnery and permission from the ecclesiastical authorities and the Venetian magistracies, which would also have to authorise building on the public ground east of the old church.

Apart from the introduction of Roman bath-style typologies inside the church that were still unknown in Venice, the most innovative feature of this building would have been the appearance on the north bank of the Grand Canal, and therefore lit by the midday sun, of the austere form of the arch that had been erected

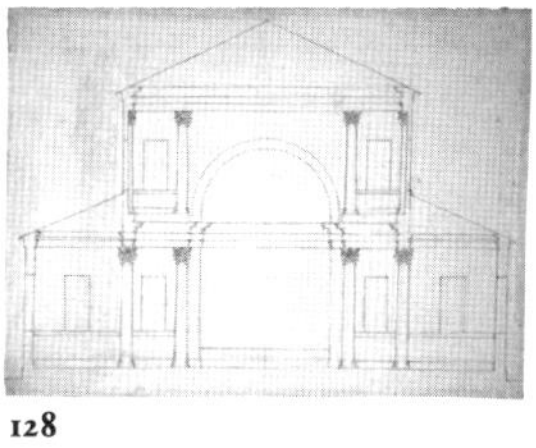

128

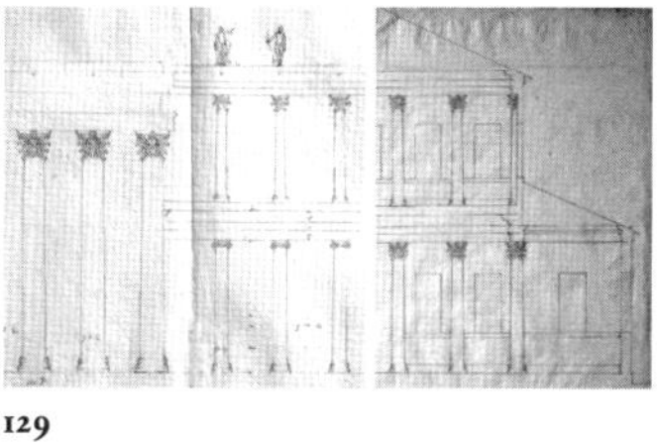

129

in Ancona by Trajan, the Venetians' favourite emperor on account of the civic virtues he demonstrated during the years when he controlled the fate of Rome. [134]

It is worth noting – in order to emphasise the link between this project and the one already devised for San Pietro di Castello – that, once more, two "wings" embellished with pilasters, which served to cover the projecting side aisles of the church, were attached to a structure based almost literally on an ancient monument. [135]

This solution – which Palladio would further develop at a later stage – did not detract from the novelty of a triumphal symbol of such figurative impact on the waters of the Grand Canal. (The self-celebratory purpose of Mocenigo's project was such an issue for the Venetian magistracies that they took steps to remove him from Venice almost immediately, appointing him as ambassador for the Republic in much the same way that Daniele Barbaro had been dispatched as ambassador to England as soon as the Venetian oligarchy realised the ambitious nature of his "scientific" undertaking.)

However, leaving aside the violation of established Venetian custom, there is something truly provocative about Palladio's *invenzione*. To anyone who knew about architecture and had followed events in this sphere in the city, Palladio's project could only be seen as a "criticism", or even as a derision of the "dwarf" triumphal arch that Jacopo Sansovino had erected for an ambitious citizen in a much less prestigious urban setting (a controversial affair with which Leonardo's father would undoubtedly have been fully acquainted as Procuratore di San Marco). [136]

THE FAÇADE OF THE CHURCH OF SAN FRANCESCO DELLA VIGNA

The confrontation, or at this point we might perhaps say the clash, between Andrea Palladio and Jacopo Sansovino was no less harsh: it came about when Palladio was asked by Giovanni Grimani to add a façade to a major church, San Francesco della Vigna, the "body" of which had been built some twenty years earlier to a design by Jacopo Sansovino.

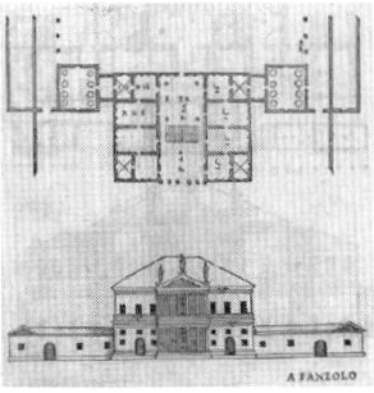

130

131

It is not difficult to pinpoint Daniele Barbaro's encouragement in this matter, simply because it was Giovanni Grimani, [137] in his capacity as Patriarch of Aquileia, who appointed Barbaro as his successor to the ecclesiastical see that the Republic was interested in keeping under its political control because it exercised spiritual power over extensive areas of the Habsburg Empire.

But the reasons that prompted Grimani to fund the cost of building the façade for the church of San Francesco della Vigna were not the same reasons that had inspired Daniele Barbaro and his brother Marcantonio to embark on the project of San Pietro di Castello. Although Grimani, too, looked to Rome and the Council of Trent, it was not in order to influence the political choices made there, as the Republic hoped, but in an attempt to extricate himself from an accusation of heresy that only the Vatican or the Council could revoke, thereby sweeping aside an impediment that would hinder his ability to manoeuvre into a position where he could attain the title of cardinal.

Palladio was indifferent to problems of this kind, which were unrelated to his specific field of interest. He resumed his reflections on the composition of a church façade, which he had started at San Pietro di Castello and Santa Lucia. His aim was to elaborate both these *invenzioni,* overcoming the contradiction clearly represented by those two "wings", which in both cases he had combined with a classical *exemplum,* in many ways diminishing its autonomy.

From his experience at Santa Lucia he retained the triumphal aspect of the façade, which was ensured by deploying paired columns a sufficient distance apart to allow a large opening, evoking a triumphal arch, to be set (ideally) between them.

Above the entablature supported by these paired columns, he placed a frontispiece – a solution that was not found in any classical *exemplum* – thereby (at least ideally) reiterating the form of a temple.

Palladio then proceeded to devise a composition based on these predeterminants involving the same basilica-like interior design

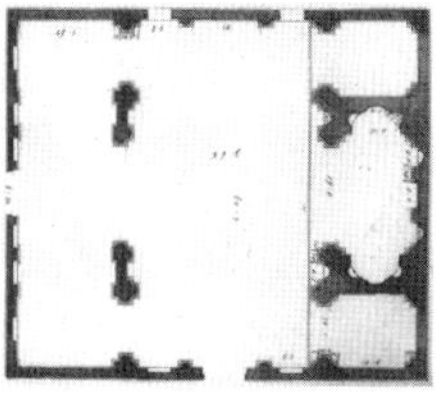

132

133

that he had started to explore in the two RIBA drawings, number XIV, I and number XIV, 9, both of which refer (in our view) to the plans for the patriarchal church of San Pietro di Castello. This, in turn, prompted him to explore the enigmatic meaning of the brief passage in which Vitruvius had described the form of the temple he had built in Fano, featuring a façade with a dual frontispiece. On the basis of this philological pretext, Palladio attributed new meaning to the "wings" that flanked the main body of the church and to the pilasters he had used to embellish them, as he had already done earlier in the project for San Pietro di Castello (by repeating on the façade the lower row of columns used to form the internal structure of an ancient basilica).

In this way, Palladio perfected the *invenzione* of a completely new type of façade, one whose legitimation did not depend on a classical *exemplum* (nothing remained of the temple at Fano) but rather on the efficacy of the analogous procedure used by the architect to arrive at his definition. [138]

The scheme of a tripartite façade with intersecting orders – to which Rudolf Wittkower alerted scholarly attention many years ago – is so well conceived conceptually and so well ordered formally that it acquired the status of a paradigm. As though to emphasise the importance of this compositional approach, Palladio repeated this *invenzione* in his design for the façades of San Giorgio Maggiore and the Redentore, thereby instituting a "tradition" to which other architects would adapt almost spontaneously, not only in Venice but also in the Veneto and in ever wider spheres of influence.

PROJECTS FOR THE BENEDICTINE MONASTERY OF SAN GIORGIO MAGGIORE

These episodes, which saw Palladio involved in building churches – however independent the projects were from one another, and however significant each project was in its own right – cannot be fully understood if they are not seen in relation to a project undertaken on a much larger scale, namely the programme for the *renovatio* of the Benedictine complex on the island of San Giorgio, right opposite the Doge's Palace. [139]

134

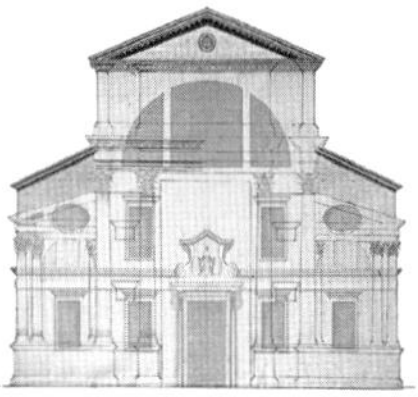

135

Perhaps the most pertinent way of putting this massive undertaking into its historical context is by recalling for a moment the figure of the man who – from the time when he returned to England (1555) – was the influential protector of the Benedictine congregation of Santa Giustina (the Cassinese congregation of which the Venetian monastery formed part).

Reginald Pole was the cardinal whose vision of the European political scene, owing to his open-minded, cosmopolitan attitude, was more in tune with the Republic's own views than that of any other contemporary churchman. Indeed, when the Farnese pope died in 1549, the Republic charged its ambassadors and all the Venetian prelates to do all they could to support Pole's candidature for election to the papal throne. [140]

Nor, on the other hand, was it coincidental that the Venetians offered this prelate renewed and unlimited credit immediately after his candidacy to the see of St Peter's had failed, given that he was appointed – almost in recompense for not being elected – to represent the new pope at the Council which was being held in Trent in circumstances that were becoming increasingly awkward for Venetian interests.

This explains why the Signoria allowed the Benedictines to embark on the renovation of their monastery within the lagoon, removing an impasse that had been created many years earlier when the Venetian magistracies had resolved not to allow any more convents to be built by a religious order that had not hesitated to abandon the city of Venice when Maximilian of Habsburg's armies had marched triumphantly through its *Stato da Terra.* [141]

No patrician was more capable of grasping the diplomatic nuances of this event than Daniele Barbaro, who had obtained the appointment to the prestigious role of Patriarch Elect of Aquileia on the strength of a request submitted by Cardinal Pole to Pope Julius III immediately after his election.

That these promises did not lead to the immediate start of renovation works on the monastery was due to the deep aversion that

136

Cardinal Carafa, later Pope Paul IV, showed for Pole – who returned to England to escape from such an insistent attack – and also for Cardinal Morone, who replaced Pole in the role of "protector" of the Benedictines of the Cassinese order. Both were disliked by Carafa for the same reason that they were so admired by the Venetian Signoria: they were open to the requests for reform formulated by the Protestant movement. It was only after Carafa's death and after Pius IV had ascended the throne of St Peter's (one of his first acts was to absolve Cardinal Morone from the accusation of heresy brought against him by Carafa) that work on the Benedictine complex of San Giorgio could finally start.

Palladio's first commission reveals the extent to which the Benedictines were determined, at this stage, to embark on a complete renewal of their monastery. According to their own decision, it was an operation that had to be completed on the basis of the building programmes which the Cassinese Congregation had approved some three decades earlier. The construction of a new refectory was the pretext for demolishing the existing refectory, together with the adjoining rooms, thereby freeing the ground required to start building a new church. [142] [143]

THE REFECTORY

This does not explain why Palladio saw this phase as a preliminary act of purely organisational value. The succession of spaces he built – passage, vestibule (*aula di purificazione*) and the refectory itself – offer a degree of solemnity, based on the vigour of their masonry structures, their volumes and the absence of ornamentation, that was unprecedented in Venice.

As for their *all'antica* nature, they revealed the essence without displaying any specific form. The passage (modelled on an example that Palladio had been able to study in Rome inside the ruins of a Roman bath house) generated the same emotion – with its vertiginous height and rough plastered walls completely devoid of *politezza*, or delicacy – as a trumpet blast that shatters the silence. The refectory is reached through the vestibule dedicated to purification, graced with two imposing hand basins. With its high

137

138

windows that prevent any view to the outside, its cross-vaulted ceiling that offers an unexpected reference to Roman baths, its dimensions and its "whiteness", the conceptual power of its design can only be grasped in relation to the volume and ornamentation of the main hall of Sansovino's *Libreria,* the only space in Venice that is comparable in terms of size and the intensity of its intellectual content.

THE CHURCH

This architectural introduction is sufficient to highlight the radical innovation – one might say metamorphosis – that Palladio brought to a project that had been drawn up three decades earlier based on an explicitly Florentine model (as is clearly borne out by the sequence of semi-cylindrical chapels that repeat on the sides of church the solution devised by Brunelleschi for the church of Santo Spirito). [144] [145]

By eliminating the chapels, narrowing the bays, widening and heightening the central nave, and including apsed transepts the same length as the central nave (as in Bramante's project for St Peter's), this monastic church acquires a majesty and a quality that radically innovate the spatial conception of the earlier solution.

The architectural language that Palladio revealed with such confident eloquence imbued every part of the *fabbrica* with formal cohesion and was regarded by every Venetian as a real "lesson": the same "lesson" that for years Daniele Barbaro had tried to teach his fellow citizens, while instead they continued to regard his warnings and appeals with diffidence and suspicion. [146]

Even the most superficial reflection on the *novitas* of such a composition clearly shows that this architecture intended to display the evidence for its form right in the centre of basin of San Marco, demolishing the structural barrier (a row of publicly owned buildings) that would otherwise have blocked its view from the west. [147]

Here, too, it is worth noting that Francesco Sansovino – who once again acted as interpreter of the conflict between his father,

139

140

141

the *proto,* and this architect who, for over a decade, had challenged his primacy on the Venetian scene – tried to undermine the importance of this operation (which Vasari admires unreservedly) by stating that it had already been commenced in the 1530s when Gregorio Cortese was the highly respected abbot of San Giorgio.

As further evidence of how this antagonism formed a gulf that profoundly divided the Venetian world of culture, one need only note the aggressive, almost violent reaction to the laconic rigour of Palladio's language by an artist protected by Titian and loved by Michele Sanmicheli "like a son"[25]: Paolo Veronese. In a space of such solemnity as the refectory, and in the silence that was mandatory within it, Veronese introduced – for the same provocative effect that one might turn on a juke box at full blast in a silent library – an enormous painting, one might say of disproportionate size, depicting the most worldly scene from Christ's life described in the Scriptures: the *Wedding at Cana.* [148] It takes up the whole rear wall of the refectory and reveals sumptuous garments, dogs, dwarves and seductive women amidst the clatter of plates and the clamour of voices and music; then – as if this were not enough to disturb the atmosphere of this sacred space – behind the uproar of this worldly celebration, he offers a glimpse of an imaginary city packed with buildings that are merely scenographic settings.

THE COUNCIL OF TRENT

Palladio refused to become involved in such rivalries.

Moreover, these were the years when the fourth session of the Ecumenical Council was fully underway. As time passed the Venetian Signoria was growing more aware of the Roman Church's determination to oppose the jurisdictional principle that lay at the heart of the Republic's constitutional regime; there was also mounting concern about the risk posed by a political break – even more so than a spiritual break – resulting from the increasingly sharp clash between the triumphal ideology of the Catholic Church in Rome and the aspirations towards religious reform

142

143

that had garnered support over the past few decades in many European "nations".

Having not deemed it necessary to send even an ambassador to the first three sessions of the Council, at this point Venice decided to send a diplomatic delegation (instigated by the Patriarch Elect of Aquileia, who had already travelled to Trent some time earlier). At the same time, however, it decided to make a statement that would assert the independence and autonomy of the Venetian Church and emphasise, as clearly as possible, the mediating role between Rome and the rest of Europe that the Republic had always played, not least because of its geographical position. At this point, it focused attention on a building of enormous symbolic status in the history of the Republic: the convent where, according to tradition, Pope Alexander III had taken refuge when the Hohenstaufen Emperor, Frederick Barbarossa, was about to overwhelm the papal army. For Venice, a *renovatio* of this ancient monastery at such a specific historical moment conjured up the role played by the Republic in the late twelfth century when it had avoided a clash between the Empire and the Papacy that would have led to a complete subversion of the balance of power in Europe.

THE MONASTERY OF THE CARITÀ
THE REFECTORY

By celebrating this event with an impressive building project, Venice officially put itself forward as a mediator between the Roman Curia and the German states.

Embarking on the renovation of the Monastery of the Carità, which came under the rule of the Augustinian canons of the Lateran Congregation, was an act whose significance was not dissimilar – in terms of the Republic's diplomatic customs – to starting to rebuild the Benedictine monastery of San Giorgio. In the same way that the Venetian magistracies had intended those works to win the loyalty of Cardinal Reginald Pole, "protector" of the Benedictine order, the new project served as proof of the Republic's full backing for the positions taken in the council debates by Cardinal Ercole Gonzaga, "protector" of the Lateran order, who now

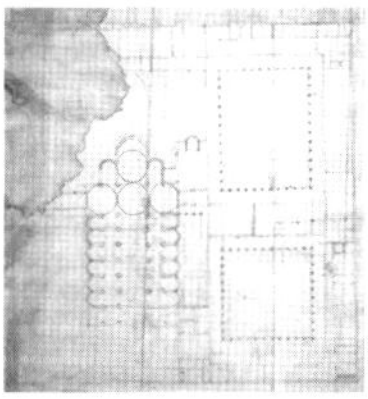

144

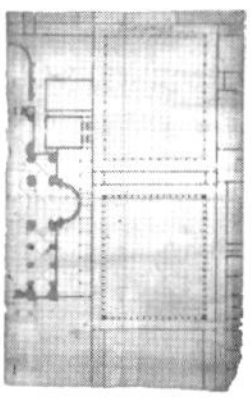

145

presided over the council meetings since Reginald Pole had left for England. Gonzaga was also committed – indeed he dedicated all the strength he could muster – to avoiding a breakdown between the central European world and Rome, between reform and the broadly self-referencing attitude that had increasingly permeated the highest echelons of the papal curia.

Proof that the renovation work on the Monastery of the Carità and the resolve with which it was undertaken were the outcome of a political design based on the shared views of the Venetian Signoria and Ercole Gonzaga is the fact that when the Council of Trent ended and the cardinal died, work stopped immediately, never to be resumed. At that point, this building project clearly lacked any *raison d'être* as an ideological and political message.

But let us take events in the right order and focus on the moment when Palladio was given this commission.

It was only fitting that the architectural language of a project bearing such a weighty message to the world should be that of ancient Rome. In accordance with the ideological approach developed for the *renovatio* of the Marcian *platea,* this was the choice that characterised the official form of Venetian architecture when it was decided to intervene in a political affair that involved both the Papacy and the Empire. In this case Venice claimed the right to be seen within Europe as the "sole remaining exemplar of the magnificence and grandeur of the Romans" (as Palladio himself put it).

It was almost inevitable, in a situation like this, that Palladio would be summoned and he was determined not to be caught unprepared. He seized this moment as an opportunity to re-work a particular topic of Vitruvius's treatise that had intrigued Fra' Giocondo three decades earlier, and which Daniele Barbaro had also had to deal with in order to complete the translation of classical writings on architecture: namely, the question of the *ancient Roman house.* Thanks to what appears to be an almost endless capacity for invention, Palladio's reflections on the subject resulted in an outcome whose grandeur was both unexpected and audacious.

146

147

148

He designed a building that was unlike anything else in Venice, both in concept and size. [149] Joined to the north of the fifteenth-century church of the Carità, it extends south well beyond the physical limit of the building that currently houses the Gallerie dell'Accademia, crosses over a public street (something that was unheard of in Venice) and continues for another hundred metres or so on the other side. The dimensions of this *fabbrica* was such that its ground plan – despite the especially reduced scale used for the illustration – exceeded the maximum page size of the *Second Book* in which it was published in 1570. [150]

Some experts have marvelled at the strict cadence on the inside of this building, recognising it as a form of monumentalism that is, in some respects, conventional. In practice, here as never before, the architect set himself the goal of modernising Roman traditions by avoiding any recourse to Tuscan-Roman architectural forms, or to representations of an *all'antica* style that could in any way be referred to an imperial matrix.

In order to avert the first of these pitfalls, the *ornamenti* used for this *casa* are in keeping with canonical precepts inside this massive building, reserving to a few erudite observers an understanding of the *exempla* evoked, which are nonetheless recognisable in the very conception of its structures. [151] Likewise, to avert the second, these were built in brick. This material – which, moreover, allowed the *fabbrica* to be completed rapidly in view of the political circumstances that had given rise to this project – was ideally seen, also in view of its low cost, as an expression of the Republican virtues of ancient Rome. Having inherited these virtues, the Republic of Venice now wished to show that it had assimilated and could express them through an operation whose content was so markedly ideological.

To gain a full understanding of the significance of this ambitious project it is necessary to compare the forms displayed inside the *fabbrica* with the restrained magniloquence and the way it presents itself outside, on the only side open to the surrounding urban fabric. The immense white expanse, which rises with almost

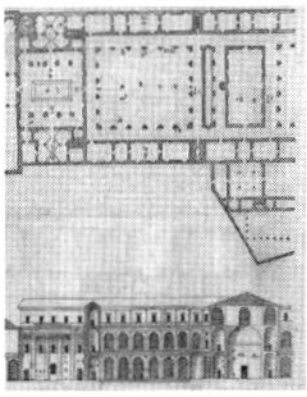

149

metaphysical solemnity above the water of a not particularly wide canal and is lined by showy entablatures of orders devoid of any other *ornamento*, conveys a message whose terseness is so surprising that – for precisely this reason – it acquires extraordinary eloquence. [152]

To paraphrase John Osborne's words when he says that Luther kept the rules so strictly that that in itself showed he was getting ready to break them, in this case we might say that Palladio's acceptance of the principle that no new architecture should alter the image of the city was so stringent that he resolved to use other ways to show the inflexible *ragione* that inspired his architecture and the cultural and political message it conveyed.

We need only ask ourselves a question to realise how an intention of this kind could be carried out. Is it possible that an undertaking of such ideological – let alone financial – importance could be condemned by the architect who conceived it not to appear on the banks of the Grand Canal and to be obscured from the view of citizens, and the world, by the delicate structure of a late Gothic church?

A ROTONDA ON THE GRAND CANAL?

It is a question that stops merely being rhetorical when one notices – after a careful examination of the drawing of this *casa* that Palladio published in 1570 – that the sole entrance to this grandiose monastery is shown as a doorway that would be opened in the southern wall of the adjoining church.

By doing so, it is not that Palladio made a mistake: namely that he did not know that the wall through which the door was meant to lead was occupied by the monumental tombs of the Barbarigo doges, or that he meant to condemn the powerful Lateran canons to enter their imposing *casa* through the courtyard of a welfare institution, in other words the *Scuola* that lay to the west. In keeping with his normally prudent conduct – above all when he wanted to convey an important message – what he meant to point out was that the question of access to the monastery he was building was one that must be shelved as pending. [153]

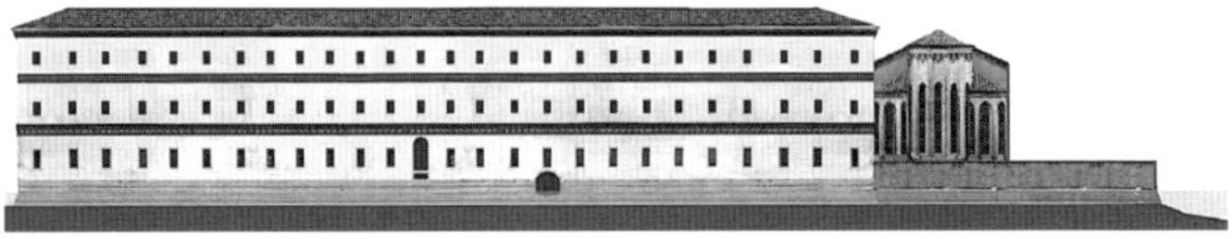

150

Indeed, by doing so Palladio sets out his thoughts in not too ambiguous terms: in place of the slender fifteenth-century church, which abutted the monastery to the north, there would be a church, or perhaps we should start to call it a temple, consistent with the huge *fabbrica* that should have risen behind it and that would convey to the city, and to the world, the message which this ambitious building operation was intended to represent.

The idea that this temple should be a *rotonda* comes almost spontaneously, given that there was no reason why Palladio – free as he was during these solitary reflections to opt for the choice he thought most suitable – should not decide to use a form he judged to be "most perfect and excellent"; the one that more than any other "is perfectly adapted to demonstrate the unity, the infinite existence, the consistency, and the justice of God", "as it alone amongst all the plans is simple, uniform, equal, strong and capacious".[26]

But over and above the conceptual precedence that Palladio attributed to the circular form – and which he expressed in terms that almost betray a sort of enthusiasm – there was a specific reason that justified this choice. This can only be understood through the realisation that if the Lateran monastery rose behind a rotunda, along exactly the same axis, it would repeat the ground plan and volume of the *exemplum* offered by the imposing Baths of Agrippa rising behind the Pantheon on exactly the same axis. [154] [155]

Therefore, in response to the question of access to the Lateran monastery, it is impossible to resist the tempting thought that Palladio might have adopted a solution that would have conjured up the entrance to the Baths of Agrippa, and considerable graphic evidence for this theme can be found among the surviving Palladian drawings.

Here too, at the Carità, behind a rotunda, there would have been a large transversal space that would have served as the entrance to the monastery along the same axis. On entering this austere *fabbrica* and moving through it in the correct order, one would experience the spatial excitement produced by the succession of

151

152

153

an atrium surrounded by a giant order of columns and a vast courtyard. In other words, it would have created the sensation of moving from a space ornamented with surprising grandeur – but which was relatively dark since it was lit by just a *lucernario* – into an open space in which the orders, superimposed according to Vitruvian principles, were bathed in sunlight and irradiated the colour of the brickwork.

The Council of Trent would have had to have ended differently for the building project to have been completed and, in front of such an imposing ancient Roman house, for there to have been a building that was intended to evoke the form of a temple that "at the time of the Republic" was dedicated to all possible forms of worship, as Palladio writes about the Pantheon. [156]

When he handed the printer the drawing to be published in his *Four Books,* Palladio may still have hoped that some event would allow him to realise this *invenzione;* but he reduced the message of his "hope" to a few lines – the two columns and two pilasters that frame a virtual door on the side aisle wall of the late Gothic church.

THE MEETING WITH GIORGIO VASARI

But we should step five years back from the date when he sent this terse message to the printers. Giorgio Vasari came to visit the building site of the Lateran monastery; Palladio accompanied him and seized the chance to explain to this distinguished visitor from Arezzo his interpretation of Vitruvius's obscure passage on the ancient Roman house: he did so with such enthusiasm that – to one who had never met him before – it was evidence of his knowledge of the "studies of the art". [157]

It was during this meeting that Vasari first came across the extraordinary figure of the intellectual and theoretician, Fra' Giocondo, whom Jacopo Sansovino had not even mentioned at their meetings, clearly in order to retain for himself the merit of having been the first to introduce an architecture based on a knowledge of classical antiquity to Venice. (Vasari was so struck by this discovery that in the second edition of the *Lives,* which he published

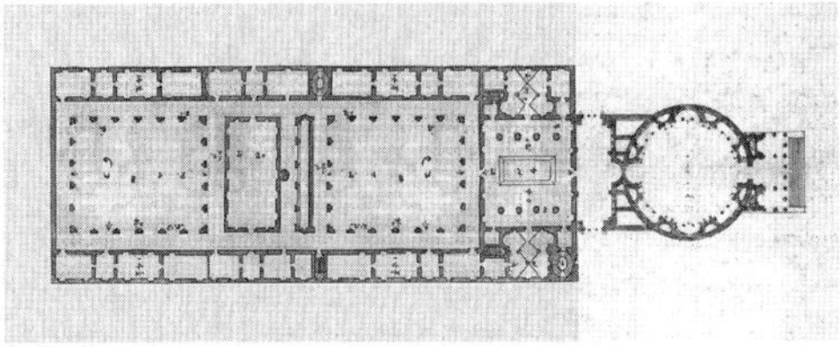

154

shortly after this visit – and in which he recorded his meeting with Palladio – he even apologises to the readers for not having mentioned the existence of this exceptional figure in the first edition.)

We can be almost certain that Palladio spoke to Vasari about Fra' Giocondo because the latter's translation of Vitruvius's treatise in 1521 made him the first to attempt an interpretation of the theme of the ancient Roman house of which this great *fabbrica*, designed to house the Lateran canons, claimed to be a correct *invenzione*. But there was also another reason. There is only one precedent in Venetian architectural history for an intervention that was foisted or attempted to foist itself on the city, as this Lateran monastery does: namely, showing complete indifference for the late mediaeval matrix of its urban fabric. This is the project that Fra' Giocondo, that cosmopolitan and erudite figure, had devised to rebuild the Rialto emporium after the serious fire that had destroyed it in 1514.

One might think it likely that Palladio (an architect whom Vasari describes as "young" in comparison to the *proto* of the Procuratia di San Marco who now seemed to him "old") drew Vasari's attention to the "beautiful drawing"[27] elaborated by Fra' Giocondo a century earlier in order to highlight this precedent.

Even though Vasari was accustomed to seeing plans and drawings, he was fascinated by the radicality of Fra' Giocondo's proposal, by the theoretical enthusiasm that animated it and by the determination with which, in practice, it contested the essence of the city's urban structure.

Proof of the influence that Palladio exercised on Giorgio Vasari during his visit to Venice can be found in the harshness with which the writer from Arezzo attacked the *proto* of the Salt Magistracy who had carried out the rebuilding work in the Rialto area, thwarting any chance of implementing the proposals put forward by Fra' Giocondo. On Palladio's part, the fact of drawing attention to this outcome is not an expression of resentment against the magistracy that had refused to employ him as *proto* some twelve years earlier, and probably not even a criticism of the ambiguous

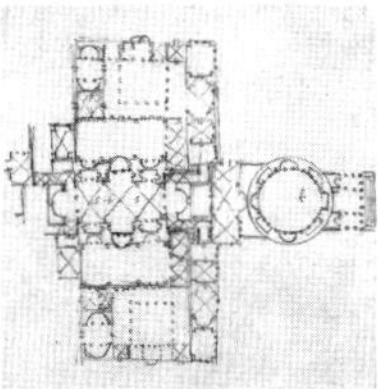

155

156

157

role played by the *proto* of the Salt Magistracy with whom Jacopo Sansovino had collaborated at various levels. Instead, it was a statement of concern: because Fra' Giocondo's failure so many years earlier was an expression of the Venetian world's resistance to any change in established practice and to any form of cultural innovation that departed from tradition in the lagoon city.

A PIAZZA DEI LATINI AT THE FOOT OF THE RIALTO BRIDGE

We will never know whether Palladio's renewed focus on the Rialto area was a consequence of his meeting with Giorgio Vasari. It is a fact, however, that shortly after it, Palladio picked up the sheet of paper on which, a few years earlier, he had sketched his proposal for a stone bridge at the Rialto, turned it over and started to draw a project on the *verso* for the area between the Rialto bridge and the *campo* of San Bartolomio.

This time it was not the bridge that occupied his thoughts (and indeed all he did now was to repeat – in a simplified form – the solution already shown on the *recto* of the sheet). Nor was he distracted from the theoretical principles governing all his work by the suggestion of Fra' Giocondo's "beautiful drawing". Once again, Palladio elaborated his design by taking a classical *exemplum* as the inspiration and basis for his composition.

Harking back to his reflections on a subject that he had already discussed with Daniele Barbaro while working on Vitruvius's *Commentaries,* he outlined a *Piazza dei Latini* ("Square of the Latins"): namely, a square that was "longer than [it was] wide"[28], surrounded by a double-storey portico, cadenced by Ionic columns at the ground level and Corinthian columns on the upper storey.

Palladio was not indulging in any visionary approach but rather developing a precise thought. This can be seen from the precision with which he set this *invenzione* in the urban context (even specifying the dimensions of the *campo* – namely the public space – that would be created behind it, to the south). But what was his real intention?

To discover this we must not divert our attention from the lines he used to express his thoughts. In his project – as can be seen on

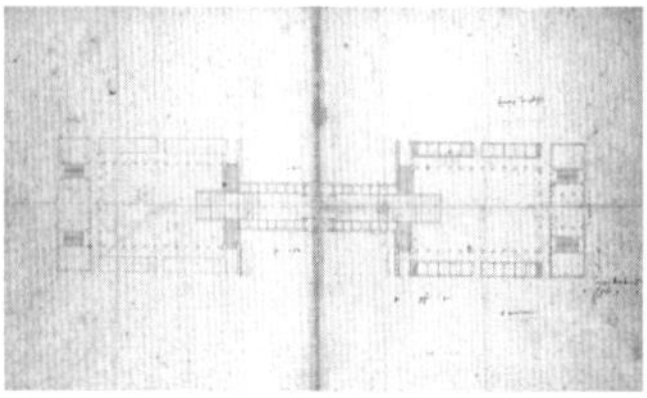
158

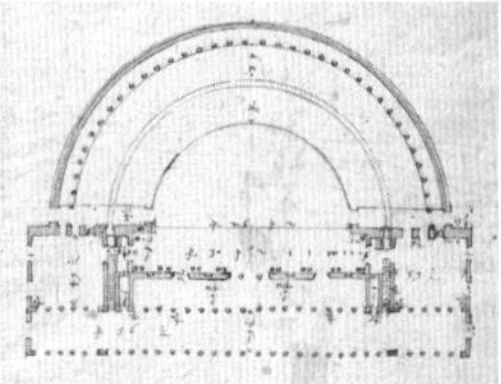
159

sheet D 25v in the Museo Civico of Vicenza – the flow of persons and goods between *campo* San Bartolomio and the Grand Canal does not cross this piazza (which we could also call a *platea* in order to link it to the Roman tradition, in linguistic as well as architectural terms). Instead it runs along two narrow streets (clearly two *calli* given that we are in Venice) that lie outside the structures containing the piazza. Moreover, Palladio specified that the new shops occupying the ground floor of the building structure should face onto these *calli* and not onto the piazza. [158]

To understand the reasons for these choices, which otherwise remained unexplained, we need to immerse ourselves in everyday Venetian life of the mid 1560s. Palladio had just emerged from an experience that had in many ways been traumatic, given that – reticent as he was in describing personal feelings – he had no hesitation in writing that, at the time, he had paid penance for all the sins he had committed until then and all those he might ever commit in the future.

A "HALF COLOSSEUM" FOR A THEATRICAL PERFORMANCE

It was certainly not the construction of those semicircular tiered steps, which looked like a "half Colosseum" from the outside, that had concerned him; nor was it the stage (which appears to have been created on the site of some houses that were being built, if it can be recognised as such from the rapid sketches on RIBA drawing XVI, 9v, on which we have already focused owing to the appearance of other "Venetian" annotations). [159]

Rather it was the unusual convergence of two spheres that until then he had perhaps kept apart: his life in Vicenza and that in Venice. It cannot have been a matter of indifference to Palladio that the theatre was created to celebrate the arrival of a young duke in Venice: Francesco Maria II della Rovere who, as well as bearing the name of the captain general who had implemented Doge Gritti's defensive strategy, was also related to the Bishop of Vicenza. Moreover, the theatre itself was being built on land that belonged to Pietro Foscari, Marco Foscari's son, or, in other words, the brother-in-law of Vettor Pisani, the patrician who had commissioned the house at Bagnolo (and who continued to act as the patron of other initiatives in which Palladio was regularly engaged).

Nor can it have been any consolation that the performance given in the theatre shortly afterwards provoked a scandal, not for the novelty of the architecture or the content of the comedy, but, on the contrary, precisely because of its success: to judge from the reports of a reliable witness like Speron Speroni, little else was talked of in Venice for weeks. Such was the throng of patricians trying to enter the "half Colosseum" that neither Cosimo Bartoli, the Medici agent in Venice, nor the Imperial ambassador, the Savoy ambassador or even the papal legate had managed to get inside.

Therefore it was the exclusiveness of such performances that had prompted severe criticism, to the extent that, from then on, no more *Compagnie di Calza* were allowed to be set up, like the *Compagnia degli Accesi* that had arranged this extraordinary event.

In a situation like this, in which institutional matters overlapped with cultural habits and social conduct, it is symptomatic to note the reaction of a brilliant man who had always boasted, until this moment, that he too had been a *Compagno di Calza*, and who had equipped the *corte* of his *casa* in Padua as a theatrical space in order to continue to give performances along the lines of those introduced in the Veneto by these *Compagnie* a few decades earlier.

A PROVOCATIVE STEP BY ALVISE CORNARO

Alvise Cornaro [160] – always driven by the desire to be the centre of attention that was one of the most distinctive traits of his character – did not hesitate to interpret the new climate created after this "scandal" and to suggest building a large theatre in Venice that would have been public. It would have taken the form of an *arena* (not a "half Colosseum", therefore, but a whole one) where a practically unlimited number of citizens could be accommodated free of charge to attend performances given in the *piazza* (this is the term Cornaro used to refer to the uncovered area at

160

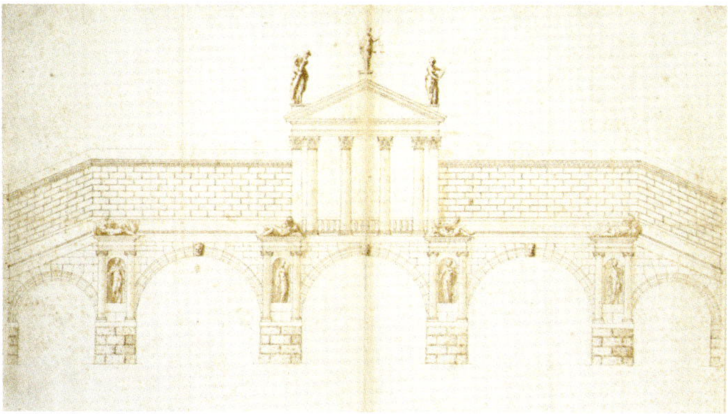

119 *Plan of the stone Bridge of Rialto with five arches,* Venice
120 Jacopo de' Barbari, *Perspective plan of Venice* (detail)

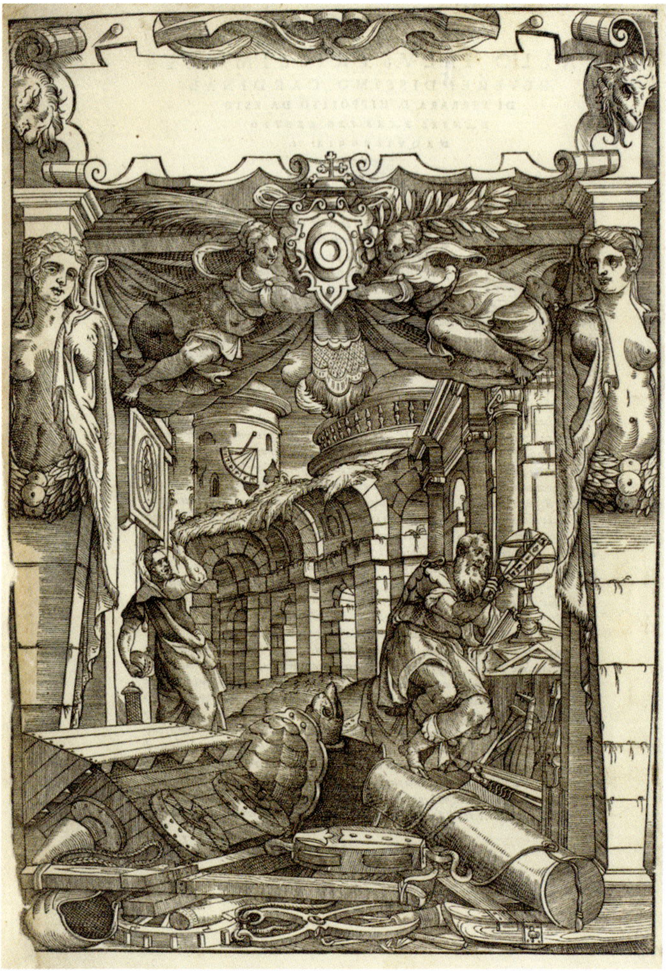

122 *I Dieci Libri dell'Architettura, tradotti e commentati da Daniele Barbaro*, 1567

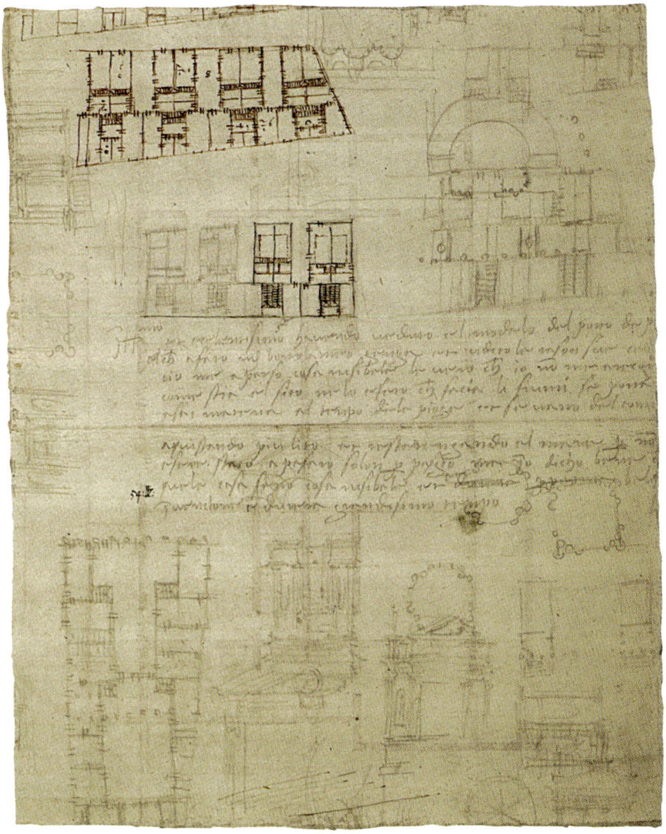

123 *Draft of a letter and sketches*

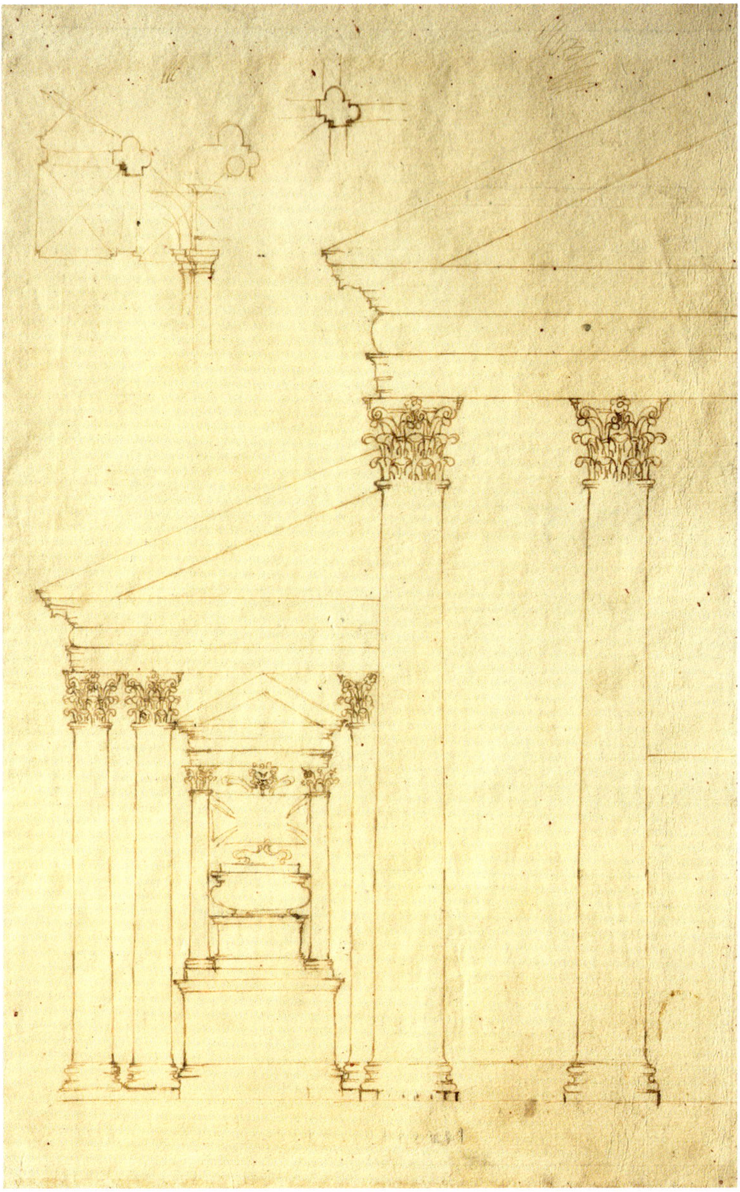

126 *Project for the facade of a church* (mirror image on right)

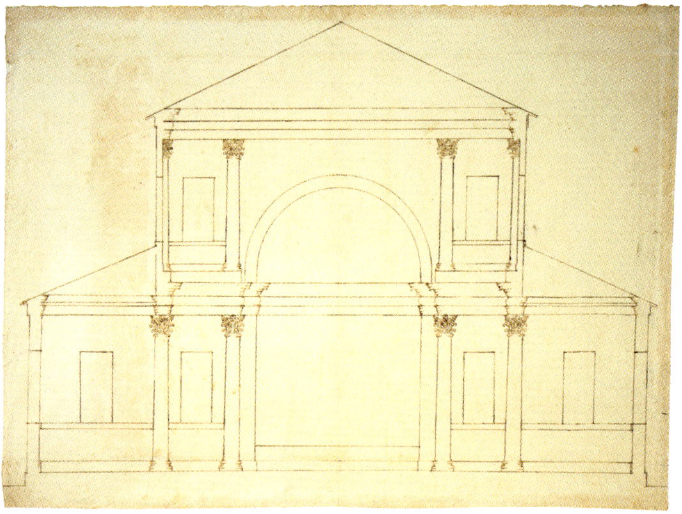

127 *Project for the Church of San Pietro di Castello. Section with view of conterfacade,* Venice (identified by Antonio Foscari)
128 *Project for the Church of San Pietro di Castello. Section with view of apse,* Venice (identified by Antonio Foscari)

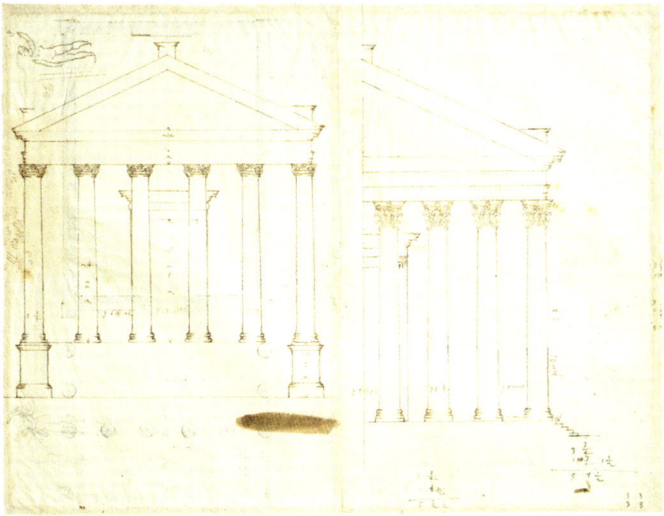

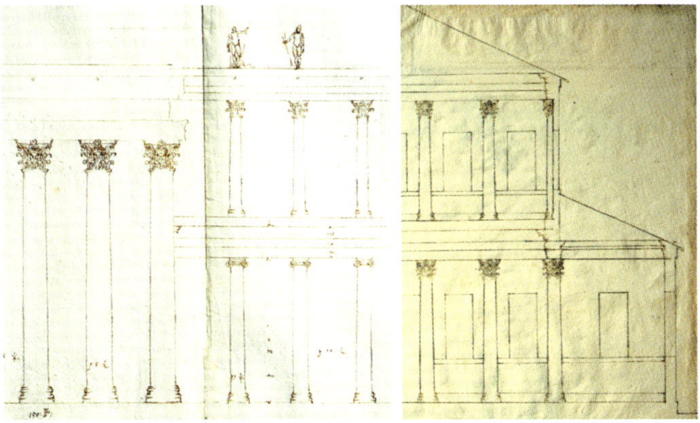

125 *Temples of Saturn and Venus*, Rome

129 Collage of the *Temple of Jupiter Serapis* and the *Cross section of a church (San Pietro di Castello)* (identified by Antonio Foscari)

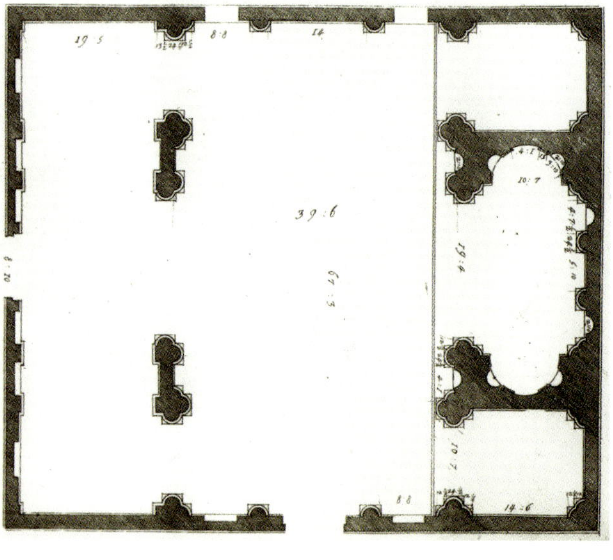

133 A. Palladio, B. Del Moro, *Project for a funerary chapel* (detail)
132 *Plan of the Church of Santa Lucia* (edited), Venice

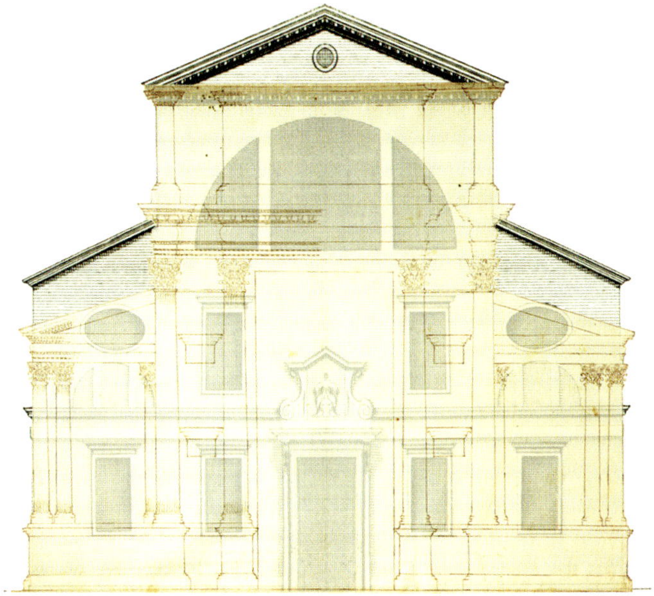

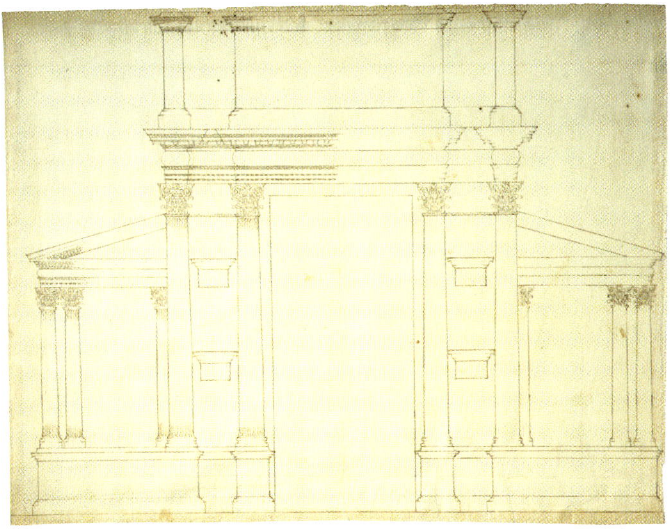

135 Antonio Foscari, Collage of the drawing *Project for the facade of a Church of Santa Lucia* and the survey by Francesco Muttoni of the facade of the Church of Santa Lucia
134 *Project for the facade of the Church of Santa Lucia,* Venice (identified by Antonio Foscari)

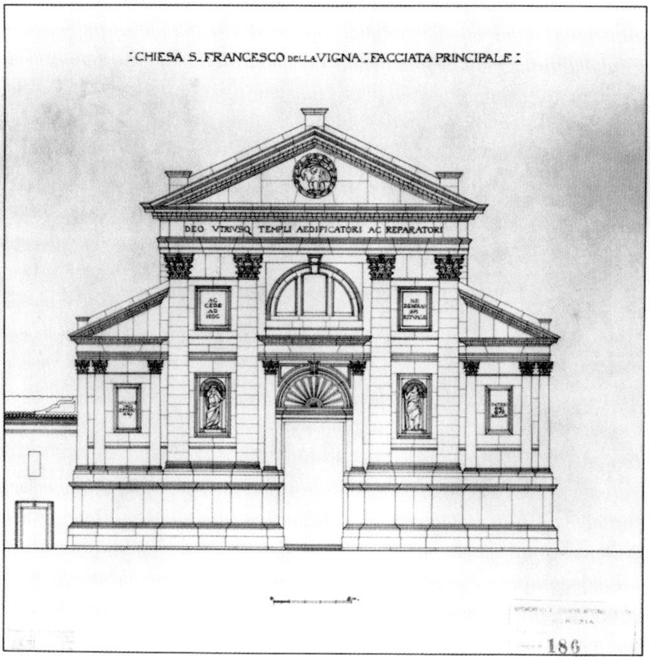

138 *Church of San Francesco alla Vigna,* survey of facade, Venice

147 *Church of San Giorgio Maggiore,* exterior (edited), Venice

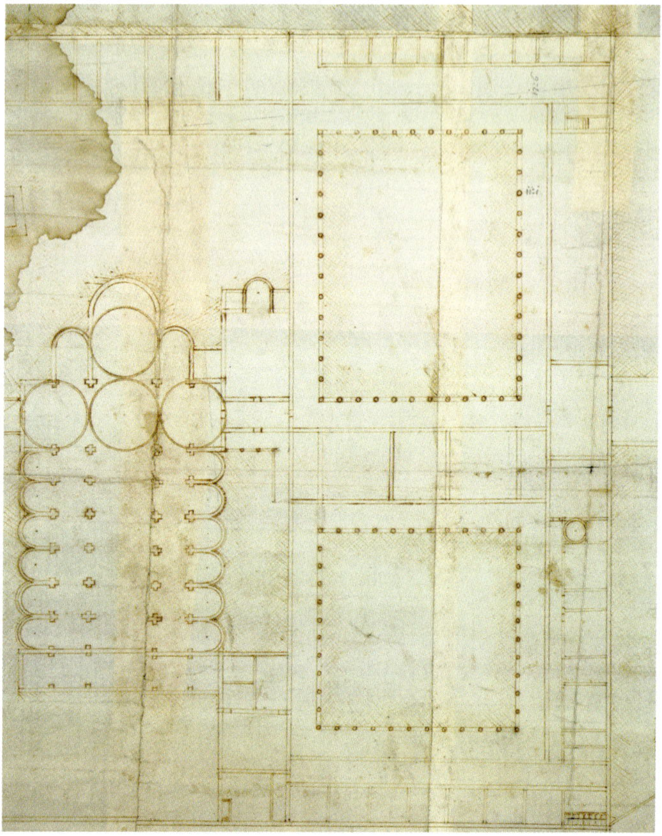

144 Anon., *Plan of the Church and Monastery of San Giorgio in Venice, before Palladio's intervention* (detail), 16th cent., Venice

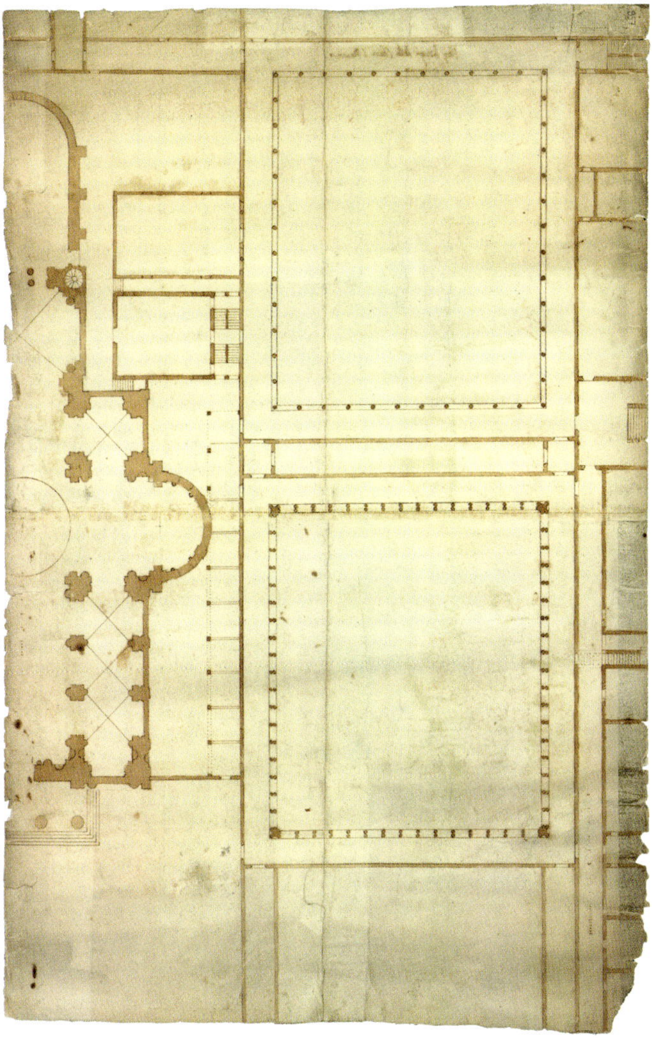

145 Anon., *Plan of the church (partial) and cloisters of the Monastery of San Giorgio Maggiore,* 15th cent., Venice

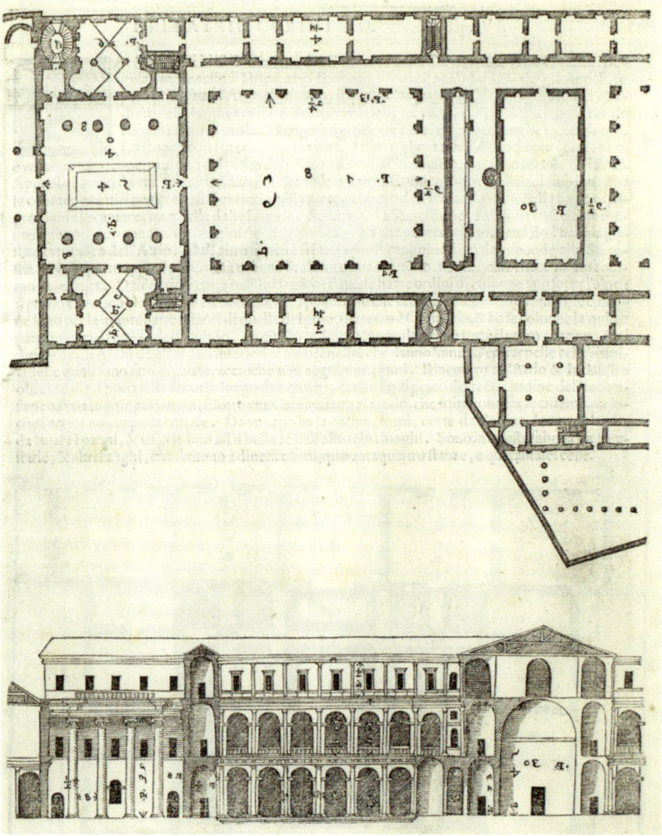

149 *Monastery of the Carità* (mirror image), Venice
151 Giovanni Antonio Canal (Canaletto), *View of Venice with the Monastery of Lateran Canons* (detail)
152 *Monastery of the Carità,* east facade facing the canal [now filled in] (edited), Venice

156 *Monastery of the Carità,* cross section of atrium, Venice

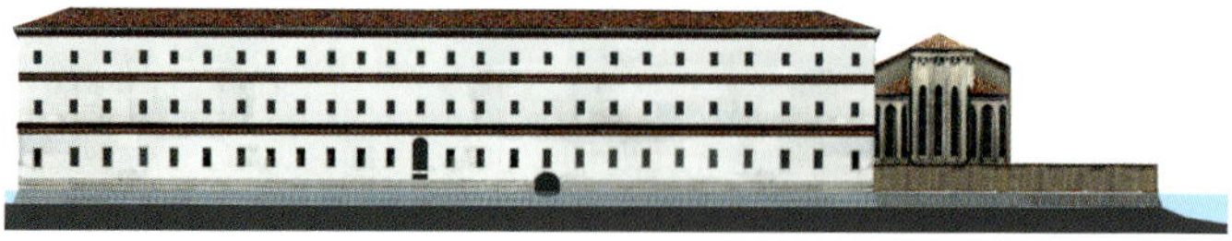

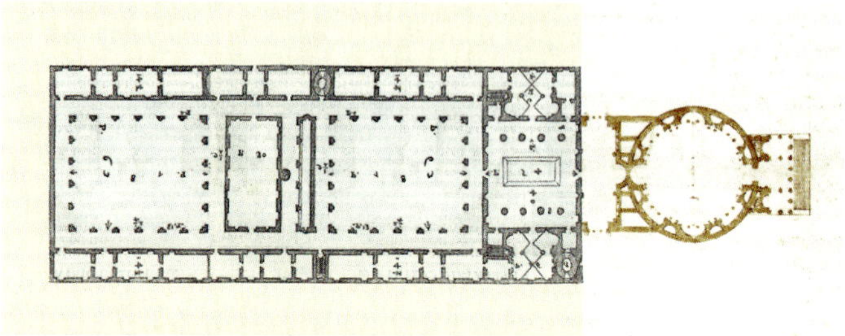

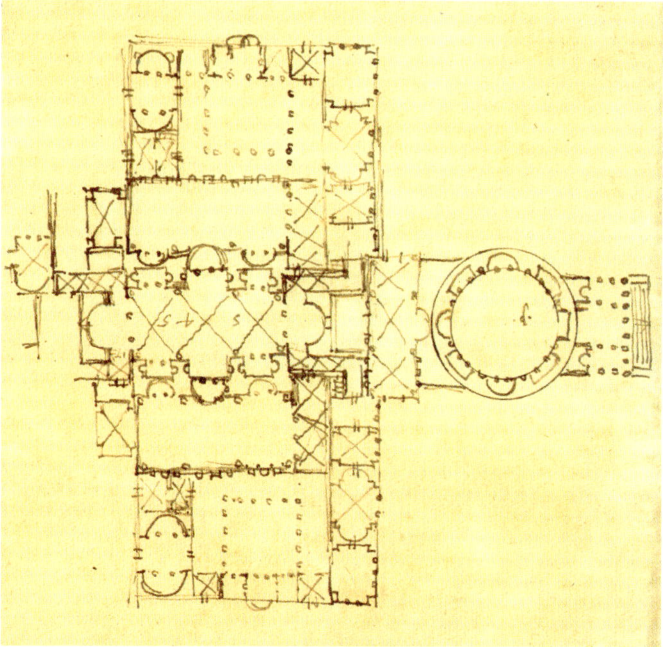

150 Antonio Foscari, collage of the *Monastery of the Carità,* Venice, eastern side, based on the Palladian design published in *I Quattro Libri dell'Architettura*
154 Antonio Foscari, collage of the *Monastery of the Carità,* plan showing Palladian project published in *I Quattro Libri dell'Architettura* with a rotunda at the northern end. The solution of the rotunda church is inferred from drawing D 33 r, Pinacoteca Civica, Vicenza
155 *Baths of Agrippa* (detail), Rome

the centre of the *arena*). This structure – which would have been a sensational evocation *all'antica* (and which some witty individual even thought could be built by transporting the Roman theatre at Pola to Venice, stone by stone) – would have been sited in the basin of San Marco, surrounded by water and therefore easily accessible for the Venetians who travelled by boat around the canals of their city.

Palladio refused to be distracted by the brilliant provocations of a man like Alvise Cornaro, whom he had come to know and even admire over the years for the intellectual autonomy that he succeeded in retaining for many years on the Venetian scene.

In reply, Palladio asserted that an *arena* is not a theatre. To make it a theatre it was not enough to call the uncovered area in the centre a "piazza". There were rules to follow when building a theatre: a dedicated *piazza* must be formed in the city, in the very heart of the city. In a city that claimed to be the "Third Rome", as Venice did, what was needed was a *Piazza dei Latini*.

ON THE PIAZZA DEI LATINI

This was because *Piazze dei Latini* or "Squares of the Latins" – as Palladio himself highlighted in the *Third Book* (repeating expressions that had appeared in the Vitruvian *Commentaries* published in 1556) – are spaces set aside to hold public events. "For this reason," he wrote, "they made the intercolumniations of the porticoes around the square two and a quarter column diameters":[29] so that the citizens who gathered here, being more crowded around the edges, could easily watch the events going on in the centre. [161] [162]

In short – instead of ephemeral and exclusive theatre structures, or improbable reconstructions of classical monuments (such as the *arena* which Alvise Cornaro imagined in the middle of the water in front of the Doge's Palace) – Palladio proposed to build a public *platea* in the heart of the city that conjured up a model used in ancient Rome. It would be a "theatre" open to the people and obviously also to the patriciate, who would have sole use of the upper loggia when attending performances, thereby

161

162

complying with that criterion of social distinction that Alvise Cornaro had also respected (indeed in his *arena* , he had assigned each social class its "place and step", adding "as though God had given it to him and nature required [...] it").[30]

What is more, at the head of the *piazza,* the Latins would have placed a *basilica,* one of the "places" – as Palladio explains – where "the judges presided under cover to administer justice and where, from time to time, very important business was conducted" and where "in our own times," he adds, the citizens can "assemble to deal with their lawsuits and business in comfort".[31]

Building on this Vitruvian idea, Palladio drew up plans in his project for an imposing edifice at the head of his ideal *piazza* at the Rialto: this would have had quite a large central *sala* on the ground floor and another two rooms leading through to the ends of the side porticoes of the *piazza.* The populace would go up two broad staircases, with two ramps – also accessible from the porticoes – to the upper floor, which would have had the same layout as the ground floor (although the central *sala* was not divided by columns but instead covered by a roof supported by exceptionally long trusses).

Palladio has left nothing to indicate what function he had in mind for such a building that, had it been built, would have occupied such an impressive position in the city. We can rule out that he intended it to house magistracies, thereby replicating the custom of the ancient Romans. (It was premature, at this time, even to think that the exercise of justice could be removed, or even separated from the Signoria's central seat of power, namely the Doge's Palace.)

If more information were available regarding the discussions that, precisely during these years, had led to the establishment of an office of *Provveditori alle Pompe* (the magistracy responsible for administering sumptuary laws), we might be persuaded into thinking that Palladio was influenced by a trend that was also becoming apparent in Venice: that the State should assume responsibility for managing performances and entertainment in order to oversee events that attracted vast audiences and might therefore have political implications that, given the rapid evolution of social custom, ran the risk of proving uncontrollable.

The large rooms that Palladio planned at the head of his *piazza* might therefore have been intended as venues for such festivities – recitals by *momarie* and performances of tragedies – as well as for serving the dinners and refreshments that usually followed public performances and were reserved to members of the Venetian patriciate and their aristocratic guests.

It seems likely, however, that Palladio gave up the idea of submitting this proposal to the Salt Magistracy, which would have had to build the project because it had sole responsibility for managing all town-planning matters and building within the Rialto area. Indeed, one can almost hear the murmur of criticism that would have met such an unexpected proposal – as if the voices have become trapped in the web of narrow streets in a city determined to resist any hint of "modernity". To many the idea of staging ephemeral events in an area of the city that was the heart of commercial and financial activities which, over the centuries, had governed the fate of European trade may have seemed provocative rather than stimulating.

A PROJECT FOR PUBLICATION: THE RIALTO BRIDGE

Palladio took these criticisms as an incentive to move on and responded with a surprisingly fresh burst of inventiveness. He abandoned the idea of the theatre, the *exemplum* of the classical *Piazza dei Latini* and the evocative concept of "twin" buildings (namely two equal structures, on either side of the Grand Canal, such as the ones he had imagined by siting a *fabbrica* on the other bank of the Grand Canal to balance the building planned beside the *campo* di San Bartolomio). Then he withdrew, ideally, from the city and moved onto the waters. There, he contrived a hanging platform to be built over the bed of the Grand Canal itself.

That this was a platform rather than a bridge is clear from the fact that it was supported by arches of equal width and height. That this platform must be seen as a different area of the city, and separate from it, can be understood from the fact that it is accessed through *porte* or gates. Moreover, that the setting can be deemed a *piazza* can be deduced from the massive size of these gates. [163]

The centre of this virtual piazza is the spot marking the intersection between the lines that Palladio – with brilliant insight – took as the *cardus* and *decumanus* of this "singular" city of Venice: the axis provided by the flow of traffic up and down the Grand Canal and the flow of people moving endlessly between the Doge's Palace and the financial hub of the Rialto.

This hanging structure, isolated from the city, was open to the city through porticoes.

Palladio knew that the Venetian citizens would see these porticoes as loggias below which they too – benefiting from a privilege that, until then, had been reserved to patricians (who had always had their own loggia at the foot of the Rialto bridge) – could come to discuss their affairs and be sheltered from the sun and the rain. Equally he knew that these porticoes-cum-loggias – this maritime emporium that was still admired as a model of efficiency – would make the city look like a theatrical setting.

But these factors played no part in determining his choices. Instead, the driving force behind every decision was the discipline he practised – namely architecture – and, in this sense, we should turn our attention to the compositional logic of this project.

The insight of designing an urban structure on two symmetrical axes intersected at right angles to each other (the ideal *cardus* and *decumanus* mentioned earlier) led to two architectural outcomes that Palladio had never before explored in such detail: a central plan composition in which the centre was a void, a virtual and intriguing *platea,* and a four-fronted structure that projected its image in all directions, interacting ideally with the entire city.

A CASA FOR LEONARDO MOCENIGO ON THE BRENTA

Palladio returned to the idea of a composition whose central concept took the form of a void, opening on the outside with two equal, paired facades, in a study he undertook for the patrician for whom he had drawn up plans to rebuild the church of Santa

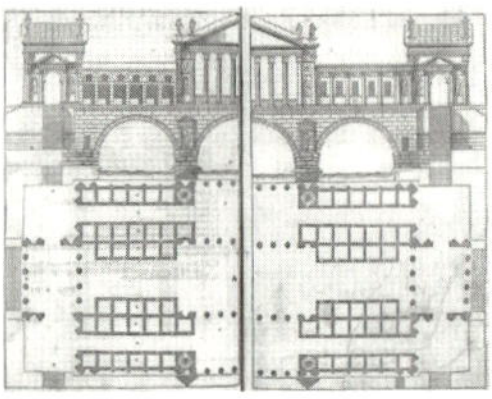

163

164

Lucia, namely the design that saw the unexpected appearance of the triumphal arch dedicated to Trajan, standing in full sunlight on the bank of the Grand Canal.

In the meantime Leonardo Mocenigo's interest in the classical world had turned into an antiquarian passion, as was perhaps inevitable in one who combined erudition with a desire for personal affirmation. His interest had blossomed during his mission to Germany, where he had been dispatched by the Signoria after his political vocation had displayed traits that were not altogether consonant with Venetian tradition. At the imperial court Leonardo Mocenigo had met a Venetian acquaintance, Jacopo Strada, who had been appointed by Ferdinand of Habsburg as court antiquarian and charged with expanding his collections of classical sculpture (as well as providing garden designs, stage sets, costumes for festivities and special equipment for tournaments).

To gratify this passion Palladio provided Mocenigo with a drawing of the Arch of Constantine so that the latter could commission a truly unique container for his collection of antique coins: "the most beautiful you would ever see", as an admiring contemporary wrote.

Leonardo Mocenigo was so firmly convinced of the importance of collecting and performance, also as an instrument or display of power, that he almost entirely gave up attending the Doge's Palace and even borrowed from his sons so that he could spend his time solely fulfilling his role as a connoisseur of antiquity.

This was the frame of mind that prompted him to ask Palladio to draw up plans for a *casa* on the banks of the Brenta Vecchia, a house that would embody the ideals to which he had decided to dedicate his life, as well as being a sort of *pendant* in the Terraferma to the Arch of Trajan that would have affirmed the standing of his family in Venice, on the banks of the Grand Canal.

Palladio scrupulously preserved the drawings for his projects and often referred to them in the belief that each offered potential that could be more fully explored. Therefore, he now returned to the proposals he had outlined many years earlier for a *casa di villa* for Marcantonio Thiene, when he was still under the strong influence of Giulio Romano's teaching. This was a *casa* whose façades opened onto two courtyards, one of which faced onto a watercourse.

Only once before – in the project for the *casa* built on Giacomo Angarano's country estate – had he returned to the theme of the courtyard in front of the *casa,* and he had done so by annexing the farm outbuildings to the porticoes flanking the courtyard rather than keeping them separate from the central house, as in the *casa* for the Thiene at Quinto where they were divided by roads also running towards the watercourse.

Here in Dolo, he preserved the double courtyard model of Quinto, while of the proposal in Angarano he retained the expanded breadth of the courtyard that exceeded the width of the *casa,* as well as integrating the porticoes surrounding its perimeter with the farm functions required to manage the country estate. [165] However, at least on one side of the *casa,* this solution created a lack of clearly defined boundaries between the owner's activities and those of the farm. In response – in another drawing – Palladio promptly rotated the main axis of the *casa* by 90 degrees, thereby creating loggias on two sides that solemnly mark its main entrances. [166]

To achieve this he had to expand the *casa,* not by changing the distributive scheme but by creating a large square courtyard inside it. It was during this last phase of the design process that the *invenzione* of a four-fronted *fabbrica* – namely with two paired and equal facades – matured, or one might say erupted.

Here, too – as with the Rialto bridge project – this almost unexpected outcome highlighted the architect's creativity and he immediately started to experiment with possible forms for the external areas, now part of the *casa,* on its two axes. This brought him almost naturally to the daring – almost visionary – proposition that would also be printed in 1570, together with the Rialto bridge project. [167]

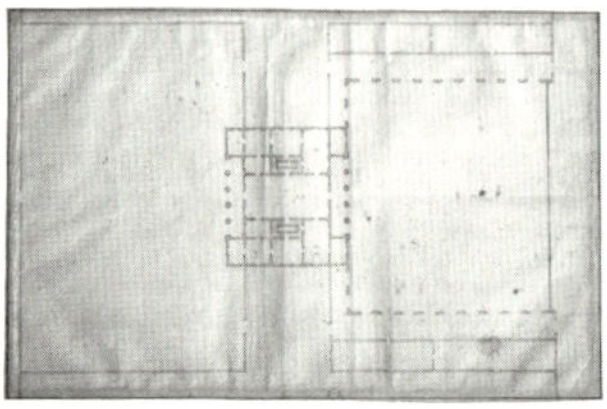

165

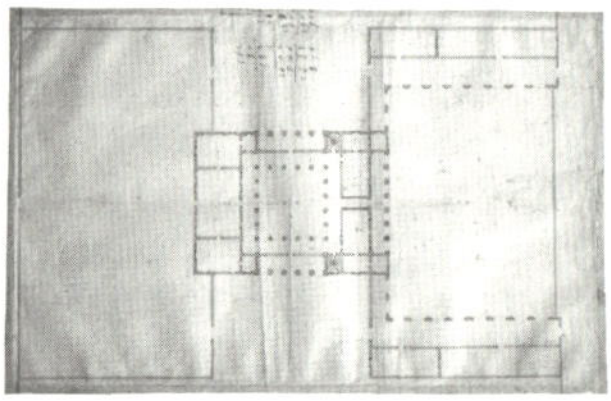

166

Everything – the opening up of the forms, the multiplication of the loggias, the use of the giant order and even the proposal of a structure whose imposing mass echoed the one at the southern end of the *Piazza dei Latini* designed for the Rialto area – pointed to the fact that Palladio had overcome the strict canons which he felt he had to respect in his projects for the Terraferma when interpreting the republican ideology of Venice.

The proposal drawn up for Leonardo Mocenigo was so disruptive in terms of the experimental impetuosity with which it was conceived and the theatricality of its layout that Palladio decided to devise a variation of the project elaborated in the early 1540s for the Thiene family at Quinto to include in his *Second Book.* [168] Moreover, it made the concept of the residence designed many years before for Giacomo Angarano look immature – at least in formal terms.

A CASA DI CITTÀ FOR GIACOMO ANGARANO

The first to realise this was Giacomo Angarano, who continued to support the architect with undiminished esteem and trust, and he clearly shared his enthusiasm for the wave of creativity that prompted such inspired designs. It was in this frame of mind, one might argue, that Angarano asked Palladio to design a new *casa:* but, this time, it would be a *casa di città.*

The dialectic between this initiative centred on Vicenza and the project for the Venetian patrician on the banks of the Brenta Vecchia is relatively clear once one realises that it was articulated in contrast.

The *casa di città* that Palladio designed for Angarano is closed, compact, and volumetrically impenetrable, in contrast to the *invenzione* designed for Leonardo Mocenigo which is open, interpenetrating the surrounding landscape and devised so that a refreshing breeze can reach the heart of the building unimpeded. [169]

The difference between these two models is not a form of eclecticism. Here again Palladio was motivated by his determination to develop his research in a new and different direction, without ever wavering in his conviction that the unity of all his work was

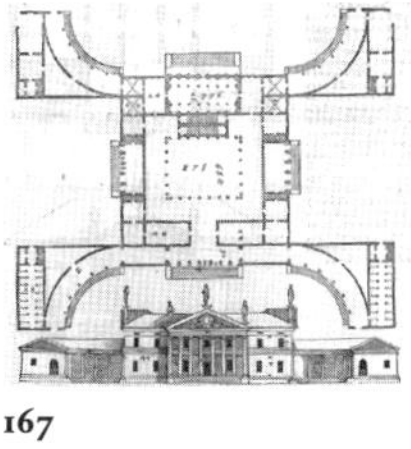
167

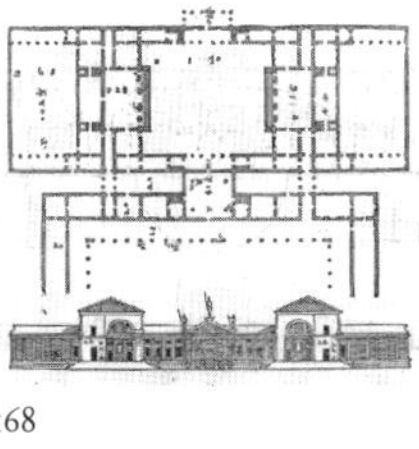
168

guaranteed by the consistency with which he used the same compositional logic and a perfectly tested linguistic code in all his projects.

When he decided to develop this project for Giacomo Angarano's *casa di città,* Palladio accepted the concept – and promptly elaborated the *exemplum* – offered by the Roman ruin at Nîmes, a drawing of which is also included in the *Fourth Book.* It is a peripteral temple, one of those which Palladio defined as *alati a torno* because they "do not have porticoes around them, but on the exterior walls of the cella there are half-columns".[32] He found this *exemplum* creatively stimulating not only for the unique model of its form but also because it was known locally as the *Maison carrée* because it was "rectangular in shape".[33]

Drawing inspiration from these two ancient models, he designed a square *casa* by distributing "half columns" on all its visible sides to form an innovative peripteral-type building without a *portico* on the front.

In the same way that the peripteral form would have set the building apart from the urban context in which it stood, the grandeur of its internal rooms would have proclaimed the status of its owner. Behind the façade of this *casa* would have been, in the same order, that succession of three rooms (including the central one "devoid of columns" on the upper floor, so that "its ceiling would rise up to the roof")[34] that make up the body of the *fabbrica* standing at the head of the *Piazza dei Latini* for the Rialto area.

In Palladio's compositional process – here, too, interpretative in every detail – the choice of the *exemplum* of Nîmes is not limited to an evocation of its peripteral form and the square layout conjured up by the name given to this Roman temple by the inhabitants of the city.

Instead the choice was a starting point to legitimise the appearance, within an urban context, of an unexpected and sensational sequence of giant Corinthian columns whose dimensions would have been accentuated by the height of the stereobate, or base,

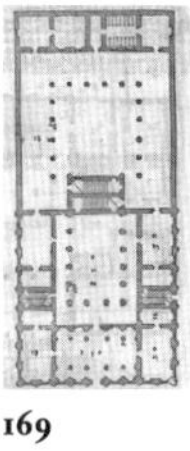

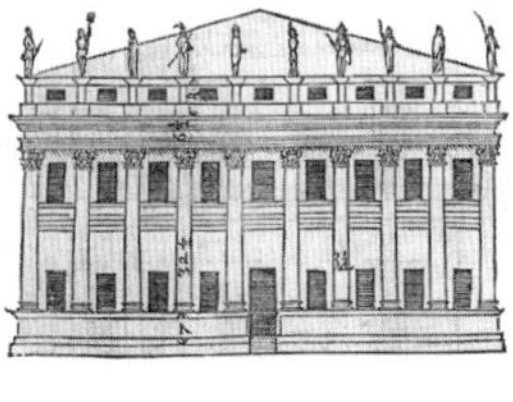

169

on which they stood: in other words an *ornamento* of the kind that, because of its grandeur, had never been used by anyone in Vicenza, or in Italy for that matter, to define the public image of a private residence.

It is hardly surprising that such an audacious *invenzione* was never realised. Its execution was blocked not only by the objections of some, indeed many of the city notables. More probably the Venetian Rectors themselves refused to countenance that a person of standing in a city of the *Dominio* could exalt his family's prestige and his personal ambitions in such a glaringly obvious manner.

A CASA DI CITTÀ FOR MONTANO BARBARANO

This principle of government did not apply only to the Angarano family but was also invoked when another Vicentine nobleman, Montano Barbarano, tried to build himself a *casa* in Vicenza that once again used the Colossal order for self-celebratory purposes. It matters little that in this case the *fabbrica* was not peripteral and had only "eight" columns on the façade. Barbarano had already embarked on works to build his new *casa* to this design when he had to modify his plans and build a *fabbrica* that also introduced an innovative image to the city – consisting of the superimposition of two architectural orders – but was to a certain extent legitimised by the precedent set by Girolamo Chiericati in the first section of the *casa* he had built at Isola. [170] [171]

Palladio only succeeded in introducing the Colossal order to Vicenza by renouncing the volume of the columns when – between the two proposals described above for Giacomo Angarano and for Montano Barbarano – he built a *casa* in Vicenza for Isabella Nogarola, widow of Giovanni Alvise Valmarana, the Vicentine nobleman who had been one of his strongest supporters during the competition to rebuild the loggias around the Palazzo della Ragione in Vicenza. [172] [173]

THE VALMARANA CASA IN VICENZA

But this project – one of the most evocative of all of Palladio's vast output – was generated using a different compositional process

170

171

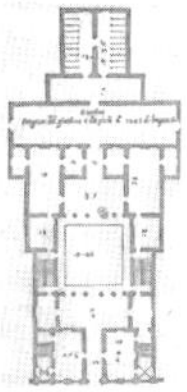

172

173

from the one that inspired the design of the *Maison carrée* "surrounded by corridors", or the reduction of this *exemplum* to a fragment (the palace façade for Montano Barbarano). This can be seen by comparing the drawing for Palazzo Valmarana with that for the palace designed by Palladio for Iseppo Porto. [174] [175]

It was that extraordinary feat, achieved two decades earlier, that Palladio – an architect for whom all compositional choices remained more or less in synchrony – "inferred" in the project he presented to Giovanni Alvise Valmarana's widow.

While the earlier project presented the visitor moving ideally along its axis with the "discovery" of a giant order inside a *fabbrica* whose façade consisted of a minor order resting on a high basement, the later design reversed this layout. The giant order was transposed onto the façade and the minor order was moved inside – again into a square courtyard.

Proof of the simplicity with which Palladio implemented this project and the open-mindedness with which he managed the consequences – even those that to others might seem to have been uncontrollable events – can be seen from the fact that the hatching of the façade for the new Valmarana *casa* "reflects" the short width of the courtyard porticoes in the *casa* for Iseppo Porto shown in RIBA drawing XVII, 3. The lack of a corner load-bearing structure and the appearance of a minor order on the façade in no way represent licences that can be seen as the architect's concessions to Mannerist ideas. They are the outcome of a compositional process that was so natural to Palladio that this is perhaps the main reason for such a surprising end result in formal terms.

Using this logic – as if to assert that the appearance of the Colossal order was not the premise of this *invenzione* but rather the consequence of a compositional process with its own unrepeatable specificity – Palladio did not use "half-columns" for this façade but instead shallow pilasters.

However, let us return to the *invenzioni* that Palladio produced for Giacomo Angarano and Montano Barbarano. In order to gain

174

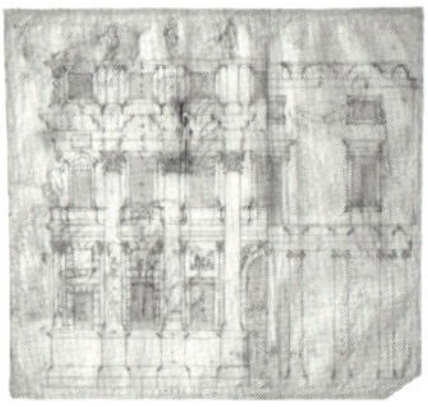

175

a clearer understanding of their significance, it is worth noting how the first *invenzione* coincided with the moment when the *Provveditori della fabbrica* of the Palazzo della Ragione finally approved – after countless hesitation – the form of the upper storey of the loggias; while the second happened before building work had started on the Capitanio in front of the Palazzo della Ragione (namely the *fabbrica* used to house the Venetian representative responsible for public security and policing in the city).

THE CONSTRUCTION OF A NEW LOGGIA IN THE PIAZZA AT VICENZA

We must first take a step backwards in order to focus on the event that resulted in this outcome – the construction of the Capitanio. It is worth noting that the Venetian Signoria had erected a *lodia magna* – in the same year that Vicenza came under Venetian rule (1404) – on the very site where this *fabbrica* would be built, using a model that the Serenissima then repeated in Udine in 1445 and in Padua in the late fifteenth century, because it perfectly expressed the concept of the rule that the Republic wished to establish in the cities of its *Stato da Terra*.

This loggia provided the setting – raised slightly above the piazza – where members of the city's ruling class could gather and meet, and which also housed the magistrates who administered justice *coram populi* (according to ancient customs still in force in a Republic where, in the absence of a written corpus of law, the formulation of judgments was entrusted to the *arbitrium* of its representative – in this case the *podestà* – in line with the judicial customs of ancient Rome). In view of its functions, the loggia took the form of a tribune (or "tribunal" to use the fifteenth-century term) and was surrounded by columns, namely by structural elements that did not obstruct – or only very slightly – the view of what was happening inside.

Above this loggia and supported by columns was the large hall used by the city Council, namely the body that expressed and represented that political autonomy which the Republican regime guaranteed to the city's inhabitants.

Therefore, in view of the institutional function of a building of this kind, it is not surprising that it had been damaged and desecrated during the conflicts of the War of the League of Cambrai, nor, however, that the Republic had arranged for its restoration after the war had ended.

This task had been overseen by Alvise Foscari (uncle of the two brothers who later summoned Palladio to Malcontenta) after he had been elected *Podestà* of Vicenza in 1520. To reaffirm the symbolic value of this structure, Foscari had called the *proto* of the Salt Magistracy of Venice to carry out the restoration work; Titian and Paris Bordon were also asked to reassert the importance attributed to justice by the Venetian Signoria in two large frescoes that evoked the statues positioned emblematically at the ends of the Doge's Palace (on the corner close to the Porta della Carta and at the opposite end beside the Ponte della Paglia): Solomon, the just ruler by definition, and Noah, the only mortal in a corrupt world whom God saved because he was "just".

But to return to the mid 1560s: after being restored in 1520, the fifteenth-century loggia was still being used as a *tribunale* and retained a sort of sacrality, in civil terms, owing to the dignity of the institutional functions it housed.

It seems likely that in 1565 it was the Venetian rectors – Marco Cornaro (Alvise's son) and the extremely wealthy Francesco Giustinian – who had the idea of building a Capitanio on the site of the loggia (which belonged to the Republic, as did the neighbouring palace that had been confiscated from the Verlato family after they had been embroiled in a plot many years earlier).

It was perhaps in response to this claim, therefore, that the Great Council of Vicenza – which understandably did not wish to lose the building in which it assembled – decided to purchase the houses overlooking the piazza west of the fifteenth-century loggia. The aim was to build another loggia on their foundations ("when the time was right" added the Council members in order not to set too immediate a deadline that perhaps they would not be able to keep).

The fact that the resolution passed by the Great Council of Vicenza states that this loggia would be "most beautiful" clearly means that they had already seen a model: it seems very probable that this is the one documented in Palladio's drawing on sheet D.19r preserved in the Museo Civico of Vicenza. [176]

If so, it would have been a hexastyle loggia embellished with fluted Corinthian columns topped by a large hall overlooking the piazza, with five windows let into its attic. From the piazza the hall was open to public view up a wide staircase (of a kind that seems to copy the model of the loggia beside the Palazzo del Capitanio in Padua) and also by another side stair that clearly led into Contrà dei Giudei.

THE CONSTRUCTION OF A CAPITANIO ON THE PIAZZA IN VICENZA

Even now, centuries later, the decision taken by the Capitano of Vicenza to start building a Capitanio on the site of the old loggia before a new loggia had been built to accommodate the leading Vicentine citizens and house the city's Great Council on the upper floor seems somewhat rushed. Moreover, it does not seem likely that Giovan Battista Bernardo had sufficient political standing to take such an important decision. Therefore, he must have at least had the support of Francesco Bernardo, his close relative, who during this two-year period held the offices first of Savio del Consiglio and then Savio di Terraferma.

Francesco Bernardo – a merchant actively involved in international markets and an expert on international diplomatic negotiations – might well have dealt with this Vicentine affair given that, as we know, he had been *Podestà* of Vicenza in the crucial years of 1548 and 1549 when the debate over the reconstruction of the loggias at the Palazzo della Ragione, which had dragged on for years, finally ended with Palladio's engagement.

If, during the course of his short term as Capitano, Giovan Battista Bernardo – possibly with Francesco's backing – started to build the Capitanio on the site of the pre-existing loggia, it was almost implicit that he would turn to Palladio for drawings of the *fabbrica*, as the architect who had been appointed in 1549 to oversee the

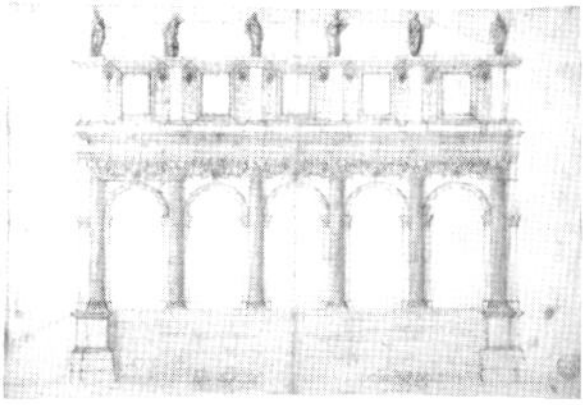

176

rebuilding of the loggias at the Palazzo della Ragione. (Moreover, he might also have been prompted to do so by his wife, the sister of Alvise Badoer, who in 1567 – just two years before Bernardo's arrival in Vicenza – had married the daughter of Leonardo Mocenigo, the patrician who had hired Palladio to build a *casa di villa* in Dolo that would equal those "of the ancients" in magnificence.)

Even the *Provveditore alle Fortezze,* the official responsible for the security of the territory to whom the Capitano had to report, would not have objected to a choice of this kind, given that this role was then held by Alvise Foscari who spent a few months every year in a *casa* that Palladio had designed a decade earlier at Malcontenta. [177]

Without this sequence of coincidences it might not even have been possible for Palladio to work on an *invenzione* in which he could finally make a triumphant display of the giant order, based on the assumption – which was undeniable on this occasion – that the Republic was fully entitled to use columns that expressed the supreme authority of the State through the figurative power resulting from their colossal dimensions. [178]

To understand how Palladio devised this *invenzione* – whose form is so well known that it hardly needs describing – it may be useful to consider the criterion he used to position the *fabbrica* within the site delimited by the Contrà del Monte to the east and the piazza to the south. [179]

That this *fabbrica* should present itself in the urban setting as a volume whose visible fronts are strictly orthogonal should be expected, since Palladio always complied with this compositional requirement in his architectural approach. However, what merits closer attention is that neither of the two facades follows the alignment of the buildings flanking the Capitanio. One (to the south) does not follow the line of façades created by the houses overlooking the western side of the piazza (an alignment that is also clearly visible in the view sketched by Marco Moro in 1850) and the other (to the east) does not follow the line of houses facing the Contrà del Monte.

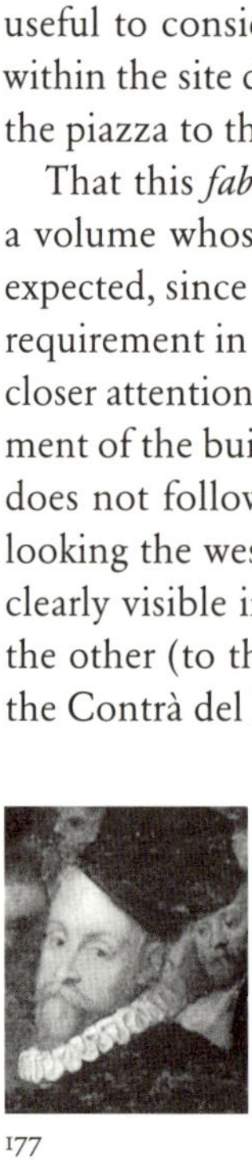

177

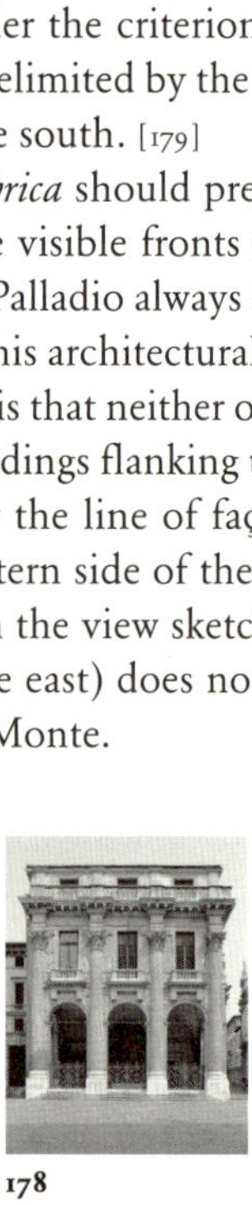

178

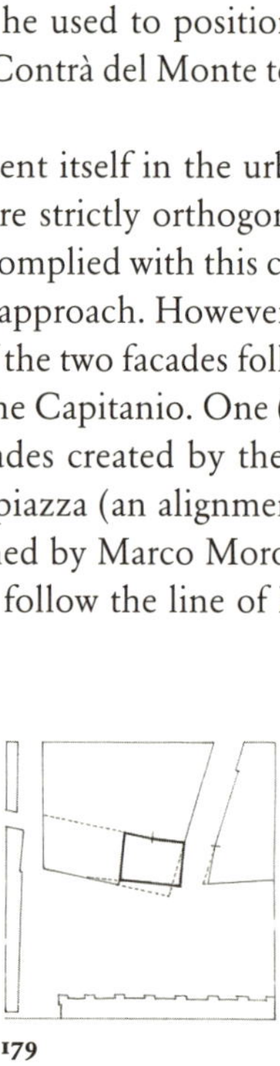

179

The architect also chose the spot where the two orthogonal alignments of the new *fabbrica* intersect with consummate skill: the flank of the *fabbrica* is sloped, making it clearly visible to anyone approaching the piazza from Contrà del Monte; the alignment of its façade – while not parallel – is less steeply inclined compared to the façade with the arcades of the loggias of the Palazzo della Ragione opposite. (A little more can perhaps be said on the subject of this alignment: it appears to have been designed to allow the *fabbrica* to be extended by five modules, precisely the number required to join it with the alignment of the houses overlooking the piazza on the western side.)

Thanks to the use of brick rather than stone as the construction material (and to the loans that Giovan Battista Bernardo granted for its construction, even after his term of office as *podestà* had ended), the building was completed very rapidly.

The speed of construction was inevitably seen as a sort of negative comment on the slow rate of progress in the construction of the loggias for the Palazzo della Ragione, which Palladio had ceased overseeing nearly twenty years earlier and which – by the early 1570s – had not produced more than four bays of the upper storey.

However, this is not the only facet to emerge from the construction of the Capitanio, providing a comparison that is not without certain implications for the works on the Palazzo della Ragione. The Colossal order of columns irrefutably announces its superiority – thanks to the Corinthian *ornamento,* as well as the size – over the Doric and Ionic orders whose canonical superimposition is a feature of the loggias.

In short, it would appear that the Vicentines may have been somewhat perplexed by the appearance of such a blatant symbol of central Republican power in their piazza, replacing a public loggia that had previously housed the hall of their Great Council. Moreover, given that the buildings facing onto the piazza as far as the Contrà dei Giudei were not purchased in the end, the loggia and hall were not rebuilt, nor would they ever be in the future.

The ground floor of the new *fabbrica* was not a real loggia, in spite of the decision to describe it as one: the massive volume of the columns and the masonry wall into which they are set keeps the whole area in the half-shadow and means that it is not clearly visible to the citizens gathering in the piazza. Indeed, Palladio – once again showing intellectual honesty – was at pains to point out that it was not a loggia but a portico.

The appearance of this *fabbrica,* with its surprising shape and function, had a huge impact on the urban scene: an impact that was not diminished or lessened by the figures with which Palladio covered its surface (perhaps somewhat mischievously), to please the eye. The thought does come to mind that this might explain why Giovan Battista Bernardo's *cursus honorum* came to such an abrupt end. The Venetian magistracies were quick to put such a controversial outcome down to his self-celebratory aims; and perhaps they did not forgive the inclusion of his name in large Latin letters on the frieze of the Capitanio (together with the Roman title of *pretore,* instead of the less honorary Capitano which was his due).

A CASA DI CITTÀ FOR ALESSANDRO PORTO

If we shift our attention from Piazza dei Signori to Piazza Castello – therefore, remaining in Vicenza – and examine that "impressive fragment" (as Lionello Puppi aptly describes it) consisting of the double bay of the *casa* that Alessandro Porto had proudly started to build at exactly the same time that work on the Capitanio was underway, we begin to realise how stimulating the architectural implications of building the Capitanio were for Palladio. [180] [181]

While working on this *invenzione,* Palladio made a daring attempt to embellish a private *casa* with a giant order. While doing so, his thoughts returned to the project for the Capitanio, with that capacity for self-criticism which he constantly reveals, and in particular to the presence of an attic above the entablature supported by the Colossal order of columns. The attic is only slightly hidden by a balustrade running along the whole length of the entablature.

180

181

Taking as his starting point a feature he had implemented while building the façade of the Venetian church of San Francesco della Vigna, Palladio decided to raise the giant columns of this *fabbrica* on very high pedestals (tall enough to contain the ground floor of the *casa*). This meant that the magnificent hall on the *piano nobile* was contained, up to its full height, within the level of the entablature. (This result removed the need for the attic; indeed the windows providing ventilation and light for the upper part open within the frieze of the entablature.)

The overall outcome of this design – which Palladio achieved by complying with the internal requirements of his compositional procedure – was so controversial that it caused hostile reactions among many members of the Vicentine ruling class and the Venetian magistracies (but also, so it would seem, lively censure among the inhabitants of Vicenza itself where the *fabbrica* was promptly dubbed the "devil's house").

It comes as no surprise, therefore, that the construction was not resumed and that when Francesco Thiene asked him shortly afterwards to build a new *casa* in Vicenza, Palladio advised him unequivocally to choose the model of two superimposed orders, following the prudent criterion used by Montano Barbarano after the failed attempt to design the façade of his *casa* featuring a giant order.

Yet Palladio was not discouraged by these failures and he concentrated all his efforts on practising a discipline that was ethical in conception, over and above being artistic.

The existential anxiety he suffered at this stage of his life was probably triggered by the pain of losing his son Leonida, who used to help him with his work, followed shortly afterwards by the death of his other son, Orazio. A number of factors point to this explanation: for example, the conciliatory attitude – completely unlike the rigour that normally characterised his behaviour – during his negotiations to define the façade of the grandiose Bolognese church of San Petronio; or his willingness to provide drawings for tombs, as if he had returned to his youthful role of stonecutter.

Also the attention he paid to the figure of Emanuele Filiberto, the prince who had recently moved the capital of his kingdom to Turin where he adopted Italian (rather than French) as his official State language and restored the University, replacing the antique communal laws with his own, may have been a clue to Palladio's growing desire to move to a new setting.

At this particular moment, Venice did not seem to offer a satisfactory outlet for his ambitions. Jacopo Sansovino's death in 1570 might finally have enabled him to obtain some official recognition from the administrative hierarchy of the State, and the almost contemporaneous death of Daniele Barbaro should have opened the way to his recognition as the leading figure in the city's cultural life. [182]

Instead, the magistracies of the Republic only engaged him as a trusted professional, providing advice on public works to be carried out in cities within the *Dominio*. It was in this capacity that Palladio, "inventore" of loggias, was dispatched to Udine to advise on the accessibility of the Sala dell'Ajace above the city's loggia, or to Brescia to launch a more ambitious plan to rebuild the loggia and the city's Great Council hall.

THE TRIUMPHAL APPARATI FOR THE ARRIVAL OF THE KING OF FRANCE

Nor were the tasks assigned to him by the Signoria for spectacular events held within the setting of Venice any more satisfying. For Palladio, the commission to prepare triumphal *apparati* for the arrival of the King of France in 1574 was a task that took him back to the years when he had made his debut in Vicenza, where he had been summoned to work on the ephemeral architecture set up for Cardinal Ridolfi's entry into the city. Moreover, when the design of the loggia he had installed behind a triumphal arch, built "according to the ancient Roman custom in imitation of the Arch of Septimius"[35], was altered merely on grounds of protocol (due to the excessively large number of patricians who intended to attend the welcome ceremonies for the young French sovereign), Palladio was sufficiently affronted not to bother attending the actual ceremony. [183] [184]

182

Likewise, being involved in restoration work on the rooms in the Doge's Palace that had been ruined by fire that same year (1574) was a task he cannot have found gratifying. He had to work as a subordinate and report to two *provveditori* (one was the same Piero Foscari for whom he had built a theatre, an occasion that had proved the only time he had ever complained in his entire life); moreover, he had to provide details of furnishings and ceiling compartments (works whose overall design did not comply with any "ragione", as he had already had occasion to remark).

To make a bad situation worse, the end of the year saw the return of the plague to Venice, decimating the population and robbing Palladio of valuable supporters. (Leonardo Mocenigo also died of the plague, after which work was suspended on the magnificent "*casa di villa* of the ancients" that should have stood on the banks of the Brenta.)

THE CONSTRUCTION OF A TEMPLE DEDICATED TO THE REDEEMER. DANIELE BARBARO'S PROPOSAL

After the death toll had risen to not fewer than forty thousand, the Venetian Signoria decided to pledge a solemn vow, taken by the Senate, to build a church to the "praise and glory" of God which would be dedicated to the Redeemer and which the doge would undertake to visit solemnly once a year. This marked the start of a project that at long last resulted in Palladio's engagement on a public work of outstanding symbolic importance, although not without carrying out a selection process of his possible rivals, as was normal in a "well ordered" regime.

But before turning to Palladio, it is worth focusing on the line taken by Marcantonio Barbaro at the solemn meeting of the Senate in late 1576 when it was decided where the church would be built and what form it would take. [185]

Bolstered by his authority as Procuratore di San Marco, Barbaro argued that the church should be round and that it should be built on a site overlooking the Grand Canal facing the church of the Carità whose Late Gothic structure obscured the northern front of the grandiose monastery of the Lateran Canons whose rebuilding Palladio had started a decade earlier.

183

184

The determination with which Barbaro defended this idea cannot have been coincidental. It is almost self-evident that he had seen Palladio's proposal to introduce an irrefutable model of the *casa degli antichi* onto the Grand Canal by means of a rotunda sited at its northern end.

He was therefore influenced by the idea of creating a duplication of this form on both banks of the Grand Canal, reinstating the intriguing proposal that Palladio himself had suggested in the drawing illustrating the placement of two *Piazze dei Latini*, in the Rialto area, on either side of the city's main waterway.

Two round-plan churches on the banks of the Grand Canal – almost at its mouth – and facing each other on the same axis would certainly have created a monumental entrance that would have radically innovated the perception of its function as a port.

The correspondence of such a unique architectural form on the northern bank of the Grand Canal with the one that (in our interpretation) should have appeared on the opposite bank would have been even more emphatic if, behind the temple in the area of San Vidal, there had been a sort of building complex, full of rooms designed to house the members of the Jesuit order, as Marcantonio Barbaro proposed.

It is precisely this last proposal that reveals the political aim Barbaro had set out to achieve, disguising it somewhat in the context of a project of primarily cultural importance.

He seized the opportunity of the debate sparked by the proposal to build a church as a pretext to try to impose on the city his vision of the political line that the Republic should follow in the European scenario taking shape at the close of the Ecumenical Council: a line that presupposed quite a close relationship between the Republic and the Church of Rome.

THE CONSTRUCTION OF THE CHURCH OF THE REDENTORE. THE SENATE'S DECISION

It is hardly surprising that this suggestion was rejected by the government of a Republic that had by now learnt to navigate its way through history without entering uncharted waters. Instead, it chose a decentralised area of the city as the site for the church: the

185

island of Giudecca which, for at least a century, had been the district preferred by intellectuals (and where the doge's wife also cultivated her interest in plants by maintaining a celebrated botanical garden). Moreover, it decided to assign the running of the church to a well-deserving religious order that, during the fatal months of the plague, had helped the poorest groups of citizens and which practised a regime of poverty with such rigour that it precluded any possibility of political involvement.

It has already been pointed out on other occasions that the construction of a central-plan church at the Zitelle, the only base the Republic had allowed the Jesuits to establish in Venice, and the construction of a *rotonda* at Maser can be seen as the proud reactions of the Jesuits and Barbaro – with Palladio's assistance – to the failure of their shared plan in late 1576. Therefore, this is not an aspect worth stressing now. [186] [187]

Having chosen the site on the Giudecca overlooking the wide canal to the north, the Senate ruled out the idea of building a traditional-type church.

Once more (as had happened years previously when – according to our interpretation – the hypothesis was first put forward to rebuild the patriarchal church of San Pietro di Castello), the construction of a church that expressed the religiosity of the State prompted the Venetian Signoria to opt for a central-plan building, whether square or round.

In response to this request, Palladio – tireless as ever – promptly drew up two solutions.

The difference between these two typologies (both of which would have had to stand on a rectangular site, given the particular shape of the area made available by the Republic) lay primarily in the type of structure covering the sacred space: the *quadrangular* solution would have been covered by a cross vault; the rotunda by a dome at the top of which would have been an *oculus*, allowing natural light into the temple.

Both solutions would have displayed an exceptional wealth of ornamentation in their interior, to a degree that was unprecedented

186

187

in any of Palladio's earlier works: such embellishment would have generated – through the medium of architecture – a degree of solemnity not unlike that produced by a concert of brass instruments of the kind held at the time to mark the doge's most important visits. [188] [189]

However, each of these forms would have had a different impact on the urban fabric. The square solution would also have offered an unavoidable landmark to anyone viewing it from a distance – and from the Piazzetta of San Marco, in particular. But a dome, like the one that would have topped the rotunda, would have been even more clearly visible owing to its geometric clarity and its height, which would have exceeded that of a four-pitched roof. [190]

The choice of the rotunda solution would have had other implications too. Irrespective of the fact that the *fabbrica* had a rectangular base (for the reasons stated earlier), it would evoke the paradigmatic form of the Pantheon and therefore presuppose the inclusion of a portico in front of it, based on the type standing in front of the famous Roman rotunda.

However, the proposal of a portico in front of the church would have necessitated a building lot of greater depth. Indeed, Palladio highlighted this need to the *provveditori* by emphasising the important role played during the doge's visit by the possibility of having a sacristy in front of the church where the highest state magistracies could gather and regroup both before entering the church and after leaving it with pomp.

In the same spirit, one might imagine, Palladio suggested building a large choir behind the altar (a choir whose circular form appears to conjure up the model devised by Antonio da Sangallo for the Roman church of San Marcello al Corso), highlighting how the solemnity of the religious celebration held in the presence of the doge would be heightened if accompanied by liturgical chants and music that had been specially composed for the occasion. [191]

These were the reflections that Palladio submitted to the *provveditori* supervising the project on the instructions of the Senate.

188

189

190

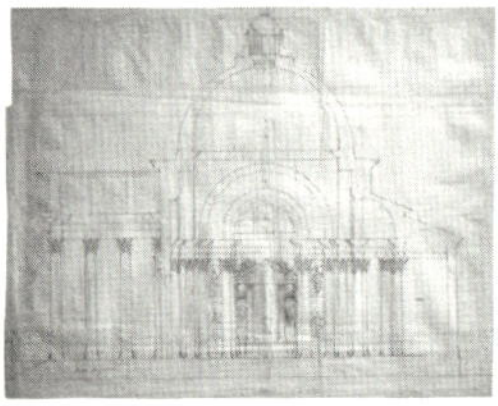

191

Yet, in consideration of the matter, it was not just these reminders that made the Signoria rapidly realise the need to amend the project they had initially been offered.

The *provveditori* knew all too well that, in its vow to build this church, the Senate had pledged that once a year the doge would lead a solemn procession, accompanied by the entire Signoria, to give thanks to the Redeemer for saving Venice from the horrendous plague.

In this sense, a church like the one that Palladio had outlined in a prompt response to the Senate's request – whether square or round – would have served almost exclusively as the point of arrival or destination of this procession, and not as the setting for a celebration of the eucharist attended not only by the Signoria but also by representatives of the highest state magistracies.

It seems wholly plausible that it was an argument of this kind (not all that different from the one that a few months earlier had resulted in changes to the form of the loggia Palladio had designed to welcome the French king to Venice) that contributed to the decision that was taken shortly afterwards to use a different architectural model for the construction of the church.

It is therefore not difficult to identify the "political" reasoning behind this initiative, which the Signoria took at a time when the memory of the epic naval battle between the Christian fleet and the Ottoman armada only a few months earlier was still very much alive in the city.

It is known – and at the time it would have been common knowledge – that, after the victory in the waters off Lepanto, sensational as it was, the Republic did not hesitate to sever, almost summarily, its alliance with the Papacy and Spain in this military campaign against the Turks. Instead it drew up a separate peace with the Sultan in which it granted the Ottoman Empire some of its most valuable maritime outposts in the eastern Mediterranean. Venice could not even begin to contemplate standing alone in the eastern Mediterranean against the Turkish counterattack, which would inevitably follow, while the pope was safely ensconced on the banks of the Tiber and the Spanish king even more secure on the far-off Iberian peninsula.

There was another consequence to this painful decision that Venice was the first to realise: the Republic would never again take part in a military adventure under the guise of a "crusade", and as a result the Holy Land would never again be reconquered by Christianity.

It was considerations of this kind that persuaded the Republic to undertake the construction of a virtual Holy Sepulchre within its own lagoon, on the Giudecca. Indeed, it marked a return to a similar question that had been debated by the Venetian Signoria in the months after Constantinople fell to the Islamic forces in 1453, leading to the start of building work on the doge's church of San Zaccaria.

THE CONSTRUCTION OF THE CHURCH OF THE REDENTORE. THE FINAL PROJECT

Even in the early fifteenth century the *exemplum* that was chosen to build a church evoking the Holy Sepulchre was the church built by Emperor Constantine's mother in Jerusalem on the site where the Cross was found on which Christ's Passion had reached its tragic conclusion: a circular building, the *Anastasis,* preceded by a basilica-like construction whose width equalled the diameter of the *Anastasis:* the so-called *Martyrion.* [192]

To some Venetians, the use of this *exemplum* was perhaps also a consequence of the influence exerted by the numerous drawings on this theme carried out by Jacopo Bellini – clearly in agreement with leading members of the Signoria. Yet for Palladio the conceptual reference was different. Like the many other connoisseurs of architecture with whom he talked, he knew that a model of this kind had been the focus of specific and new reflection by Leon Battista Alberti, an erudite diplomat with many acquaintances among Venice's ruling class; they also knew that Sigismondo Malatesta had tried to build it in Rimini at precisely the time when he had been handed control of the armed forces of the Republic. [193]

Moreover, it was to this ground plan, the one from Rimini, that Antonio da Sangallo returned when he elaborated that design for

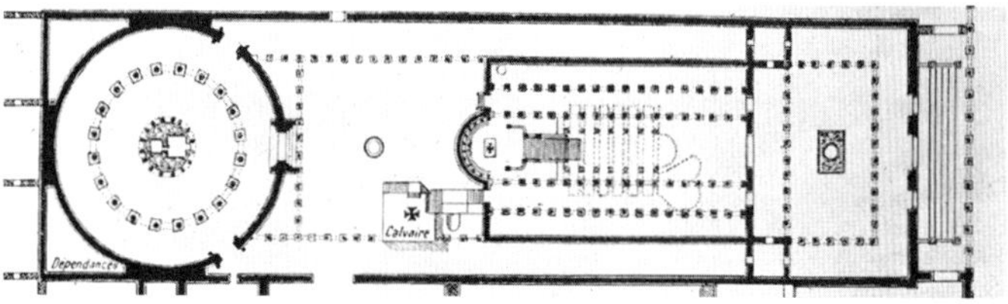

192

157 Jacopo Zucchi (attributed), *Portrait of Vasari,* 16th cent.

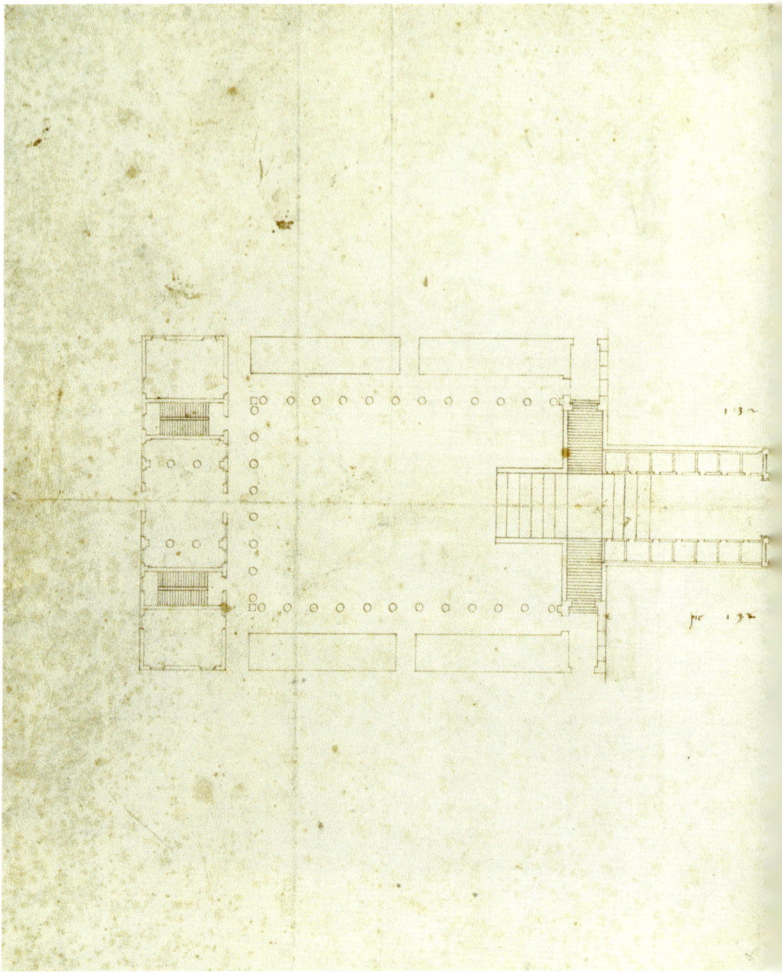

158 *Project for a new layout of the area around the Rialto Bridge,* Venice

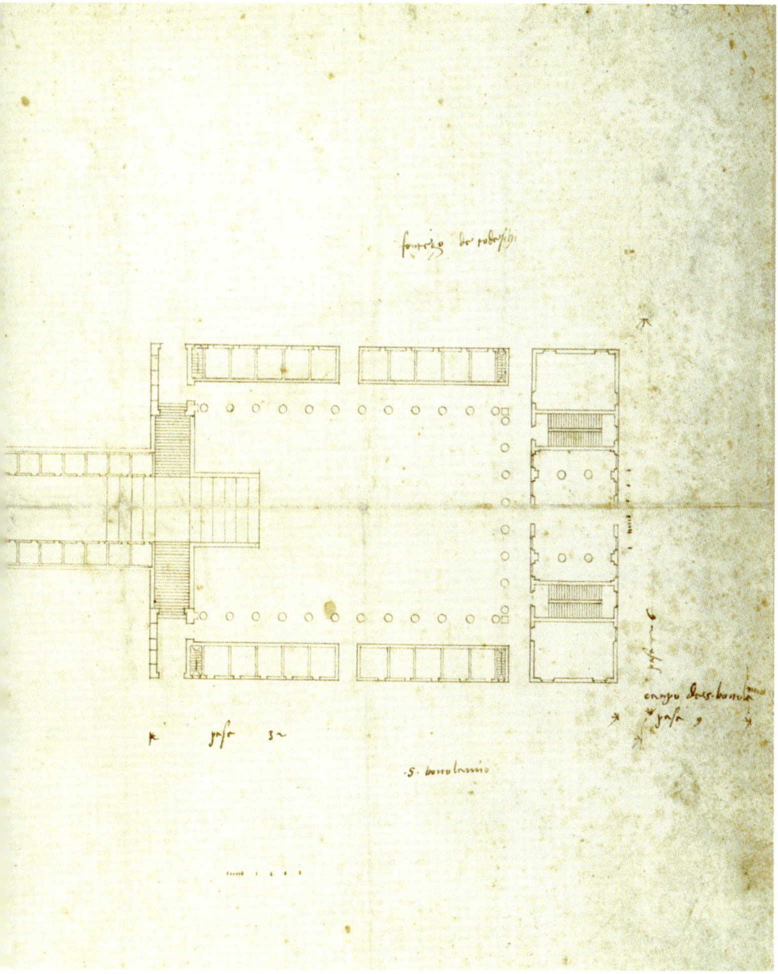

161 *Piazza dei Latini, Rialto,* Venice

162 Le Corbusier, *La construction des villes* (detail), 1915

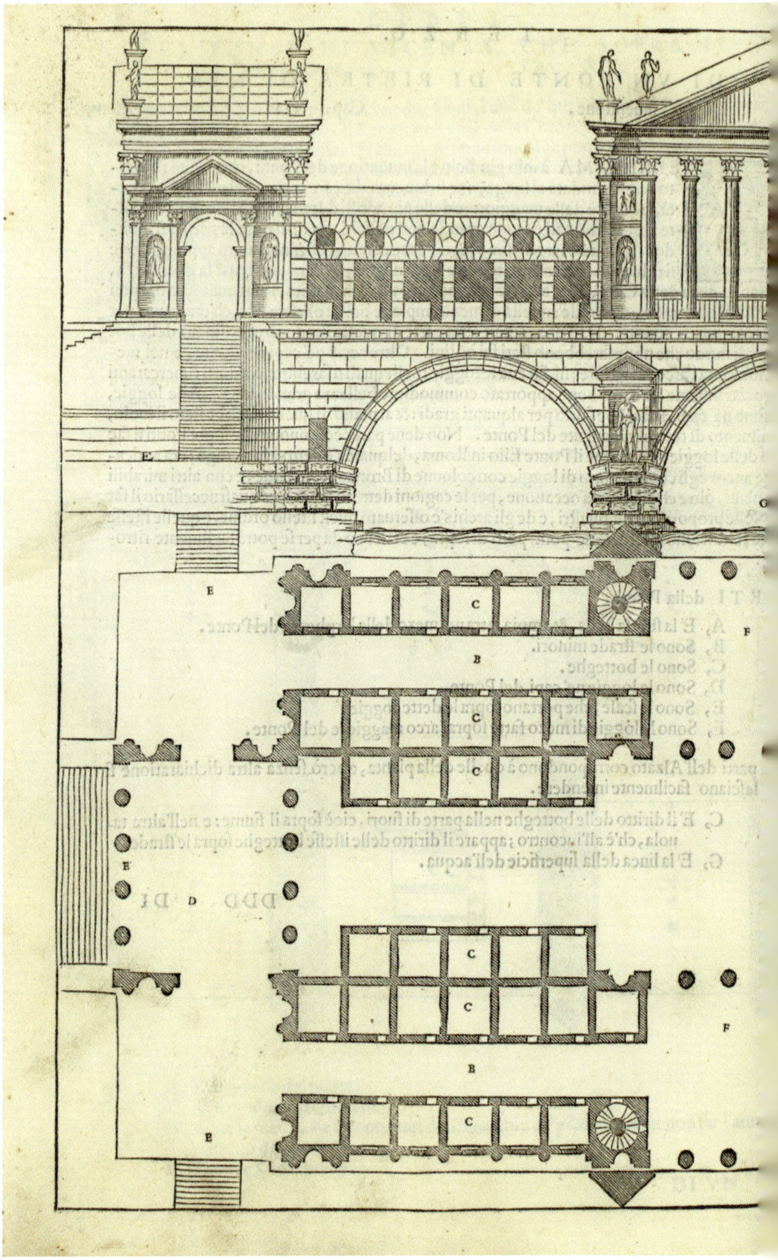

163 *Project to rebuild the Rialto Bridge,* Venice

C
E
DDD 2 D I

164 *Triumphal Arch* (above), Planimetric reconstruction by Antonio Foscari (below)

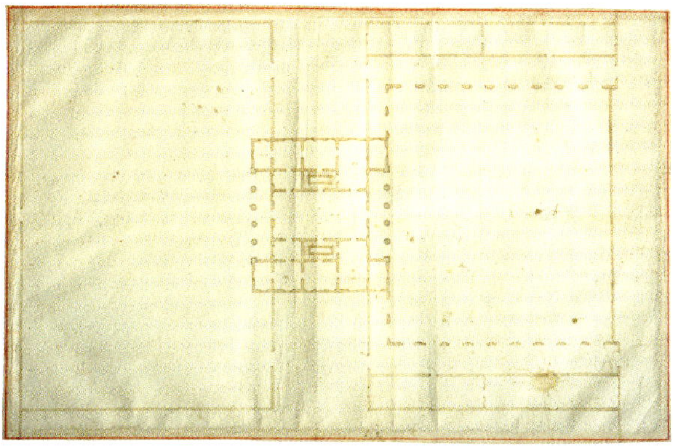

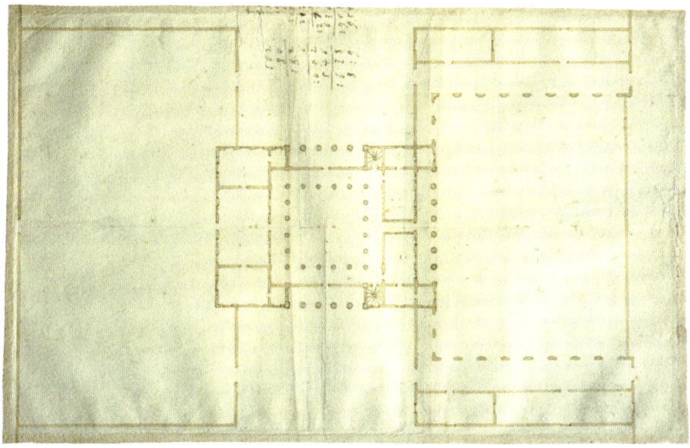

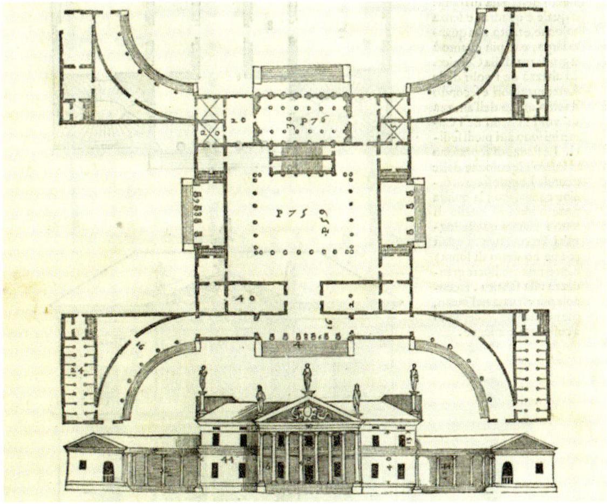

165, 166 *Villa Mocenigo,* Dolo (Venice)
167 *Villa Mocenigo* (detail), Dolo (Venice)

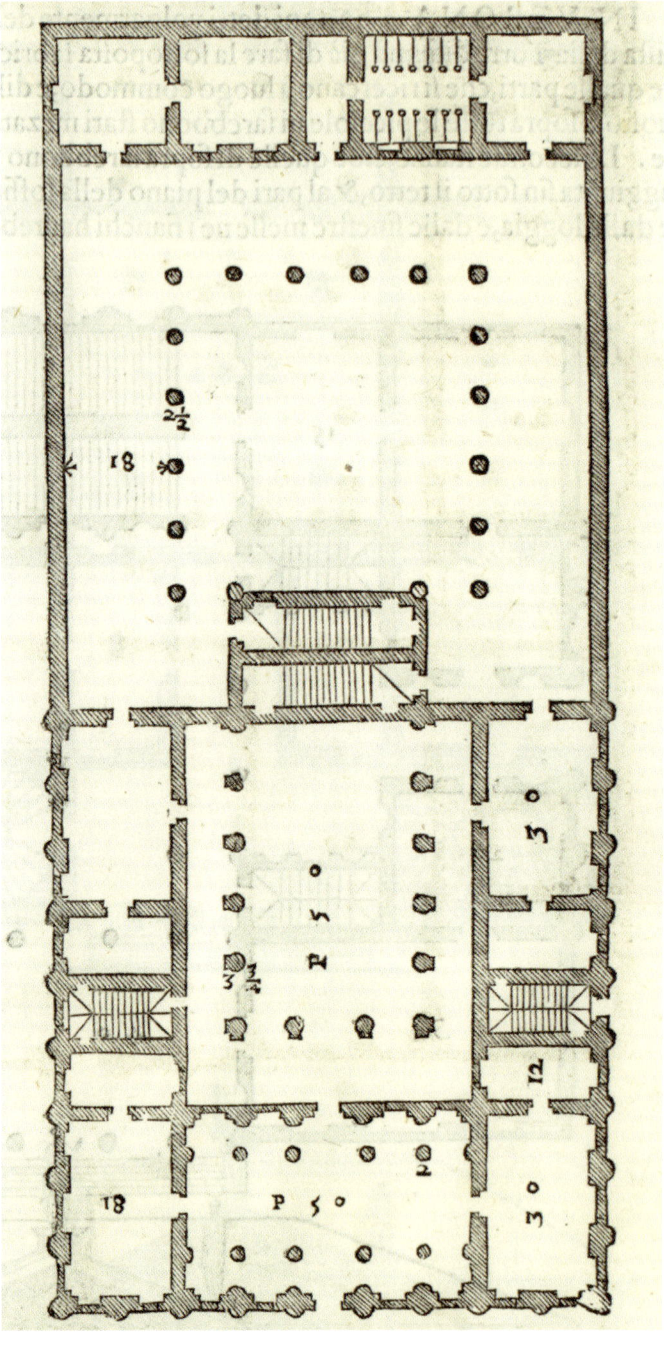

169a, 169b *Project for a palazzo for Giacomo Angarano* (detail), Vicenza

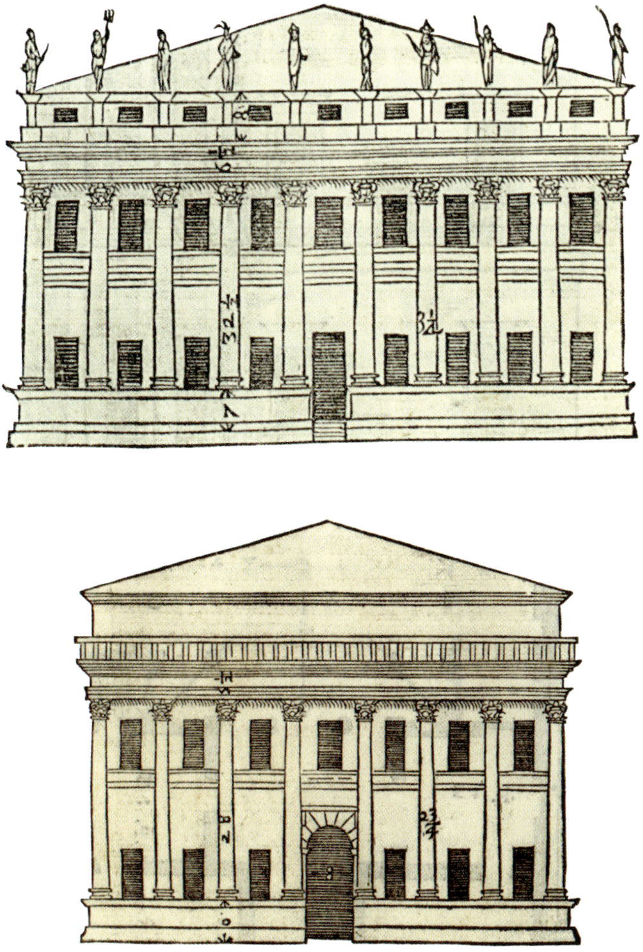

170 *Project for a palazzo for Montano Barbarano* (detail), Vicenza

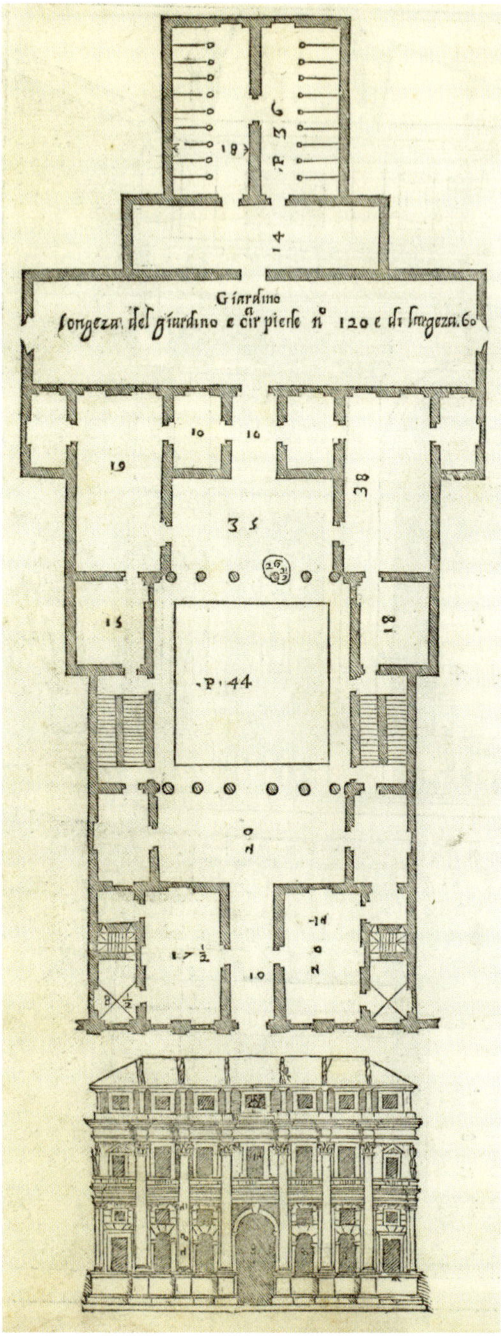

172 *Palazzo Valmarana* (detail), Vicenza

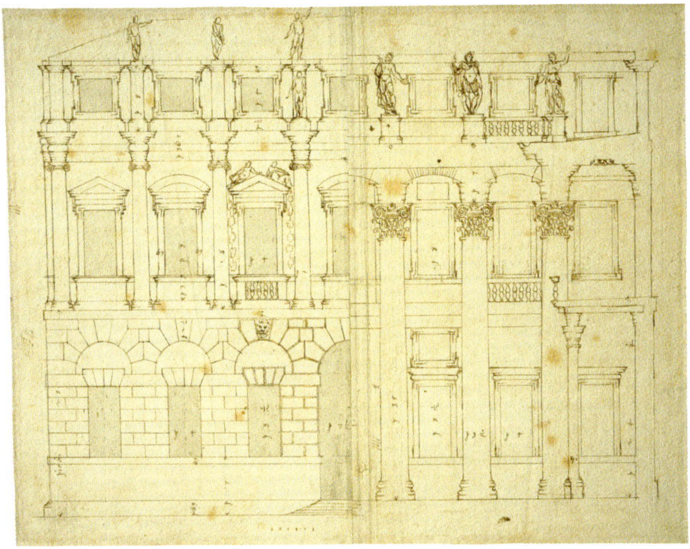

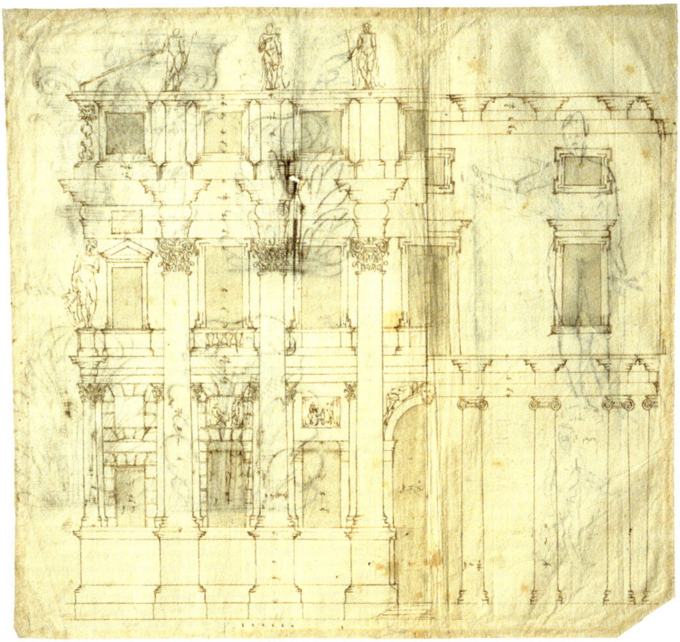

174 *Project for Palazzo Porto*, Vicenza
175 *Project for Palazzo Valmarana*, Vicenza

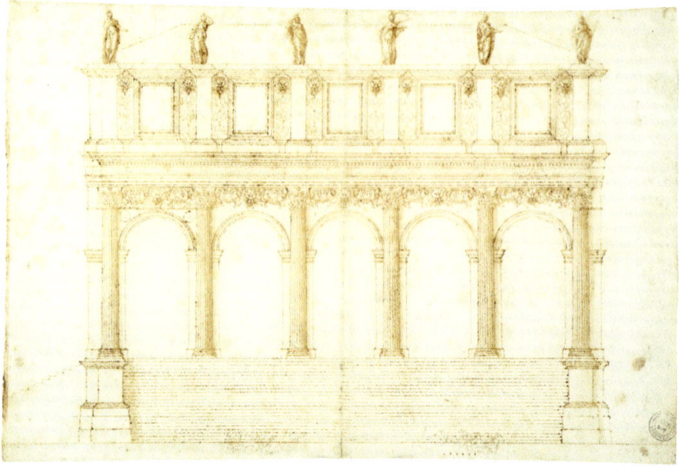

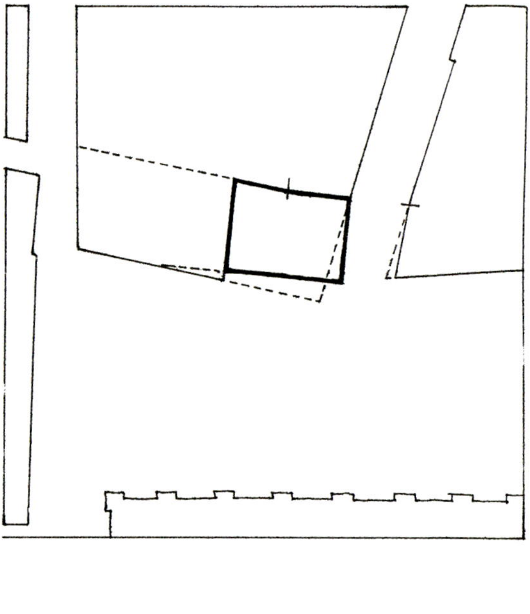

176 *Project for a loggia,* Vicenza
179 Antonio Foscari, Position of Palladio's Loggia del Capitanio in the pre-existing urban fabric

178 *Loggia del Capitanio* (edited), Vicenza

180 *Palazzo for Alessandro Porto* (edited), Vicenza

the construction of the Roman church of San Marcello al Corso featuring the unusual circular form of the choir that appears to have inspired Palladio's design for the choir behind "his" circular-plan church. [194]

What is interesting to note is that, even if it were true that Palladio returned to earlier examples, he was nonetheless ready to renounce an explicit evocation of the *forma rotonda,* since he was well aware (perhaps because of the reactions to his own project for a *rotonda*) that many members of the Republican governing class continued to harbour deep-seated aversions (the same ones that had blocked the construction of a rotunda at the end of the church of Santissima Annunziata while the Republic regime was in power in Florence) because they saw it as the evocation of an imperial *exemplum.*

He replaced the geometric typology of the rotunda with a central-plan model taken from *exempla,* thought to be classical and also located in the Po Valley: the church of San Sepolcro, for example, or the church of San Lorenzo, both of which are in Milan. These were the same *exempla* that had so attracted Leonardo da Vinci when he sketched the two evocative drawings in Paris MS B, f. 57 r and, in part, in CA, f. 733 v/271 v-d. [195]

The latter, which must be seen as a critical reflection on the San Lorenzo model, offers a clear perception of the conceptual procedure that allowed Leonardo to connect a central form, which cannot be reduced to the geometrical typology of a rotunda, to a longitudinal one. Palladio organised the building site for the construction of the church on the basis of a new project conceived using a spatial scheme of this kind. [196]

THE FIRE AT THE DOGE'S PALACE

In late 1577, when the foundations of the new building had not only been laid out but for the most part completed, the city was struck by another disaster – less fatal than the plague but no less traumatic for the Venetian oligarchy that governed the fate of the Republic: a fire destroyed almost the entire west side of the

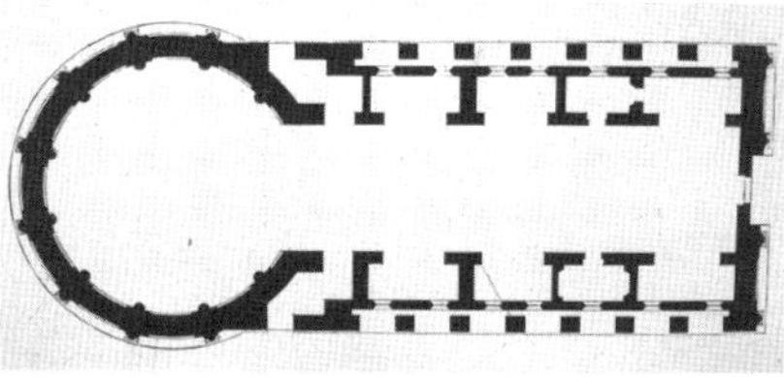

193

194

Doge's Palace, the edifice that symbolically expressed the very essence of the Republic as consecrated by history.

It is worth examining how this event affected Palladio.

A chance to work on the Palace, and in doing so to redefine the emblematic architectural image of La Serenissima, would, in all likelihood, have represented the opportunity to accomplish his hope of demonstrating the "true science of this art"[36] of which he knew he was a master, in a *fabbrica* that would become an inescapable *topos* in the eyes of the whole world.

In order to follow the course of these events while focusing on the architect, it is not necessary to retrace every step of the debate that involved the highest Venetian magistracies at this difficult time. One need only remember that the progress of the debate and its conclusion largely depended on a single assumption: that the Palace was a *fabbrica* whose form and internal layout encapsulated and expressed the constitutional structure of the Republic itself. What's more, it sanctioned the relations between the magistracies that sat inside it, and by doing so it ensured the political equilibrium that governed the administrative working of the State. Any alteration to the form of this *fabbrica* and its internal layout would therefore have had implications that could hardly be overlooked in institutional terms. This explains why the patriciate would not delegate decisions in this regard to anyone – whatever their expertise – least of all to a "technician", which is how most of the Venetian ruling class regarded an architect in the conviction that this is what he would always remain.

Palladio's summons to participate in this matter must be seen from the standpoint of a government that acted on these assumptions: he was summoned not as an architect but as an "expert", and, as such, he joined a commission chaired by a public official, the *proto* of the Salt Magistracy (which, among its other duties, was responsible for the maintenance of the Doge's Palace), together with another expert who continued to believe – as he had done a decade earlier – that his qualifications were on a par with those of Palladio.

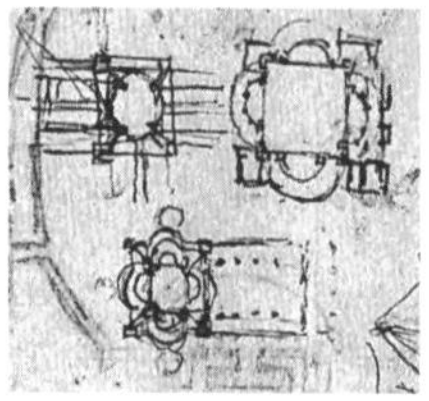

195

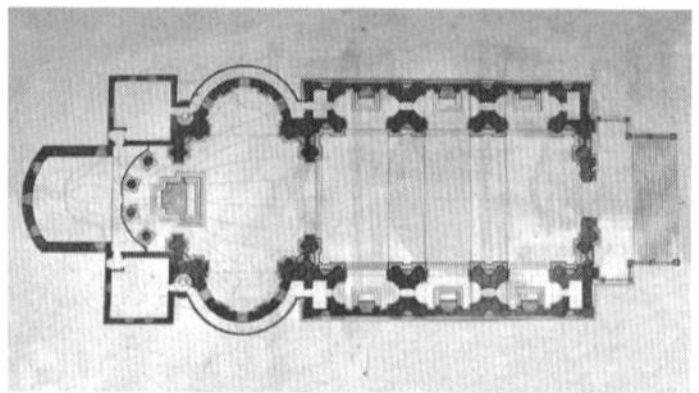

196

It was from this position, a weak one in many ways, that Palladio carried out the plan which, from the outset, aimed to launch a rebuilding process that would radically renew the image of the palace. The only important link he maintained as he focused his energies on the commission he had just joined was Marcantonio Barbaro, who was also his main contact in the project to build the church of the Redentore. But Barbaro had a different goal in mind. [199] [200]

A NEW PALACE AT TERRANOVA

Right from the opening sessions of the debate, Marcantonio Barbaro opposed every other alternative and suggested that the Great Council of the Republic – which had to move out of the palace because the enormous hall where it met for over two centuries had also been damaged, at least in part, by the flames – should be transferred to the Terranova, namely that area west of Sansovino's Mint (Zecca) where massive fourteenth-century warehouses stood on four distinct plots facing the basin of San Marco, linked by a single façade to form a compact whole.

Barbaro suggested that part of this complex – the part lying between Calle dell'Officio della Sanità and Calle dell'Officio delle Legne – should be immediately cleared and, after carrying out any alterations as quickly as possible, made ready for the Great Council meetings.

The fact that Marcantonio Barbaro was able to present a drawing almost immediately, showing his idea of the layout for the benches on which the patricians attending the meetings would be seated, highlights his conviction that the meetings of the Great Council could be held temporarily in just one of the fourteenth-century warehouses (clearly, after demolishing the floors that divided its volume vertically).

The proposal was not welcomed by many. Some may perhaps have noted that the warehouse site – even if used in its entirety – would not offer a similar area to the ample space traditionally occupied by the Great Council, and that its meetings would prove impractical.

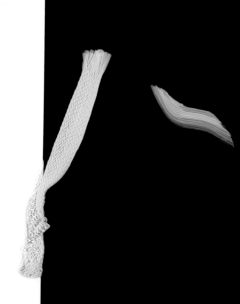

197

Stimulated by the resistance he encountered and by the criticisms raised, Barbaro – a man who did not give up easily – relaunched his proposal instead of withdrawing it, and – according to our view of events – submitted an even more challenging suggestion.

Perhaps he was contemplating a definitive move away from the Doge's Palace for the Great Council – the most "democratic" body in the Republic's constitutional system – as part of a constitutional reform. What's more, he intended to relaunch the *renovatio* process of the *platea marciana* that had been commenced by the Procuratia di San Marco in the years when Venetian Signoria was led by Andrea Gritti.

Indeed, having focused his attention on the Terranova area, he realised that by erecting a new building on these lots (as well as the *calle* running between them) it would be possible to create a hall with the same dimensions, the same orientation and the same view of the basin of San Marco as the old one.

It was the enthusiasm of this "discovery" that, in our opinion, inspired the project outlined in the large drawing preserved at Chatsworth, which Howard Burns has attributed to Palladio, rightly linking its timing to the debate on the restoration of the Doge's Palace that was held after the fire in 1577. [201]

The palace sketched on this large sheet would have occupied two of the Terranova lots: the central ones on which stood the old warehouses that had been served by a central passage accessed through a huge arch topped by the image, carved in stone, of an *andante* or walking St Mark's lion (moving virtually towards the Doge's Palace to the east). In Palladio's design the *fabbrica* would have stood three storeys high on the site of two of these lots, grouped together. In the middle of the façade of this ambitious project, he proposes a solution reminiscent of the extraordinarily high opening that led into the middle passageway in the fourteenth-century complex, and above it he placed a large *andante* St Mark's lion to reaffirm the memory of the ancient image.

According to Palladio's *invenzione*, the façade of the new *Palazzo* as this vast building must be called, since it clearly should be

198

compared with the Doge's Palace, stood further forward than the former warehouses, along the line that the end of the *Libreria* would have had if it had been extended to twenty-two bays, as Francesco Sansovino continued to assert at this time would eventually happen. The size of this shift was calculated to allow a portico to be built along the southern front. Two doorways, flanked by free columns supporting a projecting entablature, would have provided access to this portico at either end.

On the first floor, the hall destined to house the Great Council would have had a volume whose height equalled the two architectural orders that cadenced the façade above the level of the portico (in the same way that a "double height" would have contained the central halls of the imposing Venetian *case* that Palladio had published in his *Second Book*). Therefore, it would also have been the same height as the Great Council hall. This volume would have been flanked at its northern end and connected to it by a volume of equal height, within which there would have been an *anteroom* (which replicated – in more rational terms – the model of the *anteroom* that led into the eastern end of the old Council room) and a double system of stairs, accessible both from the canalside on the northern edge of the Terranova site and from the entrance on the southern front of the *Palazzo*. In this way the patricians would have been able to enter the *Palazzo* without the inconvenience of having to cross a quay – which lies to the south of the *fabbrica*, overlooking the basin of San Marco – thronged with sailors, fishermen, traders and merchants of all kinds who carried out their business there at all times of day. [202] [203]

This discussion, which saw the Venetian magistracies debate the reorganisation of the political and administrative activities of the Republic after the fire, developed so rapidly, however, that in all likelihood it had already ended before the ink had dried on this large drawing now kept at Chatsworth.

However, even this did not discourage Marcantonio Barbaro. Given that he held the office of Procuratore di San Marco (which

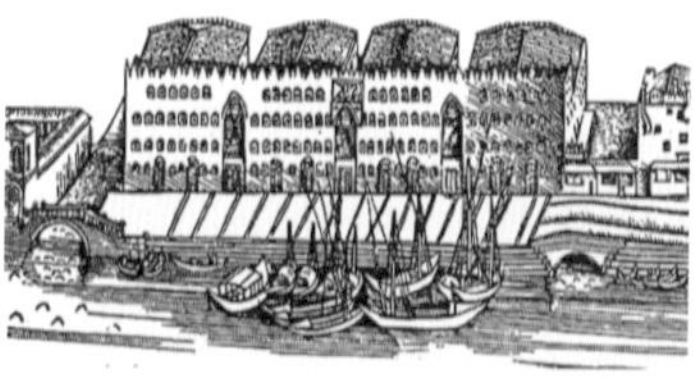

199

200

gave him specific authority to manage urban and building matters within the *platea marciana*), he realised that the reorganisation of the Terranova area might be an opportunity to relaunch the *renovatio* process of the Marcian forum, which, after thirty years of controversial management, had not yet been completed. (On a specific note, no final decision had yet been taken on the configuration of the southern end of the *Libreria*, where work had never progressed beyond the seventeenth arch, nor on the renovation, first muted years previously, of the building complex that formed the southern side of the piazza.)

A rapid sketch on the *recto* of RIBA sheet XVI, 5 (which Howard Burns rightly attributes to Palladio and links to the heated debate on the restoration of the Doge's Palace) is proof of the speed with which Palladio grasped the requests of his patron – all the more because he was a Procuratore di San Marco – and also the completeness with which he could almost instantaneously formulate a project in his mind.

Instead of using the two central lots of the Terranova site to obtain a single large building volume – like the one that would have been destined to house a hall capable of seating the Great Council and the stairs necessary to access it – he suggested using them to build two parallel parts: one overlooking the quay and the other the canal running along the northern edge of the Terranova site.

The southern part would have retained a public administrative function whose presence is borne out by the almost "triumphal" nature of its entrance and the impressive system of stairs (here again not dissimilar to that recently constructed at the south-eastern end of the Doge's Palace).

The part containing the stairs, which lies along the compositional axis, helps to divide the area between one part of the building and the other into two square courtyards surrounded by columns which, in succession, form an even number of bays (as was Palladio's habit when there were no entrances leading into a courtyard along its axes).

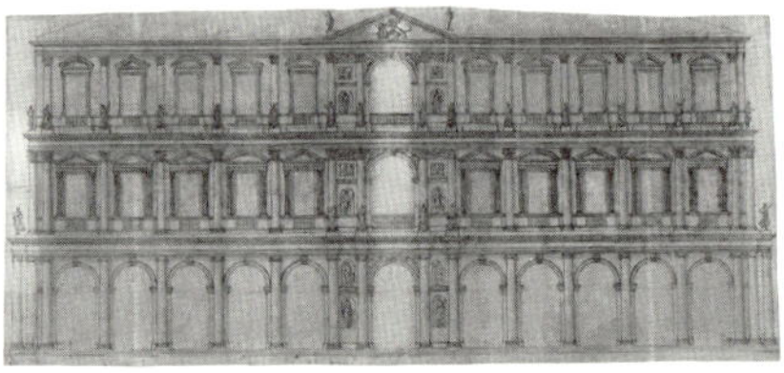

201

Intercommunicating rooms along the sides of the Palace atrium (six on each side), together with rooms on the upper levels, are set aside for the administrative functions to be carried out in this public *fabbrica*.

With the exception of these rooms, the entire ground floor is dedicated to commercial activities like those that have flourished here in the Terranova area for centuries: activities that face onto the portico running down the southern front of the *fabbrica*, overlooking the quay, or the portico on the northern side along a canal. [204] [205] [206]

In order to obtain the highest possible number of rentable commercial premises – and therefore maximise the revenue for the Procuratia – the module used for the composition of this project is smaller than that shown on the project outlined in the large drawing now kept at Chatsworth. (To be clear: Palladio adopted the module used by Jacopo Sansovino to create the shops on the ground floor of the Zecca, rather than the larger dimensions he himself had used on the ground floor of the *Libreria*.)

However, the shops and businesses that opened into the portico running along the southern front of the *fabbrica* are of the kind that had been used for at least a century by the shops fringing Piazza San Marco. (In spite of the speed with which he drew this sketch, Palladio was still at pains to show how they were structured on two floors linked by a small staircase.)

Those opening under the northern portico (a portico that would not have been unlike that of the *fabbriche nuove* which had just been finished at Rialto) are of the type that Jacopo Sansovino had designed on the ground floor of the palace built for Giovanni Dolfin overlooking the Grand Canal.

However, in this quick sketch, Palladio did not draw this sector of his project; perhaps because he wanted to avoid showing how, here again, he would have insisted on giving the *fabbrica* a perfectly orthogonal structure (in spite of the shape of the lot) even at the price of forgoing a few shops. (There would have been fifty-four shops, as he knew well – because he noted the number in

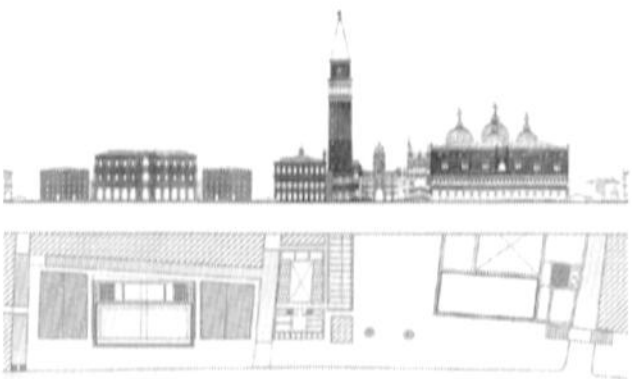

202

203

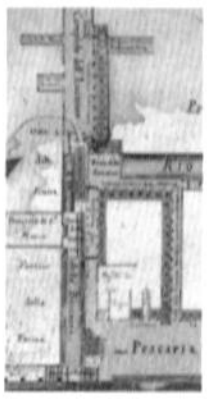

204

the centre of the sketch – if instead he had proceeded to make full use of the site's development potential and made an exception to this principle.)

These notes are enough to convince us that Marcantonio Barbaro – backed up by Palladio's proposals – was following a line of reasoning that had now moved beyond the question of rebuilding the Doge's Palace, and instead was almost entirely focused on a building venture that would assure the highest possible economic return for the Procuratia di San Marco.

It was a return that could have been increased still further by deciding to include not just two but all four of the fourteenth-century Terranova warehouses in a single renovation project. This would have allowed the full depth of the lots to be used, forming four buildings at right angles to the quay (two on the outside, overlooking the two canals that border the Terranova area to east and west). Together these four buildings would have formed three large internal courtyards. [207]

Palladio expressed this concept in extremely concise terms, drawing another sketch (on a still smaller scale) on the bottom edge of the same sheet on which he had traced in summary, but completely clear detail the ground plan of the scheme we have just tried to illustrate. He did not bother with specifics, knowing full well that the proposal had little chance of being taken into consideration by the Venetian magistracies and that his patron – who was aware of the work he was carrying out at the Benedictine monastery of San Giorgio, where the large cloister that would become known as "the cypress cloister" was then being built – did not need much explanation to understand the type of buildings that were spread out, almost suspended, between each of the three courtyards. [208] [209]

The positioning of this sketch on the edge of the sheet of paper precludes any idea of the layout that Palladio might have given to the southern façade of the *fabbrica*. But it does not take much to convince us that, on this side too – as on the other – there would have been a portico and, in the centre of the portico, a projecting

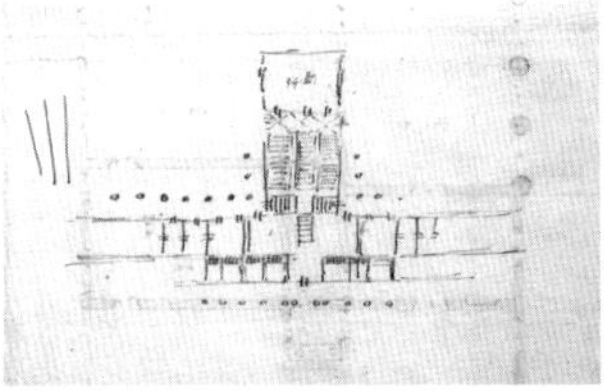

205

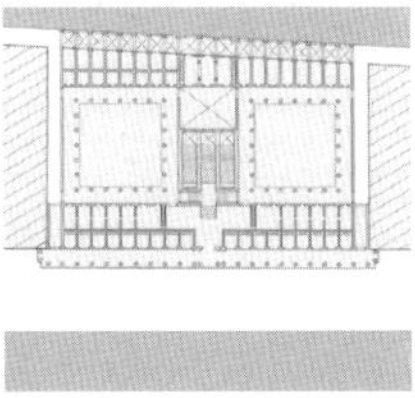

206

block that would have housed (as in the case of Palazzo Thiene and in the first project for Girolamo Chiericati's *casa* in Vicenza) the most representative functions of a building complex like this, which would have unexpectedly opened up the area of the Marcian forum.

Although Palladio had drawn the design for the façade of the *Palazzo* conceived by Marcantonio Barbaro with such accuracy on a large sheet of paper – these sketches on which we have dwelled in some detail – he traced them with the same speed and pressing rhythm, it seems, that might be needed to keep a conversation going. However, during these busy days he lacked the time – and maybe even the mental capacity – to translate these proposals into fully finished projects because his mind was entirely focused, both practically and intellectually, on a goal that only a man with an imperturbable faith in his profession could have had the strength to pursue alone.

THE PROJECT TO REBUILD THE DOGE'S PALACE

As a member of the commission onto which he was co-opted as an expert – heedless of the fact that he was in the minority – he focused all his energies on backing an extreme thesis: that radical building work must be undertaken on both sides of the Doge's Palace facing the city – one overlooking the basin of San Marco and the other facing the Piazzetta. Such an intervention would have changed the very image of the *fabbrica* that for over two centuries had symbolised the power of the Venetian Signoria in the eyes of the world.

We can get a fairly clear idea of the nature of Palladio's goal simply by examining the reaction of those who rejected any suggestion to rebuild the old palace on the one hand, and on the other those who were excited by his proposals but – being unwilling to accept them in full – tried to reduce their scope.

But a better option is to try to identify it directly, to start with by reading the report that Palladio decided to write in order to defend his "reasons" before the three Provveditori specifically appointed by the Senate (Alvise Zorzi, Giacomo Foscarini

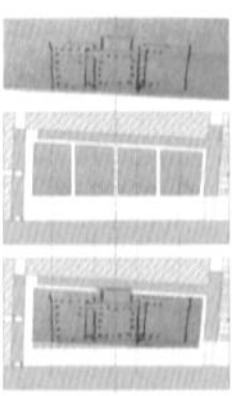

207

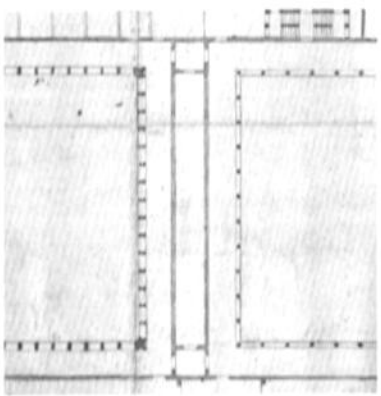

208

209

and Piero Foscari), when he realised that he had to balance and clarify his thoughts that until then he had evidently expressed too radically, prompting criticism and objections. In this statement, the only thing that Palladio did not explain – for reasons of prudence – was the architectural outcome to which his reasoning led.

Indeed, he knew all too well that some – possibly many – would regard this outcome as "scandalous". Therefore, instead of expounding it as the primary aim of his action, he tried to make it appear as the result of a series of technical arguments and theoretical considerations that demonstrated its necessity at a practical level and sanctioned its legitimacy in conceptual terms.

The arguments of a technical nature were a number of technical errors in the original construction of the palace, the cracks in a number of antique capitals, the oxidation of the *catene* installed in the fourteenth century to restrain the horizontal strains that the building had to withstand and, above all, the physical and chemical alterations to materials caused "by the violence of the fire".[37]

The theoretical considerations, on the other hand, concerned the Venetian building practice against which he had already argued forcibly some twenty years earlier when he was helping Daniele Barbaro to edit the *Commentaries* that were then published in 1556. In particular, Palladio disputed the building concept that, for centuries, had been practised in a physical environment, the lagoon, where it was impossible for buildings not to undergo sometimes major settling over time, given the instability of the ground beneath them.

Based on this two-pronged line of reasoning, Palladio asserted two concomitant theses with all the energy he could muster, and an analysis of these will enable us to understand the key presuppositions on which his proposal was based. He asserted that the outside walls of the palace, from the loggia upwards, could not be preserved and that the palace roof also needed to be rebuilt *ex novo*.

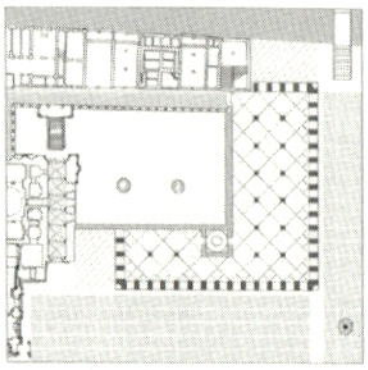

210

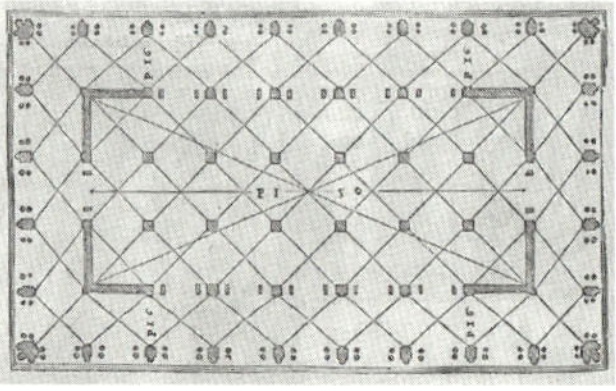

211

The reaction of one of the experts working on the same commission that Palladio had just joined can help us to understand another aspect of his thought.

Since the said expert complained of the severe consequences that would ensue, also in economic terms, from the renovation of the ground floor of the old palace, it can be inferred that Palladio had initially not refrained from suggesting the creation of a huge "covered square" on the ground floor of the palace. This solution resembled the one ideally outlined for the ground floor of the Palazzo della Ragione in Vicenza in the drawing he had published in his *Third Book.* Clearly, here too, he was counting on being able to evoke the structural layout and architectural model of the Portico di Pompeo. [210] [211] [212]

To forestall the criticisms that a proposal of this nature could hardly have failed to arouse, he took a prudent approach in his report by writing that an intervention of this kind could be limited to the eastern side of the palace. In order to fend off another kind of criticism that had clearly been put forward by someone else, he noted that to avoid any mixing between patricians and citizens walking in the covered *piazza* at the same time, it would be enough to build a wall to separate the spaces assigned to each of the two social classes.

The reaction of the other two members of the commission to which he had been appointed – the *proto* of the Salt Magistracy and the other expert working alongside him – seems to reveal yet another aspect of Palladio's initial proposal: it would appear that, at a preliminary stage, he planned to move the large rooms used by the Great Council and the *Scrutinio* so that they rested directly on the platform supported by the piers which he planned to erect on the ground floor. By eliminating the first storey, he would have linked the palace to that type of building that he himself had illustrated in the *Third Book,* in the section on *contemporary basilicas.*[38]

It is impossible to understand, except as a result of the intellectual pressure exerted by Palladio on those he was dealing with and

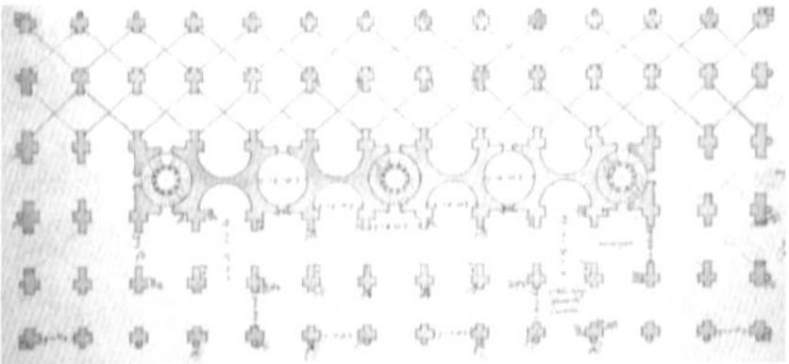

212

213

his powers of persuasion, how Antonio da Ponte [213] and Andrea Moroni could, at a certain point, have stated that, also in their opinion, "the first architect who built the palace had no intention of rising above the second order".[39]

In his statement Palladio did not insist on this point since he had clearly been too emphatic at the preliminary stage. By this stage he was convinced that the conceptual essence of the *invenzione,* which was becoming increasingly clear in his mind, would not be substantially altered by keeping the "first order" (the one forming the first storey of the old palace). As an indication that he had already revised his original idea on this aspect, he limited himself to stating that the *stanze* del Piovego and the other offices on the first floor could be laid out, when the works were finished, as the Signoria thought best: namely, his project no longer required them to be moved elsewhere.

With these introductory comments in mind, we can try to analyse Palladio's project more closely.

For this purpose, it is extremely useful that he himself offers us a cleverly worded, concise description: the *grossissimi pilastri* ("very massive piers") providing the supporting structures of the façades would have created fourteen bays *per banda,* namely on both sides of the palace.

This information – expressed so concisely – meant that the old palace would have been shortened on both sides (the old building had seventeen bays on the side facing the quay, and one more, eighteen, on the side overlooking the Piazzetta).

Knowing Palladio's way of thinking, it cannot be ruled out that the choice of fourteen as a number might be an evocation of the temples dedicated in classical times to Mars and Neptune, the two divinities standing at the head of the Scala dei Giganti in the Doge's Palace, ideally representing the identity of the Republic.

(If Palladio had instead chosen to dedicate his palace to Neptune, it is worth recalling that it is precisely this god who appears in the waters of the basin of San Marco, in front of the Doge's

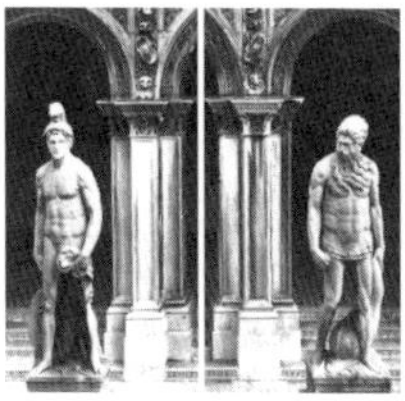

214

215

Palace, in that spectacular aerial view of the city attributed to Jacopo de' Barbari that for decades had been presented to the world as the official image of Venice.) [214] [215]

Leaving aside any conceptual suggestion, this choice was informed by quite different reasons, albeit extremely practical ones. A fourteen bay extension to the southern front of the palace would have left the measurements of the vast Sala del Maggior Consiglio unchanged: built after the 1310 constitutional reform of the Republic, for the Venetians these measurements had acquired a genuinely sacred nature. (It was this mystery of this sacred nature that Girolamo Savonarola hoped to fathom when he gave orders for the measurements of the Venetian council room to be copied precisely in building the huge hall to be used by the general assembly of citizens which he hoped would assume responsibility for governing the Florentine Republic.)

It cannot be ruled out that the reduced length of the palace on this side was not an old proposal, given that the construction of the imposing stone façade had been interrupted at a certain point on the banks of Rio della Paglia, which runs along the east side of the palace. Moreover, from Palladio's point of view, this was a choice that would have allowed the creation of a sort of quay facing Rio della Paglia where citizens and lawyers could have disembarked with convenient access to the rooms where the courts dispensed justice, without having to cross the quay in front of the Doge's Palace. [217] [218]

On the other side of the palace, facing west, this reduced length would have enabled the creation of a "void" over which a new triumphal entrance could have been built. This would have formed the backdrop for the opening that – "with great prudence, judgement and excellent advice had been designed by the wise predecessors" of Marcantonio Barbaro[40] – the Procuratori di San Marco were preparing to open between the *torre* of San Marco and the northern end of the *Libreria*. [216]

It is not so much on the form of this triumphal entrance that we should focus (although it is worth noting that, with the

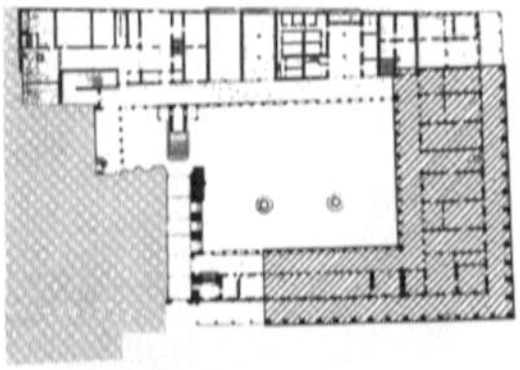

216

addition of a reworking of the Arco dei Gavi in Verona in the centre, it might have been similar to the kind Guido Beltramini has interestingly suggested that Palladio used to mark the entrance to the commercial area planned for the Rialto, which would have been built on a hanging platform over the bed of the Grand Canal).

Instead, what is worth highlighting is that the redefinition of this stretch of the palace overlooking the *platea* of San Marco would have been an operation that, once again, had enormously important constitutional implications, for two reasons. It was through this opening that the people – rightful heirs of the ancient communal assembly – witnessed the doge's coronation (which took place at the top of the stairs positioned inside the palace on the same axis as the gateway) and legitimised his rule through their approval. Secondly, this opening would have allowed a glimpse of the sumptuous stone façade of the palace wing where the doge lived and the Senate and College, the supreme governing bodies of the Republic, were housed.

But we should not digress too far from Palladio's *invenzione* for the section of the old palace that he had undertaken to rebuild from scratch.

By defining its dimensions as fourteen bays *per banda,* namely on each of the sides facing the city, Palladio made an unequivocal statement regarding the square nature of its geometric plan. Likewise, by creating substantial returns at the end of each façade (equivalent to six modules at the south-eastern corner and at least three at the north-western corner), he drew attention to the almost imperative volumetric autonomy of this *fabbrica.*

As Palladio saw it, therefore, the Doge's Palace would have been a completely separate entity, standing apart from the rest of the Marcian forum. In other words, it would have become the figurative fulcrum of a Venice that would have presented a radically new image of itself to the world.

But how did Palladio define this proposal in architectural terms?

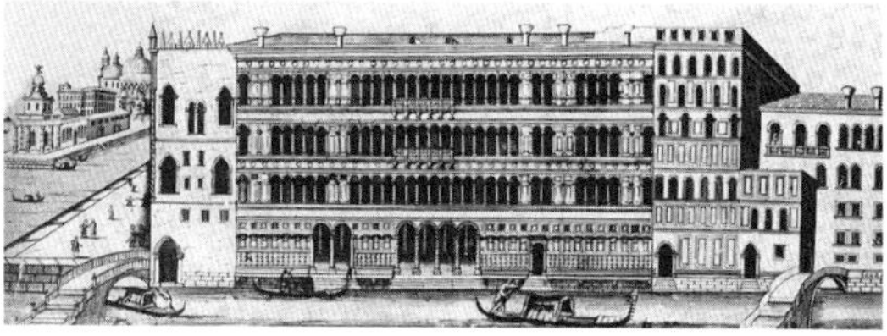

217

We already know that Palladio retained the modular intervals of the arcades in the old palace. This is not surprising because it was the only way he could use the solid foundations of the columns that bore the weight of the fourteenth and fifteenth century edifice. What's more, by doing so he could preserve the vaulted structures that supported the first floor of the palace.

In order to provide sturdier supports than the ancient columns (which could not have carried the enormous weight of the heavy wall he intended to build above them) and to get rid of their late Gothic form, he encased them in *grossissimi pilastri,* or very massive piers. (This was the same solution that Giulio Romano had suggested in order to strengthen the lower storey of the fifteenth-century loggias surrounding the Palazzo della Ragione.)

These piers were topped by vaults – "fourteen on each side", as we know – so that this composition, this succession of *grossissimi pilastri* and *volti,* created a sort of powerful basement on which Palladio planned to erect a wall described as being *gagliardissimo* or very strong (like the one that had stood for centuries on the opposite side of the palace enclosing its inner courtyard).

A wall of this size could clearly not be supported by the stone structures of the first-floor loggia. Therefore, the loggia, with all its colonnades, capitals and pierced transennae, had to be absorbed into the bulk of the wall. From the level of the loggia upwards, this wall therefore had to be built *ex novo* in Palladio's opinion, because the section of the old one was too slender and also because it had been built with a marked inward slant in keeping with a building custom that had been used in Venice for a century or more and which Palladio forcefully condemned.

At this point, it is easy understand why Palladio argued with all the force he could muster that it was necessary to rebuild the roof structure of the palace *ex novo* because it too, in his opinion, had been irreparably damaged by the fire. Moreover, it would not have been possible to erect the external walls of the palace, starting from scratch, without having first removed the roof.

In the report he submitted to the official of the Salt Magistracy, this is where Palladio stopped. He says nothing about his opinion for the architectural arrangement of the façade: a façade about which we only know – to date – that it comprised fourteen modules, corresponding to the bays divided by the *very massive piers,* linked by *vaults* to form its basement.

We are helped to understand the nature of Palladio's proposal once again by a technical expert who was clearly impressed by the firmness of Palladio's convictions, prompting him to press his case with every representative he met during these days of extreme emotional tension. However, he lacked the strength or intellectual generosity that would have allowed him to back Palladio's action without reserve and give it his full support. Having been swayed by the criticisms that were clearly raised by others, he only accepted Palladio's proposal in part. He accepted the idea of creating *piers* on the ground floor, and the fact that this sequence would form a sort of basement. He accepted the idea of walling up the first floor loggia and letting windows into this new wall. He was ready, too, to divide the façade above the basement into fourteen modules. But he restricted this intervention to the height of the first storey of the palace and suggested that the form of the fourteenth-century loggia could be replaced by a sequence of Ionic pilasters that would support an entablature. Above this entablature, however, he did not dare to suggest altering the antique structure and the original image of the existing palace.

This project by Guglielmo de Grandi – which discards two key aspects of the Palladian programme, namely the rebuilding of the façade walls from the loggia upwards and the re-roofing of the palace – is clearly a "reduction" of Palladio's project.

Jutting out from the *gagliardissimo* wall, Palladio would have gloriously erected columns using the order that, more than any other (as we now know), he saw as an expression of the State's sovereign authority: the Colossal order. [219] [220] [221]

The diameter that these columns would have had can be gauged from the fact that the ground floor piers – to which Palladio

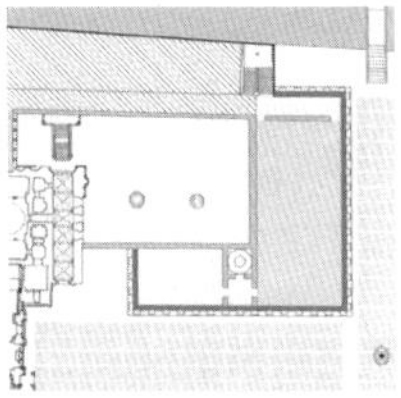

218

219

deliberately draws our attention – would have been of a size that merited the use of the superlative *grossissimi* ("very massive"). Not only did they have to incorporate the fourteenth-century stone columns, they also emerged from the straight line of the old façade to support these columns.

In short, by proposing the use of a Colossal order on the perimeter of a "four-corned" or quadrangular edifice raised up on a basement, with the additional of a heroic dimension, Palladio returned to that peripteral design he had conceived to embellish the perimeter of the *casa di città* designed for Giacomo Angarano, the Vicentine nobleman whom he "loved above all others". He did so in the sure knowledge that, on this occasion, no one could object that the triumphant impetuosity of such an audacious choice could be deemed offensive to the Republican regime since it would be used by the Venetian Signoria itself to define the form of the palace in which it exercised its supreme authority.

Here again (as in the *fabbrica* he had built in Vicenza to affirm the presence in the city of a representative of the political power of the Venetian Signoria), this majestic *ornamento* would have been built in brick to evoke and exalt, in the same vein, the Republican virtues of ancient Rome of which Venice was, in Palladio's opinion, the sole surviving example.

Within a remarkably short period (a timescale that would have been possible thanks to the use of brick and the availability of "infinite numbers of workmen") a sort of ideal *Maison Carrée* would have been constructed on the *platea* of San Marco. The grandiose dimensions and volumetric autonomy of this building would have upset the spatial organisation of the *foro marciano* that Jacopo Sansovino had used as the premise for that Tuscan-Roman style *renovatio* that had occupied at least forty years of his work as *proto* of the Procuratia di San Marco. [222]

Even the *Libreria,* his masterpiece, would have been dwarfed in comparison: the basement of the new palace would have been as high as the library's first storey; the Corinthian order of its grandiose columns would have topped the superimposed storeys

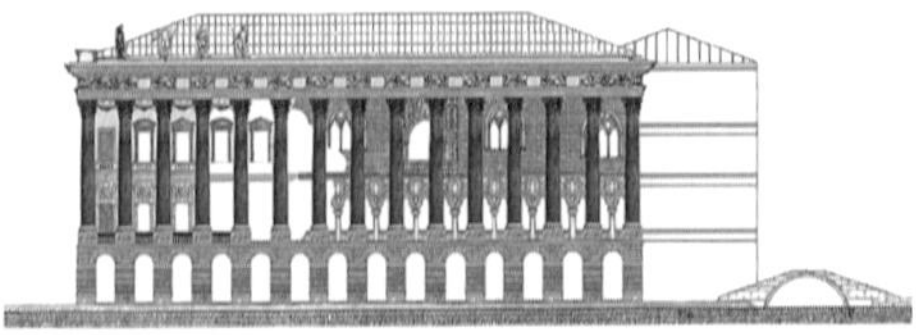

220

221

of Doric and Ionic orders that characterised the canonical composition of its façade; the use of a poor material – brick – would have been a reference to the conspicuous use of stone and ornate decoration, one of the library's most visible features (and one that Palladio had already described, somewhat polemically, as "very rich").

But aside from these aspects, all of which can be regarded as pertaining to the specific exercise of architectural regulations, the Palladian palace – had it ever been built – would have been seen as the symbol of a historic change in the very essence of the Republic: an attempt to overcome the dichotomy between the *Stato da Mar* and the *Stato da Terra* that had connoted the Republic up to that time, or – in more generic terms – a renunciation of that identity as a city-state which the form of the fourteenth-century palace had exalted to the highest degree in a European setting.

In this sensational *invenzione* the son of Pietro della Gondola, who was born in Padua during the dramatic and turbulent events of the League of Cambrai and who, day after day – throughout the span of his long life – had experienced history in the making, was therefore expressing his awareness that a historic cycle was coming to an end (indeed, this actually happened before long, in the same year that Palladio died, through a constitutional reform of the State.)

Palladio's sense of failure in this venture, which consumed almost all his intellectual and human energies, can perhaps only be gleaned from the almost perverse joy with which Giannantonio Rusconi – the architect who for twenty years had claimed to be his rival on the Venetian scene (and whom Palladio had recently beaten once again in the competition launched by the Signoria to choose the architect who would be given the task of constructing the church of the Redentore) – lists one by one the reasons why the old palace structures could be preserved and repaired at little cost. It can also be intuited – so distinctly as to be almost cruel – in the Senate official's decision, barely concealing his irritation, to stop taking minutes of the reasons for rebuilding

222

the palace that Palladio continued to expound and support with unabated zeal.

This marked the end of an affair that emerges quite clearly from reading the documents that record the salient phases. That there remains an echo of Palladio's proposals among those architects who have learnt from his skill (an echo also perceived by Le Corbusier, who likewise revealed an extraordinary capacity to understand classical architecture) is a theme that would be worth developing. But what is important to stress here is that when the debate ended, the tensions and expectations remained high and the contrasting proposals, which had clashed, influenced one another and finally filtered down, re-emerged in numerous discussions between the Venetian magistracies that involved all the components of the patriciate. [223] [224] [225] [226]

When the clamour of this debate finally began to die down, a series of operations was finally undertaken that served to make good the hope (or fear) of making radical changes to the form of the palace and, hence, to the regime of the State and focused on this unique setting, the *foro marciano,* which represented or rather acted as the physical embodiment of that regime. After years of being closed, the building site of the *Libreria* was reopened and soon after this the Procuratori di San Marco resolved to leave their old offices and move in front of the Doge's Palace, thereby succeeding in proudly claiming the authority due to their institutional role.

This move prompted the start of construction work on new *case* for the Procuratori along the southern side of the piazza, in accordance with an urban design conceived by Sansovino twenty years earlier. But more was to come: building work also started on the new prisons – on the other side of Rio della Paglia – transferring those which Palladio had intended to remove from the ground floor of the palace in his plans to form the "covered square" that would have allowed access to the eastern end.

Palladio would not have time to see all of this, nor the formidable ideological clash between "young" and "old" that ripped

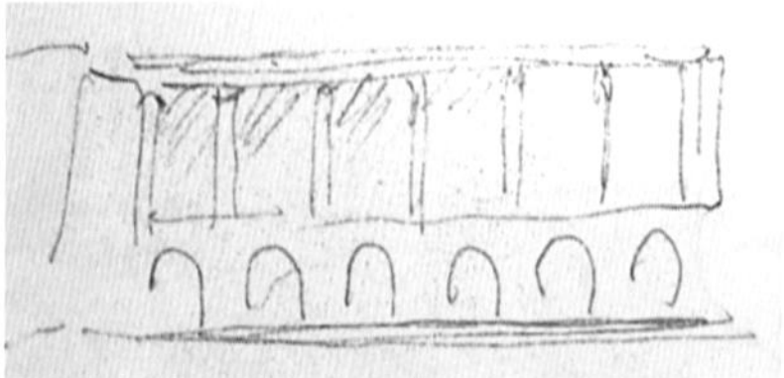

223

224

the patriciate apart at the start of this process, rekindling debate among the factions of the Venetian oligarchy that until then had seemed united. His energies were completely absorbed by the building site for the Redentore that was now a hive of activity.

THE CHURCH OF THE REDENTORE

It was by now quite clear to everyone – even just from the increased size of the lot on which Palladio was building – that the type of church being built was now different to the scheme that had been initially devised.

It cannot be ruled out that there was also a pragmatic component involved in the choice of the *exemplum* of the Holy Sepulchre (the same that Giovanni Rucellai, too, had utilised when he commenced work on a simulacrum of the Holy Sepulchre in San Pancrazio with the advice of Leon Battista Alberti). This component aimed to ensure a flow of pilgrims to the church at a time when the breakdown of relations with the Ottoman Empire after the dramatic sea battle between Christian and Islamic forces in the waters of Lepanto made it virtually impossible to travel to the Holy Land to visit the sacred sites of Christian tradition, above all, the Holy Sepulchre.

But, without doubt, a choice of this nature had also been influenced by questions of protocol.

Clearly, the Senate – the Venetian magistracy that had proposed the vow to the Redeemer and was bound to ensure its absolute respect – realised that a central plan church whose diameter occupied the limited breadth of the site available for its construction would not comply with the ceremonial requirements arising from the decision to hold a solemn annual procession through the city, culminating here on the Giudecca, in order to give thanks to the Redeemer. [227]

Unless a variation was introduced to the initial proposal, once the doge had entered the church and had taken up position in the middle of the central area – as he clearly would – the members of the Signoria accompanying him on this public occasion would not have been able to stand beside him during the service without

225

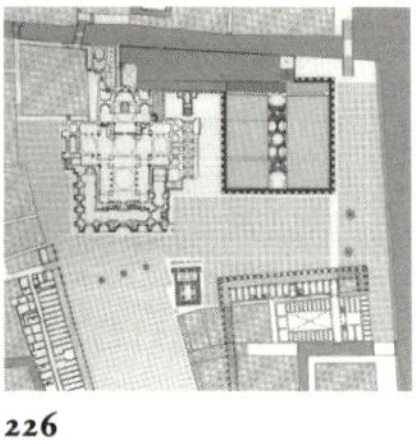

226

turning their backs on the altars planned in the side parts of the church. Moreover, only a few members of the highest state magistracies would have been able to attend the religious ceremony because the space reserved to them, standing behind the doge, was too restricted.

In the new plans for the church, the doge would walk forward to take his place at the heart of this central plan edifice, under the dome, enveloped by the light flooding in through by twelve windows (six on each side, on two levels) set into the side apses opening on its flanks.

Before him was the altar, and behind it, not an apse but columns placed in a circular alignment (a solution used by Bramante, but also evoked by Leonardo da Vinci in his small drawing for the Milanese church of San Lorenzo, as mentioned earlier). The senators would therefore flank the doge, filling the two side apses that reproduce the perimeter of the virtual apse behind the altar as if seated on tribunes. (This, too, is instinctively reminiscent of Leonardo: he was the first to suggest using these side apses as theatrical tribunes in an intriguing drawing – Paris MS B, f. 55r – in which he develops some thoughts on the central plan of San Lorenzo.) [228]

By arriving at this solution, Palladio provided a satisfactory response to the ceremonial requirements of the Republic (one that would be replicated without any changes a century later when the Venetian Signoria appointed Baldassarre Longhena to build a church dedicated to the Madonna to celebrate the end of another outbreak of plague).

The large longitudinal space behind the doge was reserved during the religious ceremony for the representatives of the magistracies who accompanied him on the procession.

Rather than evoking the plan of a basilica, this space was based on an unexpected and vigorous proposal of a Roman bath model with Colossal columns placed around its perimeter, giving Venetians the perception of architecture on a scale that no one had ever seen in the city before. But, through the rhythmic sequence

227

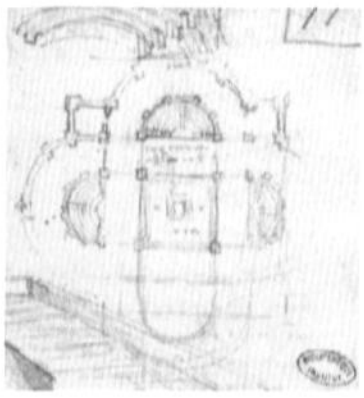

228

of large and small bays along its walls, the so-called "rhythmic travée", it also served as a reminder of the lesson Leon Battista Alberti had left for later generations when he started to build the great church of Sant'Andrea in Mantua and as a sort of Venetian echo of the model used by the Jesuits for their church in Rome, based on a design by Vignola.

This church dedicated to the Redeemer was therefore the sum of the architect's knowledge, ordered with an expertise that testified to his utmost maturity: a maturity that in no way – at no moment of this long creative process – curbed his freedom of thought and his actions.

To convince us of this, we need only consider how the monk's choir runs along the axis of symmetry of the edifice, behind the altar, and ends with a curved wall that in its own way echoes the curved line of the columns behind the altar. Or how the choir, with its surprising spatial dimensions, is flanked by two rectangular rooms used as a sacristy and two small turrets, whose cylindrical shape is unique and may perhaps truly be seen as evoking Islamic minarets.

In this compositional process, illuminated by knowledge, everything is architecture.

The procession led by the doge, which wound its way from the Doge's Palace and, for a long stretch, passed over a floating route supported by boats (according to an age-old Venetian custom, also providing scope for social entertainment), attracted and distracted the Venetians who followed this spectacular event while staying in their boats at least until the Signoria reached the banks of the Giudecca. Here every one of them looked up at the church façade, seen against the light: a vast expanse of white stone on which are imprinted (so to speak) all the enigmas that the church contained.

This white stone façade – whose form is hierarchically governed by the measurements of the virtual prostyle temple – reveals the width of the large rectangular space behind it; its columns announce the presence and dimensions of the columns that embellish the perimeter of this immense internal space; its attic solicits expectation of a central event that will become evident further on, on its axis; its "wings", which project on either side of the tetrastyle pronaos, allow those who know about these things to infer the existence of side chapels; while its overall configuration reveals the definitive outcome of the elaborate research into intersecting frontispieces that Palladio had commenced while working on his design for the façade of San Francesco della Vigna. [229]

In short, this vast white page marked by eloquent signs is unfurled like a manifesto in the urban scenario, a compendium of messages, not all of which are decipherable (as is so often the case in masterpieces). It is the proof that Palladio was truly – as he himself knew – "moved and inflamed by my profound studies of *virtù* of this type."[41]

As we cross the threshold of this church, our senses are alive to the fact that we are being handed a sort of testament. [230]

What surprises us and envelops us more than anything else is the light. It brings us to understand that this virtually metaphysical element is almost the essence of Palladio's architecture. Without it the spatial qualities of any room and the plasticity of any form cannot be perceived. Without light, a light that changes constantly in intensity and orientation throughout the day, these spaces would become static – like a photographic image – crystallised in a proportionate logic that obeys virtually only abstract principles.

This light dispels any form of mysticism and enters the church through the large thermal windows opened in rapid succession along the length of the building, above the entablature supporting the vault, and also through the windows in the walls of the side apses that form the central body of the *fabbrica*.

It illuminates the whiteness of an architecture that refutes any ornament not derived from its own internal disciplinary logic.

"Purity of colour," writes Palladio, highlighting the conceptual necessity of this whiteness, is "supremely pleasing to God": in architecture, he continues, as in "life".[42]

229

230

It is into this whiteness that the figure of this man, Andrea, almost disappears. During his lifetime he concealed his identity with a pseudonym; neither do we know where he died, nor where he is buried. His life is embodied in his work. In this sense Palladio has truly realised his wish for "fame, continuous praise, and reverence in the memories of those who will come after us". [43]

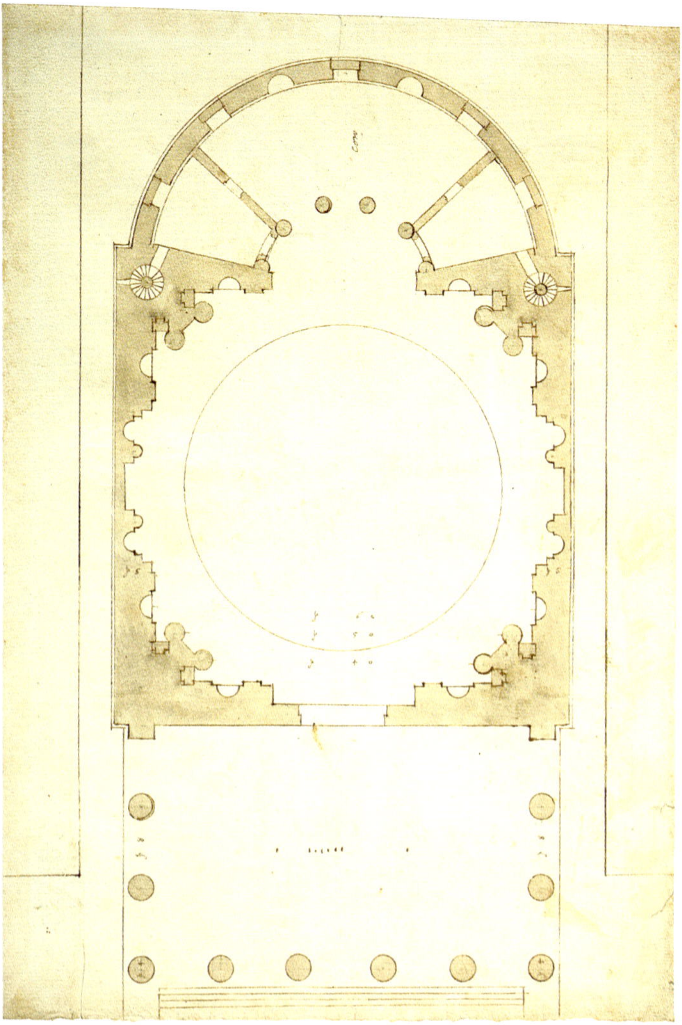

189 *Plan showing rotunda solution [Church of the Redentore]*, Venice

190 *Elevation, Church of the Redentore,* Venice

191 *Section, Church of the Redentore,* Venice

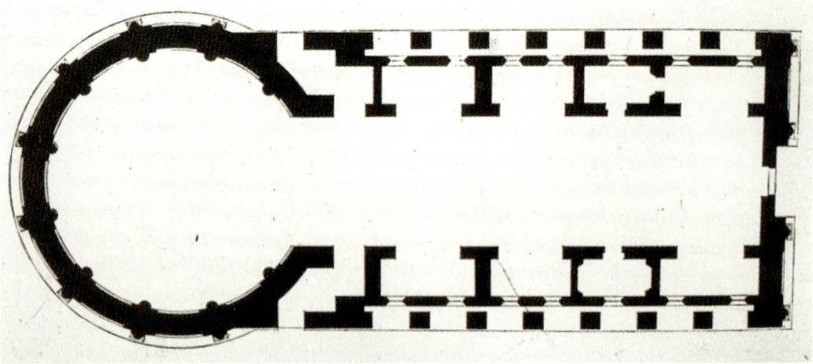

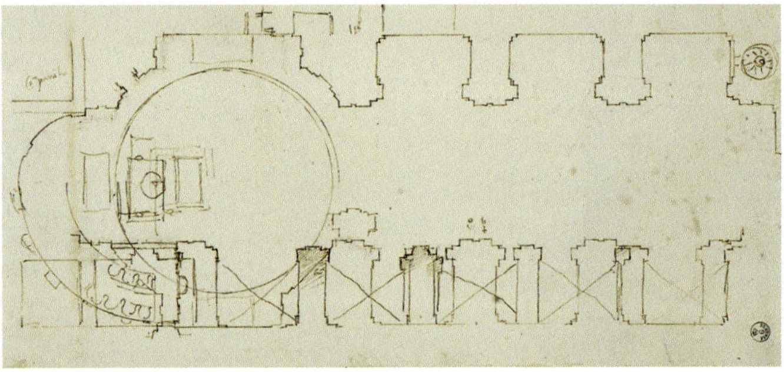

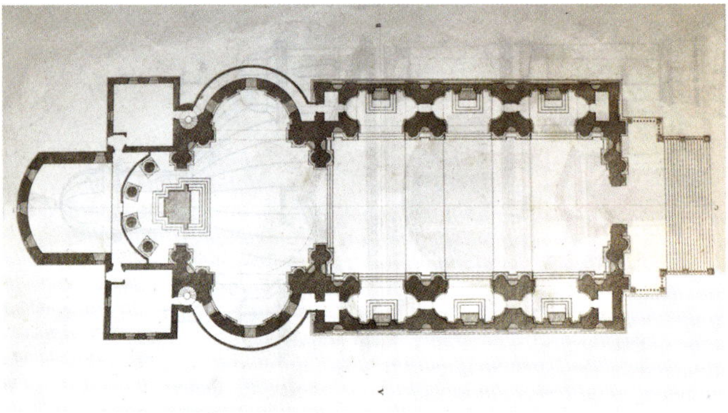

193 Leon Battista Alberti, *Model of Temple for Sigismondo Malatesta, Rimini, reconstruction, C.L. Ragghianti* (detail), 1965
194 Antonio da Sangallo il Giovane, *Studies for San Marcello in Rome* (detail), c. 1519
196 L. Cicognara, A. Diedo and G. Selva, *Plan of the Church of the Redentore* (detail), 1838, Venice

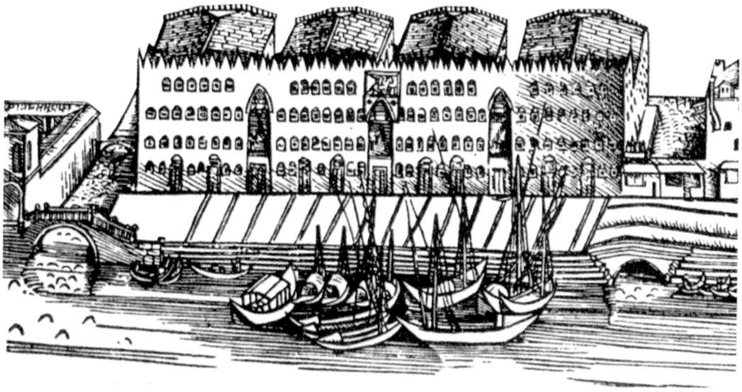

199 Jacopo de' Barbari, *Public warehouses on the Terranova*, detail of a perspective plan of Venice
200 Domenico Lovisa, *View of the Molo at San Marco and the Granaries from Palazzo Grimani* (detail)

201 *A new Palazzo to be built on the Terranova,* Venice (identified by Antonio Foscari)

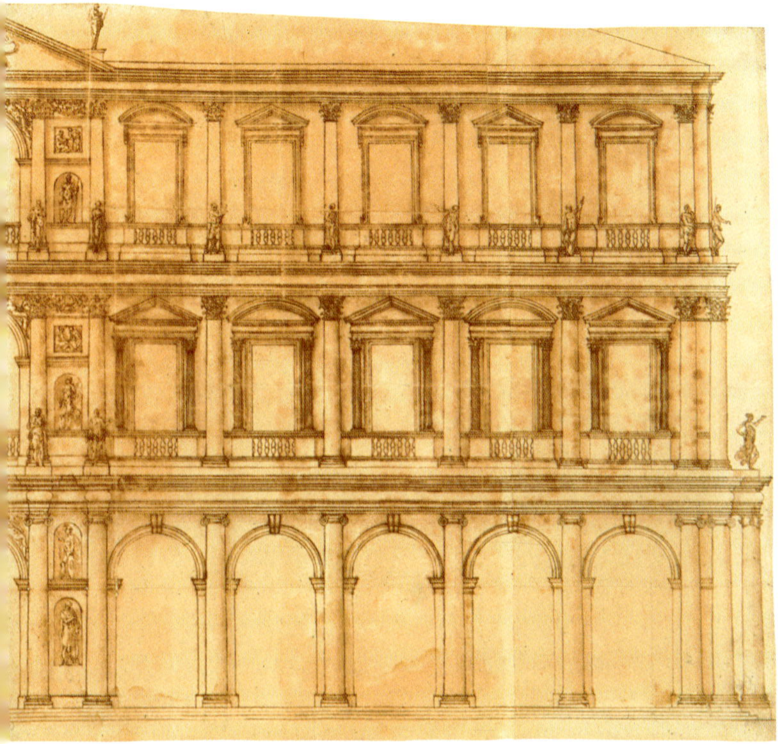

202 Antonio Foscari, The palace shown in the drawing by Palladio in the Devonshire Collection, Chatsworth, placed on the Terranova site. Front view and location plan. The drawing of the façade in the area of St Mark's overlooking the Basin is taken from *Piazza San Marco. L'architettura la storia le funzioni,* Marsilio, Padua 1970 (edited)

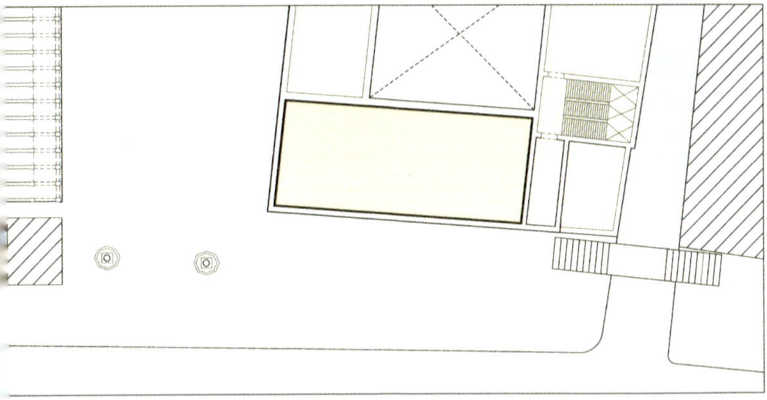

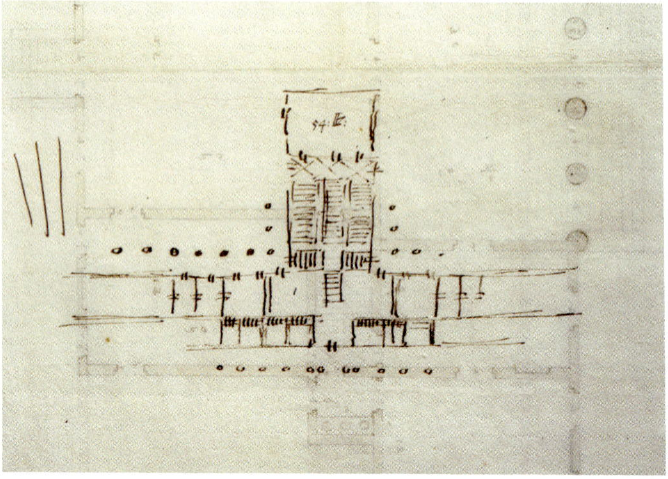

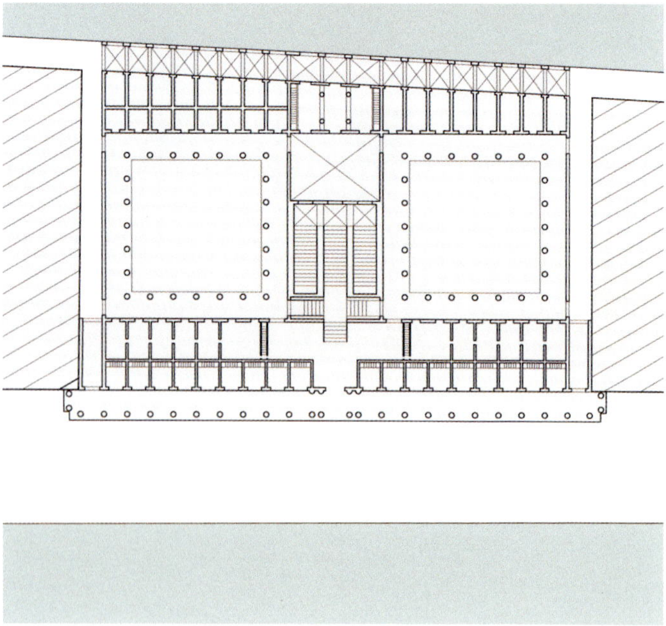

205 Palladian design for the construction of a palace on the Terranova site (detail) (identified by Antonio Foscari)

206 Antonio Foscari, reconstruction of the Palladian project for a building on the Terranova site (based on indications given in RIBA, XVI, 5)

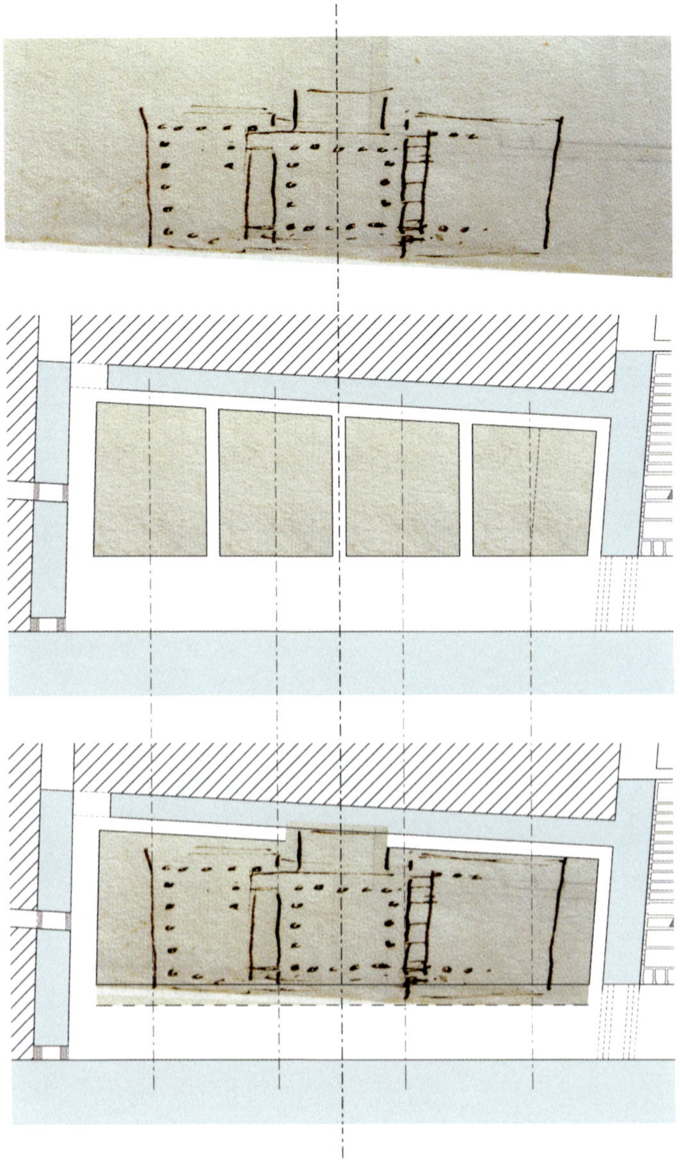

207 Antonio Foscari, Palladian design showing an alternative solution for the construction of a palace on the Terranova site (detail from drawing RIBA, XVI, 5), above, and its location plan, below (identified by Antonio Foscari)

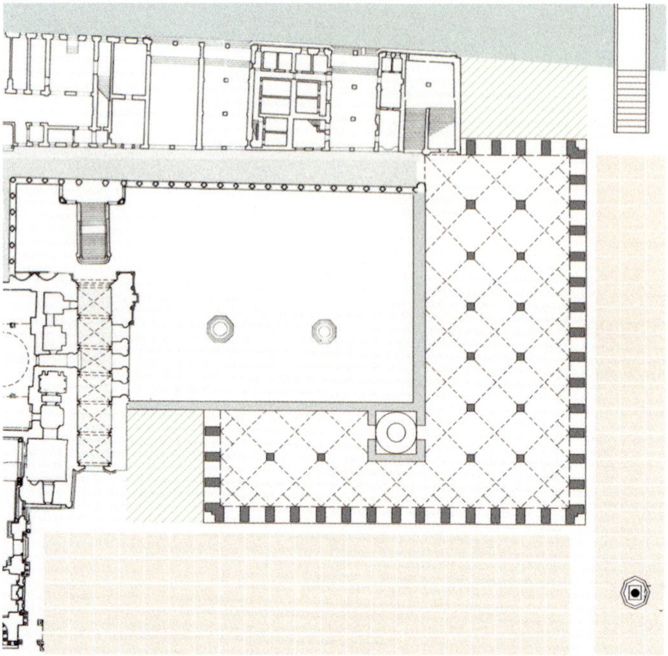

210 Antonio Foscari, reconstruction of the Palladian project to build the Doge's Palace, Venice: the ground floor

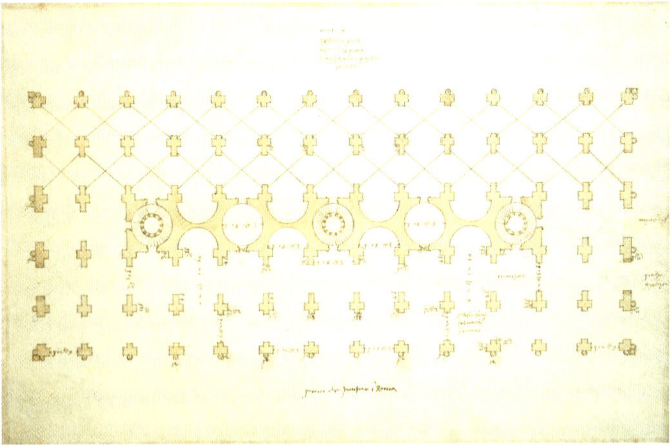

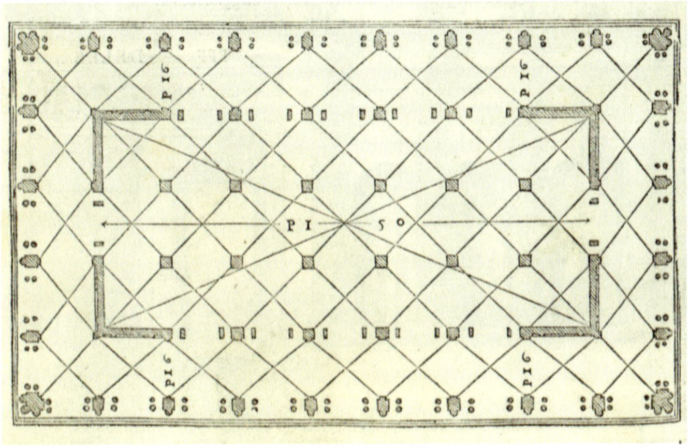

212 *Crypta Balbi (Portico di Pompeo)*, Rome

211 *Ground floor plan of Palazzo della Ragione* (detail), Vicenza

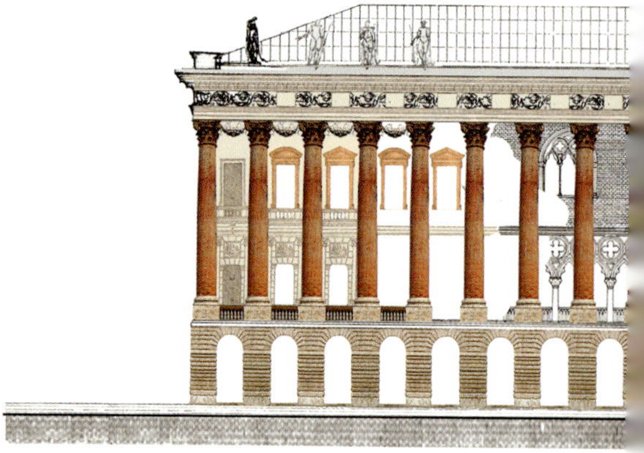

219 *The Doge's Palace,* southern elevation, drawing from *Piazza San Marco. L'architettura la storia le funzioni,* Marsilio, Padua 1970
220 Antonio Foscari, Reconstruction of the Palladian project to build the Doge's Palace, Venice: southern elevation

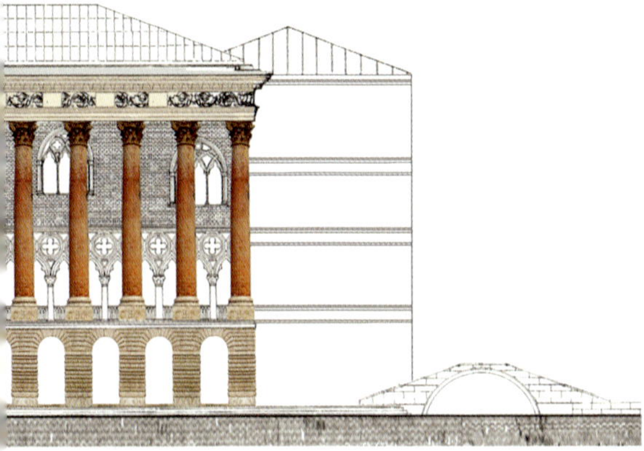

222 Antonio Foscari, Eastern façade of the *foro marciano* showing the Palladian Ducal Palace, as in our reconstruction. The Doge's residence and the Senate Hall can be seen on the second floor between the Doge's chapel of San Marco and the Palace. A new triumphal entrance (based on the Palladian solution illustrated in drawing D. 20 r, Pinacoteca Civica, Vicenza) has been sited between the church and the Palace

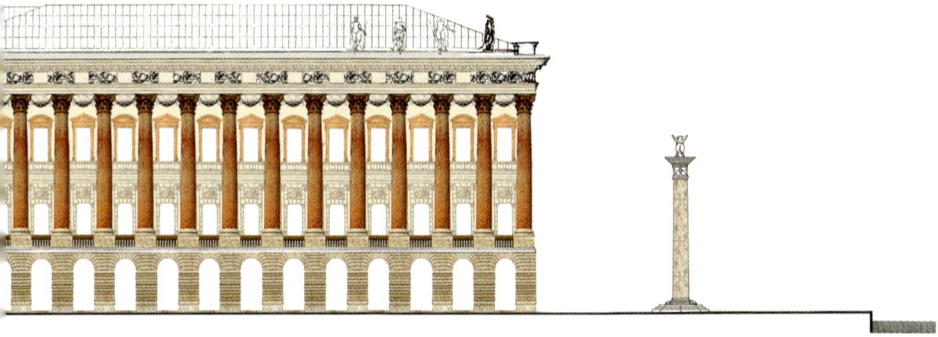

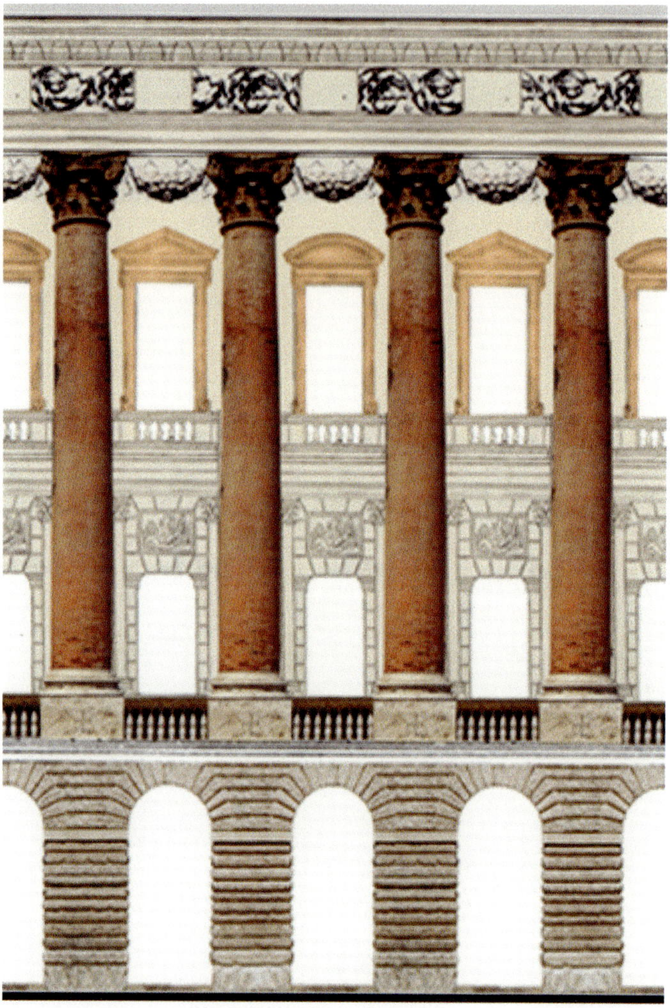

221 Antonio Foscari, reconstruction of the Palladian project to build the Doge's Palace, Venice: detail of the façade. The basement is an elaboration of the Palladian solution for the courtyard of Palazzo Thiene, Vicenza; the columns are based on the model of the Corinthian columns for the Loggia del Capitanio, Vicenza; the division of the façade between the columns is based on the façade solution in between the pilasters on the façade of Palazzo Valmarana, Vicenza, using the design published in *I Quattro Libri dell'Architettura,* II, p. 17. The design of the windows on the upper floor corresponds to those in the Chatsworth drawing from the Devonshire Collection. The cornice follows the exemplum of the Temple of Jupiter Serapis, as shown in RIBA, XI, 24.

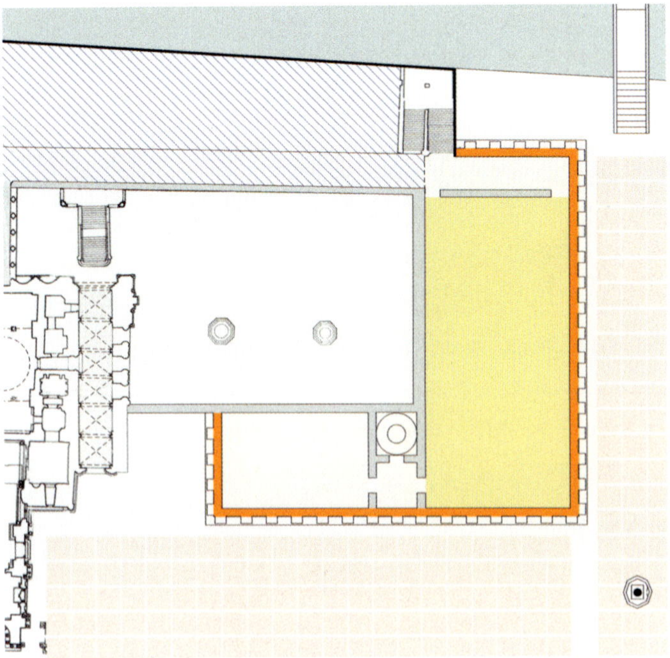

218 Antonio Foscari, reconstruction of the Palladian project to build the Doge's Palace, Venice: the level of the Great Council Hall [Sala del Maggior Consiglio]

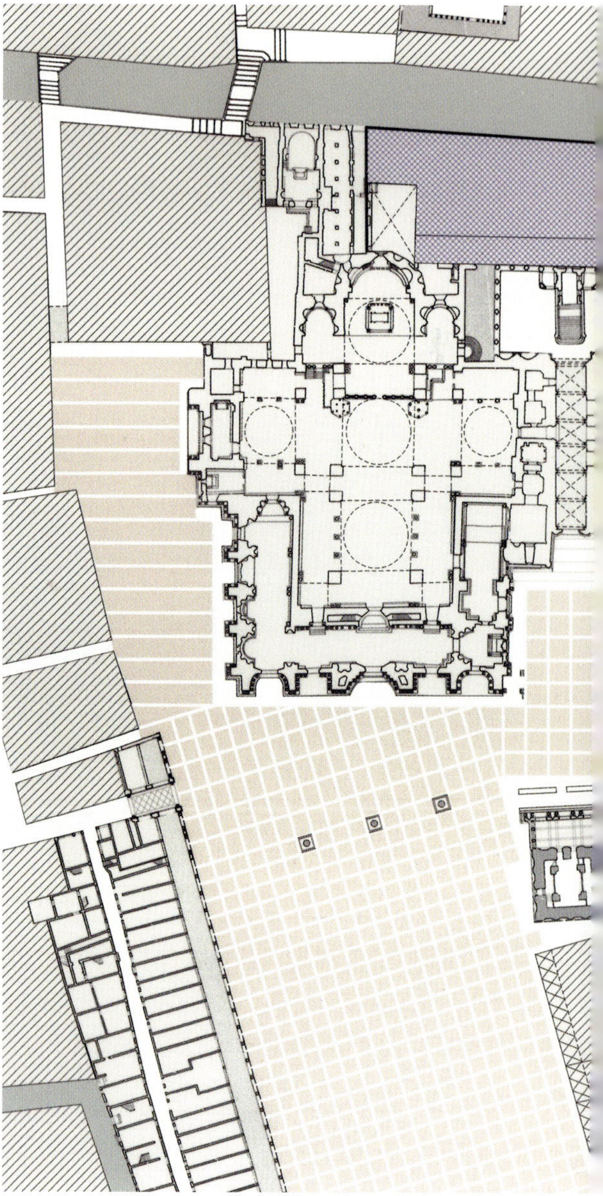

226 Antonio Foscari, reconstruction of the final design by Palladio for the Doge's Palace, showing the façade facing the Piazzetta and the Molo divided into "fourteen bays". The system of vertical connections within the building is based – purely for illustrative purposes – on Palladio's drawing of the ground floor of the Crypta Balbi, RIBA, XI, I

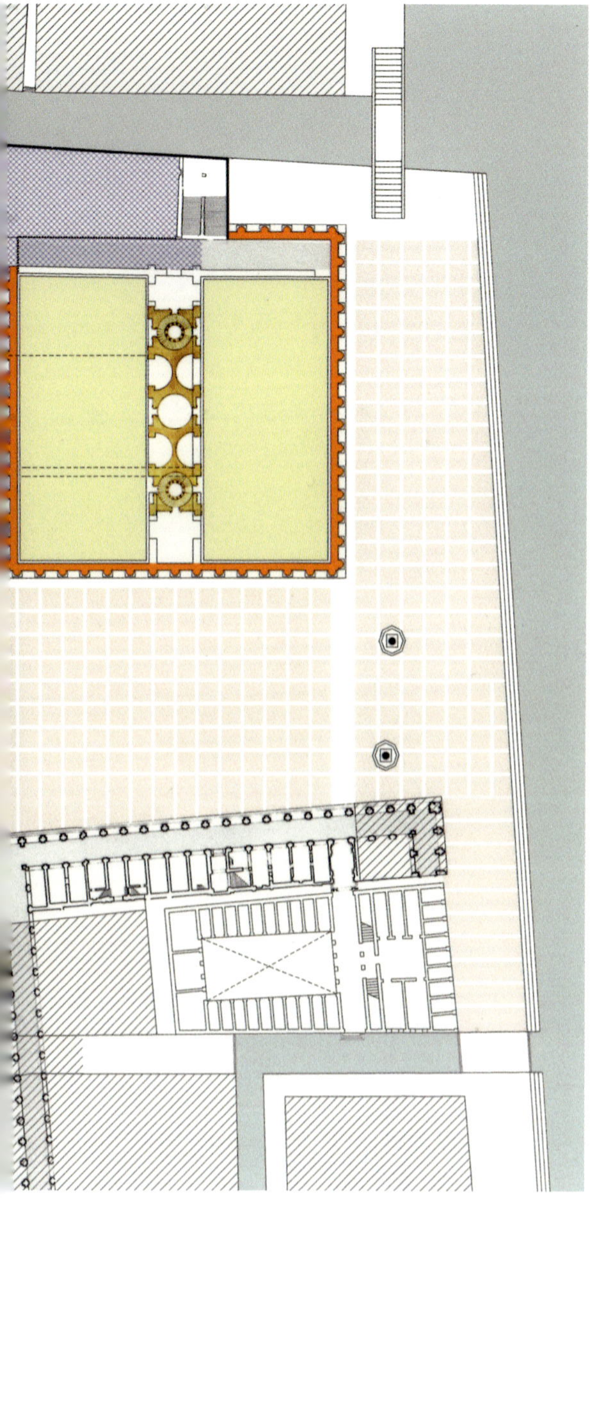

229 L. Cicognara, A. Diedo and G. Selva, *Facade of the Redentore* (detail), 1838, Venice

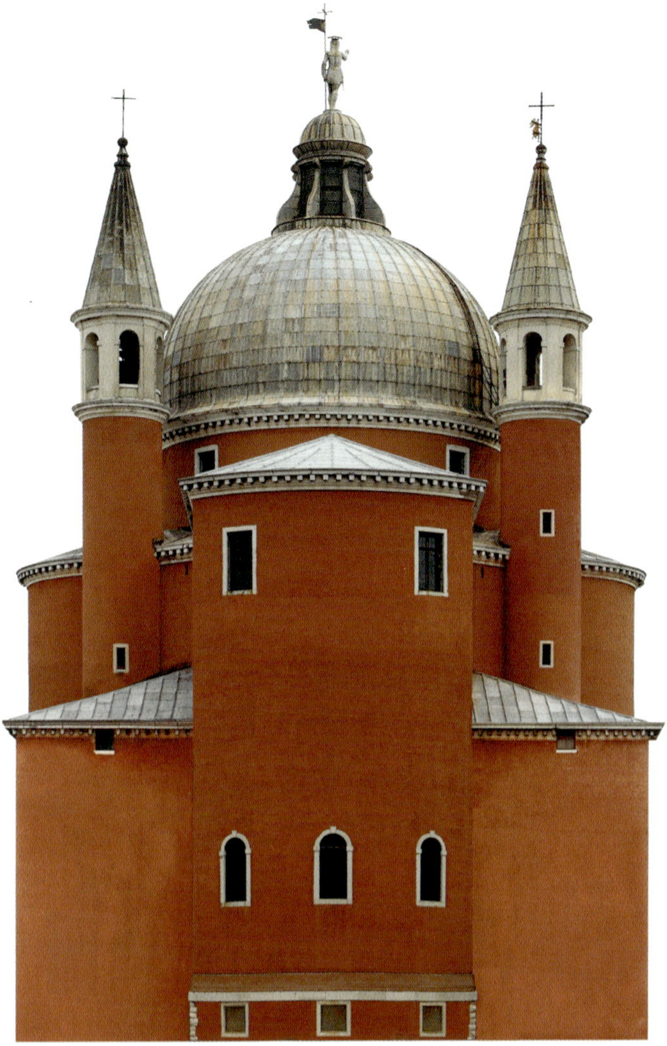

230 *Church of the Redentore,* view from the south, Venice

APPENDIX

NOTES

Translator's note: Page references to Andrea Palladio (A.P.), *I Quattro Libri dell'Architettura* are taken both from the original treatise published in 1570, and (in brackets) from Andrea Palladio, *The Four Books on Architecture,* translated by Robert Tavernor and Richard Schofield, paperback edition, The MIT Press, Cambridge Massachusetts 2002.

1 Archivio di Stato Venezia (A.S.V.), *Notarile. Testamenti,* Marco Foscari, Venice 1551
2 A.P., *I Quattro Libri dell'Architettura,* Venice 1570, II, p. 12 (p. 88)
3 A.P., *op.cit,* IV, p. 73 (p. 285)
4 A.P., *op.cit.,* IV, p. 88 (p. 300)
5 A.P., *op.cit.,* I, p. 3 (p. 3)
6 A.P., *op. cit.,* III, p. 42 (p. 203)
7 A.P., *op. cit.,* I, p. 5 (p. 5)
8 A.P., *op. cit.,* I, p. 3 (p. 3)
9 A.P., *op. cit.,* I, p. 5 [p. 5)
10 A.P., *op. cit.,* II, p. 50 (p. 128)
11 A.P., *op. cit.,* II, p. 53 (p. 131)
12 A.P., *op. cit.,* I, p. 60 (p. 66)
13 A.P., *op. cit.,* III, p. 9 (p. 168)
14 A.P., *op. cit.,* III, p. 7 (p. 165)
15 A.P., *op. cit.,* II, p. 63 (p. 141)
16 A.P., *op. cit.,* II, p. 61 (p. 139)
17 A.P., *op. cit.,* II, p. 61 (p. 139)
18 A.P., *op. cit.,* II, p. 45 (p. 121)
19 A.P., *op. cit.,* II, p. 60 (p. 138)
20 A.P., *op. cit.,* II, p. 19 (p. 94)
21 A.P., *op. cit.,* II, p. 19 (p. 94)
22 see note (5)
23 A.P., *op. cit.,* II, p. 3 (p. 77)
24 A.P., *op. cit.,* IV, p. 6 (p. 216)
25 *Le Opere di Giorgio Vasari con nuove annotazioni e commenti di Gaetano Milanesi,* Florence 1973, vol. VI, p. 369
26 A.P., *op. cit.,* IV, p. 6 (p. 216)
27 *Le Opere di Giorgio Vasari con nuove annotazioni e commenti di Gaetano Milanesi,* Florence 1973, vol. V, p. 271
28 A.P., *op. cit.,* III, p. 35 (p. 197)
29 A.P., *op. cit.,* III, p. 35 (p. 197)
30 G. Barbieri, "Co'l giudizio e con la mente esperta ecc.", in L. Puppi (ed.), *Andrea Palladio. Il testo, l'immagine, la città,* Milan 1980, pp. 17–2631 A.P., *op. cit.,* III, pp. 38–42 (pp. 200–3)
32 A.P., *op. cit.,* IV, p. 8 (p. 217)
33 A.P., *op. cit.,* IV, p. III (p. 323)
34 A.P., *op. cit.,* II, p. 75 (p. 153)
35 M. Della Croce, *L'Historia della publica et famosa entrata in Venezia del Ser.mo Enrico III re di Francia e di Polonia, Venezia 1574,* in A. Magrini, *Memorie intorno la vita e le opere di Andrea Palladio,* Padua 1845, p. 190
36 A.P., *op. cit.,* III, p. 3 (p. 161)
37 A.P., "Scrittura per il ristauro del Palazzo Ducale abbruciato nel 1577", in G. Lorenzi, *Monumenti per servire alla storia del Palazzo Ducale di Venezia,* Venice 1868, vol. I, p. 423
38 A.P., *I Quattro Libri dell'Architettura,* Venice 1570, III, p. 42 (p. 203)
39 A. da Valle and P. dal Ponte, "Scrittura per il ristauro del Palazzo Ducale abbruciato nel 1577", in G. Lorenzi, *Monumenti per servire alla storia del Palazzo Ducaledi Venezia,* Venice 1868, vol. I, p. 430
40 A.S.V., *Senato Terra, filza 81, 17 September, 1580.* Published in P. Selvatico, *Sulla architettura e sulla scultura in Venezia dal Medioevo ai nostri giorni,* Venice 1847, pp. 345–46.
41 see note (5)
42 A.P., *op. cit.,* IV, p 7 (p. 217)
43 A.P., *op. cit.,* I, p. 3 (p. 3)

GLOSSARY

***acroterium* (acroterial):** ornament placed at the apex of a building, or at the end of a pediment.
all'antica: in accordance with the architectural canons of ancient Roman architecture.
apostolic *nunzio:* papal ambassador.
apparato effimero: theatrical architecture erected for a special event.
appartamento: a suite of three rooms reserved – in Palladio's interpretation – for the use of a single person.
Arengo: a popular assembly endowed with sovreign power.
ars aedificatoria: literally, the art of building.
delenda memoria: the forced erasure of the memory of a censured political event or person.
Bucintoro: state galley reserved for the Doge's use (almost an emblem of his sovreignty).
bugnato: form of rustication with projecting blocks separated by deep joints.
calle: Venetian term for the narrow pedestrian streets in the city.
Casa degli Antichi: a definition used by Palladio to indicate the building typology of ancient Roman residences, according to his interpretation.
casa di villa: a residence in the countryside.
casa dominicale: the owner's house on an estate.
Commentaries: an accompanying body of critical commentary to Vitruvius's *Treatise.*
commodità: Palladio's definition of the domestic functions required in a residence.
compagni: partners who jointly manage a business.
Compagnia degli Accesi: the name of the Company of the Hose led by Girolamo Foscari
***Compagnie di Calza* (Companies of the Hose):** temporary associations of young patricians mainly dedicated to the organisation of events and performances.
***conservatore* (position in the Accademia degli Uniti):** general secretary, manager.
corte (*cortile*), pl. *corti* (*cortili*): open space inside a house or palace.
Dominio: Venetian expression to indicate the Republic's dominions in the Po Valley.
edificatore: Palladian expression used to refer to the patron of a work.
exedra: external architectural space, generally semi-circular in plan.
exemplum: an example, paradigm
fabbrica: a Palladian expression, synonymous with *costruzione,* building.
foro marciano: Piazza San Marco, in Venice.
fraterna: a Venetian legal institution that obliged brothers to manage their family assets jointly.
***Gonfaloniere* of the Church:** Commander of the Papacy's armed forces.
imago: public image.
instauratio Rei publicae: political imposition of a Republican regime.
intercolumniation: the space between adjacent columns.
invenzione: a Palladian expression, synonymous with project.
Libreria: the public building destined to house codices and to be used for other general cultural purposes.
lodia magna: literally "large loggia".
loggia: a meeting place, open to the exterior, supported by columns or pilasters.
lucernario: rooflight used to provide natural toplighting.
Maggior Consiglio: the supreme body of Republican government, composed of a large number of patricians.
Maison carrée: a contemporary name for the Roman temple at Nîmes, with a peripteral form.
momarie: theatrical performances following in a late medieval tradition.
Odeon: structure designed for listening to music.
officina: a workshop; the term was also used for groups undertaking intellectual research.
opus quadratum: Roman wall built using square stones.
ordinare: Palladian expression, synonymous with compose, design.
ornamento: Renaissance term used to indicate the elements of the architectural orders.
Palazzo della Ragione: literally the Palace of Justice, namely a building where the magistrates sat to administer justice.
Patriarch: a religious position second only to the pope in the ecclesiastical hierarchy of the Church of Rome.
Pax veneziana: the peace maintained by the Venetian state within its mainland territories.
per banda: on each side of the building.
peripteral: of a building whose perimeter is surrounded by columns (or half-columns).

piano nobile: the main floor of an aristocratic house.
Piazza dei Latini: Palladio's definition of the type of squares used in ancient Rome, according to his interpretation.
Piazzetta: the piazza to the west of the Doge's Palace in Venice.
platea marciana: St Mark's Square in enice.
podestà: political representative of the Venetian government.
portego: central hall of the Venetian house.
portico: space open to the outside, supported by columns or pilasters.
Pretore: Latin expression for the political representative of central power in a particular province.
Procuratia di San Marco (Procurators of St Mark); the supreme magistracy of the Republic, responsible – among other matters – for managing the buildings around St Mark's Square and St Mark's itself.
Procuratore di San Marco: a member of the Procuratoria di San Marco (see above).
pronaos: the vestibule leading into the cella or main body of a temple.
proto*, pl. *proti:* from *protomagister: chief technician of a Venetian magistracy.
Provveditore alla Fortezze: political figure appointed to oversee the State fortifications.
Provveditore alle Pompe: political figure appointed to manage all State events and to enforce laws curbing private manifestations of wealth.
Provveditori della Fabbrica: commissioners responsible for the technical and financial management of a major building site.
RIBA: Royal Institute of British Architects
ragione: literally, "justice",
renovatio: renovation process inspired by the canons of Romanitas.
***Res publica*/Republic:** the constitutional regime of the Venetian State based on the ancient communal regime and strenuously defended over the centuries – until 1797 – against the trend towards absolute monarchies in the rest of Europe (starting with the Papacy). In safeguarding their Republic and in their determination to prevent any authoritarian evolution, the Venetians almost always referred back to the ancient Roman Republic, blaming its civil wars for causing its crisis and allowing the consequent establishment of an imperial regime. Protecting the republican regime was, for Venice, also a way to ensure that the city's laws and legal system was as consistent and compatible as possible with its commercial economy and the network of maritime traffic that had underpinned its power and wealth over the centuries.
rio, pl. rii: Venetian waterway, generally not very wide.
Romanism: ideological pro-papal stance.
sala: large hall, generally used for representative functions.
Salt Magistracy (Magistrato del Sal): Venetian magistracy that supervised the financing and execution of public works.
Savio del Consiglio: a high-ranking member of the Signoria, equivalent to a minister.
Savio di Terra Ferma: a member of the Signoria responsible for governing the "Stato da Terra".
La Serenissima: a term used to refer to the Venetian Republic.
serliana: type of window opening whose popularity is attributed to Sebastiano Serlio.
Signoria: the councillors and the heads or *capi* of the three criminal courts who flanked the doge in the government of the Republic.
sprezzatura: expression used by Baldassar Castiglione to indicate an attitude of intellectual detachment or ironic superiority.
Stato da Mar: Venetian expression used to define the Republic's maritime empire (stretching from the Adriatic as far as the eastern Mediterranean).
Stato da Terra: Venetian expression used to define its mainland territories under Republican jurisdiction.
Terraferma: Venetian expression to indicate lands or possessions on the mainland.
tetrastyle: comprising four columns.
villa: Latin term for a country estate or farm, widely used in the sixteenth century.
Water Magistracy (Magistrato delle Acque): Venetian magistracy responsible for all water use and hydraulics (sea, lagoon and rivers).

LIST OF ILLUSTRATIONS

In the following, the term "edited" describes the process used to clarify a concept or isolate an image from surrounding text or background, while "collage" is the product of a combination of two or more drawings [or images] to which the author (A.F.) has added a further layer of graphic intervention.

di Andrea Palladio, Vicenza 1778, II,plate XXXVIII, photo © Centro Internazionale di Studi di Architettura Andrea Palladio, Vicenza

23 Lonedo di Lugo (Vicenza), Villa Godi (edited), Centro Internazionale di Studi di Architettura Andrea Palladio, Vicenza, photo © Centro Internazionale di Studi di Architettura Andrea Palladio, Vicenza

24 *Villini giovanili, projects*, RIBA, XVII, 2 r, Library Photographs Collection, Royal Institute of British Architects, London, photo © Library Photographs Collection, Royal Institute of British Architects, London

25 Cristofano di Papi dell'Altissimo (attributed), *Portrait of Cardinal Niccolò Ridolfi*, 16th cent., 65.5 × 51cm, Sale at Christie's New York (1989)

26 Cornaro Odeon, ground floor plan, in Lionello Puppi (ed.), *Alvise Cornaro e il suo tempo*, Comitato Nazionale per le Celebrazioni nel quarto Centenario della morte di Andrea Palladio, Palladio 1580–1980, exh. cat., Comune di Padova, 1980, p. 49, photo © Comune di Padova

27 Bagnolo (Vicenza), *Project for Villa Pisani, preliminary study* (detail), RIBA, XVI, 19 c, Library Photographs Collection, Royal Institute of British Architects, London, photo © Library Photographs Collection, Royal Institute of British Architects, London

28 Bagnolo (Vicenza), *Project for Villa Pisani*, RIBA, XVII, 1, Library Photographs Collection, Royal Institute of British Architects, London, photo © Library Photographs Collection, Royal Institute of British Architects, London

29 S. Serlio, *I Sette Libri dell'Architettura*, v. 1, c. 120 recto (detail), coll. CONS. 720 SER, Fondazione Querini Stampalia, Venice, photo © Fondazione Querini Stampalia, Venice

30 Bagnolo (Vicenza), *Project for Villa Pisani*, RIBA, XVII, 17 (detail), Library Photographs Collection – Royal Institute of British Architects – London, photo © Library Photographs Collection – Royal Institute of British Architects – London

31 Bagnolo (Vicenza), *Project for Villa Pisani*, RIBA, XVII, 2 v, Library Photographs Collection, Royal Institute of British Architects, London, photo © Library Photographs Collection, Royal Institute of British Architects, London

32 Bagnolo (Vicenza), *Project for Villa Pisani*, RIBA, XVII, 18 r, Library Photographs Collection, Royal Institute of British Architects, London, photo © Library Photographs Collection – Royal Institute of British Architects – London

33 Giulio Romano, *Battaglia di Ponte Milvio* (detail), c. 1525, Musei Vaticani, Città del Vaticano, photo © Pontificia Commissione per i Beni Culturali della Chiesa, Città del Vaticano

34 Giulio Romano (and Raffaellino del Colle?), *The Madonna and Child with Saint John the Baptist* (detail), The Walters Art Museum, Baltimore, photo © The Walters Art Museum, Baltimore

35 Alessandro Buzzaccarini draughtsman, Fioravanti Penuti engraver [from the watercolour by Marino Urbani], *Interior of the Arena at Padua* (detail), in *Cenni storici sulle famiglie di Padova e sui monumenti dell'Università*, Padua, Minerva, 1842, Esemplare Biblioteca Civica, Padua, BP 1368, photo © courtesy of Comune di Padova, Assessorato alla Cultura, Padova

36 G. Valle, *Pianta della Città di Padova* (edited), 1784, coll. C. GEOGR. M. 008, Fondazione Querini Stampalia, Venice, photo © Fondazione Querini Stampalia, Venice

37 Luvigliano (Padua), G.M. Falconetto, *Villa dei Vescovi* (edited), 1529–1535, Centro Internazionale di Studi di Architettura Andrea Palladio, Vicenza, photo © Centro Internazionale di Studi di Architettura Andrea Palladio, Vicenza

38 Pontecasale (Padua), J. Sansovino, *Villa Garzoni*, 16th cent., photo © Biggi, Venice

39 *La Villa, di Palladio Rutilio Tauro Emiliano, tradotta nuovamente per Francesco Sansovino, …, in Venetia, 1560*, frontispiece (detail), Biblioteca Nazionale Marciana, Venice, photo © Biblioteca Nazionale Marciana, Venice

40 *Studies of Military Formations*, printed sheet (detail), Worcester College, Oxford, photo © Worcester College, Oxford

41 Piazzola sul Brenta (Padua), Villa Contarini, Casa di villa with *two entrances*, RIBA, XVII, 15 Library Photographs Collection, Royal Institute of British Architects, London, photo © Library Photographs Collection, Royal Institute of British Architects, London (identification proposed by A.F.)

42 Piazzola sul Brenta (Padua), Villa Contarini, *Project for a* casa di villa *with five bays*, RIBA, XVI, 18 r, Library Photographs Collection, Royal Institute of British Architects, London, photo

© Library Photographs Collection, Royal Institute of British Architects, London (identification proposed by A.F.)

43 Piazzola sul Brenta (Padua), Villa Contarini, Project for a casa di villa with five bays, RIBA, XVI, 16 c, Library Photographs Collection, Royal Institute of British Architects, London, photo © Library Photographs Collection, Royal Institute of British Architects, London (identification proposed by A.F.)

44 Piazzola sul Brenta (Padua), Villa Contarini, *Project for a* casa di villa *with five bays,* RIBA, XVII, 27, r, Library Photographs Collection, Royal Institute of British Architects, London, photo © Library Photographs Collection, Royal Institute of British Architects, London (identification proposed by A.F.)

45 Piazzola sul Brenta (Padua), Villa Contarini, *Project for a* casa di villa *with five bays,* RIBA, XVI, 16 b, Library Photographs Collection, Royal Institute of British Architects, London, photo © Library Photographs Collection, Royal Institute of British Architects, London (identification proposed by A.F.)

46 Pojana (Vicenza), *Villa Pojana, preliminary studies,* RIBA, XVI, 4 r (detail), Library Photographs Collection Royal Institute of British Architects, London, photo © Library Photographs Collection, Royal Institute of British Architects, London

47 Finale (Vicenza), Villa Saraceno, A. Palladio, *I Quattro Libri dell'Architettura,* II, p. 56 (edited), Centro Internazionale di Studi di Architettura Andrea Palladio, Vicenza, photo © Centro Internazionale di Studi di Architettura Andrea Palladio, Vicenza

48 Cessalto (Treviso), Villa Zeno (edited), 1973, D. Birelli, Photoservice Electa, photo © Photoservice Electa

49 Antonio da Sangallo il Giovane for Raphael, *Project for Villa Madama* (detail), Florence U 314 A, Polo Museale della città di Firenze, photo © Polo Museale della città di Firenze Florence

50 Anon., *Portrait of Cardinal Ercole Gonzaga* (detail from *Deposition*), 16th cent., Church of Sant'Egidio, Mantua

51 Tiziano Vecellio, Portrait of Giulio Romano (detail), c. 1536, 102 × 87 cm, Collezioni Provinciali, Mantua

52 Antonio del Pellegrino, for Donato Bramante, Ground plan of Palazzo dei Tribunali in Rome, U 136 A (detail), Florence, photo © Gabinetto Fotografico della S.S.P.S.A.E e per il Polo Museale della città di Firenze

53 Giulio Romano, *Palazzo Te,* ground floor plan, Stiftung museum kunst palast, Dusseldorf © Stiftung museum kunst palast, Dusseldorf

54 Quinto (Vicenza), Villa Thiene, A. Palladio, *I Quattro Libri dell'Architettura,* II, p. 13 (detail), Centro Internazionale di Studi di Architettura Andrea Palladio, Vicenza, photo © Centro Internazionale di Studi di Architettura Andrea Palladio, Vicenza

55 Quinto (Vicenza), Villa Thiene, facade, A. Palladio, *I Quattro Libri dell'Architettura,* II, p. 14, Centro Internazionale di Studi di Architettura Andrea Palladio, Vicenza, photo © Centro Internazionale di Studi di Architettura Andrea Palladio, Vicenza

56 Rome, *Baths of Caracalla, reconstruction,* RIBA, VI, II, r (detail), Library Photographs Collection Royal Institute of British Architects, London, photo © Library Photographs Collection, Royal Institute of British Architects, London

57 Rome, *Baths of Agrippa, reconstruction,* RIBA, VII, 6, v, Library Photographs Collection Royal Institute of British Architects, London, photo © Library Photographs Collection, Royal Institute of British Architects, London

58 Rome, Pantheon, A. Palladio, *I Quattro Libri dell'Architettura,* IV, pp. 76–77, Centro Internazionale di Studi di Architettura Andrea Palladio, Vicenza, photo © Centro Internazionale di Studi di Architettura Andrea Palladio, Vicenza

59 Rome, *Mausoleum of Romulus on the Via Appia,* RIBA, VIII, I, r, Library Photographs Collection Royal Institute of British Architects, London, photo © Library Photographs Collection, Royal Institute of British Architects, London

60 Palestrina (Rome), *Temple of Fortuna, plan,* RIBA, IX, I, Library Photographs Collection, Royal Institute of British Architects, London, photo © Library Photographs Collection, Royal Institute of British Architects, London

61 Palestrina (Rome), *Temple of Fortuna,* RIBA, IX, 9, Library Photographs Collection, Royal Institute of British Architects, London, photo © Library Photographs Collection, Royal Institute of British Architects, London

62 Verona, *Roman theatre,* RIBA, IX, 4, Library Photographs Collection Royal Institute of British Architects, London, photo © Library Photographs Collection, Royal Institute of British Architects, London

63 *Monumental structure of the Palazzo della Ragione*, aerial photo (detail), Centro Internazionale di Studi di Architettura Andrea Palladio, Vicenza, photo © Centro Internazionale di Studi di Architettura Andrea Palladio, Vicenza
64 Antonio Nani, *Portrait of Doge Francesco Donà* (edited), in *Serie dei dogi di Venezia intagliati in rame da Antonio Nani*, Venice, Tipografia di Giambattista Merlo, 1840, Biblioteca Nazionale Marciana, photo © Biblioteca Nazionale Marciana, Venice
65 Venice, Sansovino's Loggetta (detail), photo Naya, Venice, photo © foto Naya, Venice
66 Anon., *Veduta della* Zecca (edited), from *Il volo del turco*, St. P.D. 8114, neg. M5475, Museo Correr, Venice, photo © Musei Civici Veneziani, Venice
67 Angarano, Bassano del Grappa (Vicenza), Villa Angarano, A. Palladio, *I quattro libri dell'Architettura*, II, p. 63, Centro Internazionale di Studi di Architettura Andrea Palladio, Vicenza photo © Centro Internazionale di Studi di Architettura Andrea Palladio, Vicenza
68 Tiziano Vecellio, *Portrait of Daniele Barbaro* (detail), 1545, 85.8 × 71.1 cm, National Gallery of Canada, Ottawa, photo © National Gallery of Canada, Ottawa
69 Vicenza, *Project for the loggias of the Palazzo della Ragione*, RIBA, XVII, 22, Library Photographs Collection Royal Institute of British Architects, London, photo © Library Photographs Collection, Royal Institute of British Architects, London
70 Vicenza, *Project for the loggias of the Palazzo della Ragione*, RIBA, XIII, 9 r, Library Photographs Collection Royal Institute of British Architects, London, photo © Library Photographs Collection, Royal Institute of British Architects, London
71 Vicenza, *Project for the loggias of the Palazzo della Ragione*, RIBA, XIII, 8, Library Photographs Collection Royal Institute of British Architects, London, photo © Library Photographs Collection, Royal Institute of British Architects, London
72 Vicenza, Palazzo della Ragione, detail of the corner, A. Palladio, *I Quattro Libri dell'Architettura*, III, p. 43, Centro Internazionale di Studi di Architettura Andrea Palladio, Vicenza, photo © Centro Internazionale di Studi di Architettura Andrea Palladio, Vicenza
73 Paolo Caliari, known as Veronese, *Iseppo Porto* (detail), 1551–52, 212 × 135 cm, Galleria degli Uffizi, Florence, Collezione Bonacossi, no. 16, photo © S.S.P.S.A.E. and Polo Museale della città di Firenze, Florence
74 Vicenza, *Project for Palazzo Porto*, RIBA, XVII, 12 v, Library Photographs Collection Royal Institute of British Architects, London, photo © Library Photographs Collection, Royal Institute of British Architects, London
75 Vicenza, *Project for Palazzo Porto*, RIBA, XVII, 9 r, Library Photographs Collection Royal Institute of British Architects, London, photo © Library Photographs Collection, Royal Institute of British Architects, London
76 Vicenza, *Project for Palazzo Porto*, RIBA, XVII, 3, Library Photographs Collection Royal Institute of British Architects, London, photo © Library Photographs Collection, Royal Institute of British Architects, London
77 Vicenza, *Elevation of Palazzo Civena*, RIBA, XVII, 14 r (detail), Library Photographs Collection Royal Institute of British Architects, London, photo © Library Photographs Collection, Royal Institute of British Architects, London
78 Model of Palazzo Thiene (detail), Centro Internazionale di Studi di Architettura Andrea Palladio, Vicenza, photo © Centro Internazionale di Studi di Architettura Andrea Palladio, Vicenza
79 Vicenza, *Project for Palazzo Chiericati*, RIBA, VIII, 11 r (detail), Library Photographs Collection Royal Institute of British Architects, London, photo © Library Photographs Collection, Royal Institute of British Architects, London
80 Vicenza, *Project for Palazzo Chiericati*, RIBA, XVII, 8, Library Photographs Collection Royal Institute of British Architects, London, photo © Library Photographs Collection, Royal Institute of British Architects, London
81 Vicenza, *Study for the facade of Palazzo Chiericati*, RIBA, XVII, 5, Library Photographs Collection Royal Institute of British Architects, London, photo © Library Photographs Collection, Royal Institute of British Architects, London
82 Paolo Caliari, known as Veronese, *Daniele Barbaro*, c. 1566, Rijksmuseum, Amsterdam, photo © Rijksmuseum, Amsterdam
83 Ulisse Aldrovandi, *Orbis stellatus seu orbis astrifer, a Daniele Barbaro iconem habui*, from *De Piscibus libri V, et de cetis lib. Unus, Bononiae, apud Bellagambam*, 1613,

plate 43, (edited), coll. 16A17, Biblioteca Panizzi, Reggio Emilia photo © Biblioteca Panizzi, Reggio Emilia
84 Fano (Pesaro and Urbino), Basilica, facade and cross section, *I Dieci Libri dell'Architettura, tradotti e commentati da Daniele Barbaro,* Venice 1567 Libro v, pp. 220–221, Centro Internazionale di Studi di Architettura Andrea Palladio, Vicenza, photo © Centro Internazionale di Studi di Architettura Andrea Palladio, Vicenza
85 Malcontenta di Mira (Venice), Villa Foscari, known as *La Malcontenta* (detail), photo © Private collection
86 Malcontenta di Mira (Venice), Villa Foscari, known as *La Malcontenta* (detail), photo © Archivio Osvaldo Boehm
87 Malcontenta di Mira (Venice), Villa Foscari, known as *La Malcontenta* (detail), photo © AFI
88 Malcontenta di Mira (Venice), Elevation of an unbuilt *fabbrica* (collage by A.F. of RIBA, XVII, 6 and survey by Erik Forssman), photo © Library Photographs Collection, Royal Institute of British Architects, London and Erik Forssman (identification of RIBA, XVII, 6 proposed by A.F.)
89 Paolo Veronese, *Miracolo del bambino morso da un serpente e risorto da San Pantalon [Miracle of San Pantalon]* (detail), 1587, Church of San Pantalon, Venice, photo © Curia Patriarcale di Venezia, Venice
90 Rome, *Mausoleum of Romulus on the Via Appia,* RIBA, VIII, 1 r, Library Photographs Collection Royal Institute of British Architects, London, photo © Library Photographs Collection, Royal Institute of British Architects, London
91 Malcontenta di Mira (Venice), Villa Foscari, A. Palladio, *I Quattro Libri dell'Architettura,* II, p.50, Centro Internazionale di Studi di Architettura Andrea Palladio, Vicenza, photo © Centro Internazionale di Studi di Architettura Andrea Palladio, Vicenza
92 Richard Norris, *Facade of the Malcontenta,* Victoria and Albert Museum, London, photo © V&A Images/Victoria and Albert Museum, London
93 Tiziano Vecellio, *Portrait of Doge Francesco Venier* (detail), 1555, 113 × 99 cm, Museo Thyssen Bornemisza, Madrid, © Museo Thyssen Bornemisza, Madrid
94 Rome, Temple of Fortuna Virilis, A. Palladio, *I Quattro Libri dell'Architettura,* IV, p. 49, Centro Internazionale di Studi di Architettura Andrea Palladio, Vicenza, photo © Centro Internazionale di Studi di Architettura Andrea Palladio, Vicenza
95 Rome, Temple of Fortuna Virilis, A. Palladio, *I Quattro Libri dell'Architettura,* IV, p. 51, Centro Internazionale di Studi di Architettura Andrea Palladio, Vicenza, photo © Centro Internazionale di Studi di Architettura Andrea Palladio, Vicenza
96 Vancimuglio (Vicenza), Villa Chiericati, Centro Internazionale di Studi di Architettura Andrea Palladio, Vicenza, photo © Centro Internazionale di Studi di Architettura Andrea Palladio, Vicenza
97 Piombino Dese (Padua), Villa Cornaro, A. Palladio, *I quattro libri dell'Architettura,* II p. 53 (detail), Centro Internazionale di Studi di Architettura Andrea Palladio, Vicenza, photo © Centro Internazionale di Studi di Architettura Andrea Palladio, Vicenza
98 Piombino Dese (Padua), *Villa Cornaro,* 1973, D. Birelli, Electa Editrice, photo © Electa Editrice
99 Piombino Dese (Padua), *Villa Cornaro,* photo c. 1910, Cornaro Gable Piombino collection, photo © Raccolta Cornaro Gable Piombino
100 Piombino Dese (Padua), Bridge, *Villa Cornaro,* Cornaro Gable Piombino collection, photo © Raccolta Cornaro Gable Piombino
101 Montagnana (Padua), Villa Pisani, A. Palladio, *I Quattro Libri dell'Architettura,* II, p. 52 (detail), Centro Internazionale di Studi di Architettura Andrea Palladio, Vicenza, photo © Centro Internazionale di Studi di Architettura Andrea Palladio, Vicenza
102 L. Cicognara, A. Diedo and G. Selva, Palazzo Cornaro at San Maurizio (detail), 1838, *Le fabbriche e i monumenti più cospicui di Venezia illustrati,* vol. I: c. 121, Fondazione Querini Stampalia, Venice, photo © Fondazione Querini Stampalia, Venice
103 L. Cicognara, A. Diedo and G. Selva, Palazzo Grimani at San Luca (detail), 1838, *Le fabbriche e i monumenti più cospicui di Venezia illustrati,* vol. I: c. 123, Fondazione Querini Stampalia, Venice, photo © Fondazione Querini Stampalia, Venice
104 Venice, *Invenzione* for a palazzo, A. Palladio, *I Quattro Libri dell'Architettura,* II, p. 72 (detail), Centro Internazionale di Studi di Architettura Andrea Palladio, Vicenza, photo © Centro Internazionale di Studi di Architettura Andrea Palladio, Vicenza
105 Venice, *Invenzione* for a palazzo, A. Palladio, *I Quattro Libri dell'Architettura,* II, p. 71 (detail), Centro Internazionale di Studi di Architettura Andrea Palladio,

Vicenza, photo © Centro Internazionale di Studi di Architettura Andrea Palladio, Vicenza
106 Antonio Calligaris, *Rete di seriole della Brentella nel territorio di Fanzolo [Netting Fish in the Brentella Canal near Fanzolo]* (detail), *Mappe Antiche*, b. 34/2 fg. no. 326/b. photo © Concessione no. 6/2010, Archivio di Stato, Treviso
107 Fanzolo (Treviso), *Villa Emo*, A. Palladio, *I Quattro Libri dell'Architettura*, II, p. 55 (edited), Centro Internazionale di Studi di Architettura Andrea Palladio, Vicenza, photo © Centro Internazionale di Studi di Architettura Andrea Palladio, Vicenza
108 Campiglia (Vicenza), *Villa Repeta*, A. Palladio, *I Quattro Libri dell'Architettura*, II, p. 61 (detail), Centro Internazionale di Studi di Architettura Andrea Palladio, Vicenza, photo © Centro Internazionale di Studi di Architettura Andrea Palladio, Vicenza
109 Maser (Treviso), *Villa Barbaro*, A. Palladio, *I Quattro Libri dell'Architettura*, II, p. 61, Centro Internazionale di Studi di Architettura Andrea Palladio, Vicenza, photo © Centro Internazionale di Studi di Architettura Andrea Palladio, Vicenza
110 Maser (Treviso), *Villa Barbaro*, Nymphaeum (edited), 1973, D. Birelli, Electa Editrice photo © Electa Editrice
111 Fratta Polesine (Rovigo), Villa Badoer, A. Palladio, *I Quattro Libri dell'Architettura*, II, p. 48 (detail), Centro Internazionale di Studi di Architettura Andrea Palladio, Vicenza, photo © Centro Internazionale di Studi di Architettura Andrea Palladio, Vicenza
112 Fratta Polesine (Rovigo), *Villa Badoer*, Portico (detail), 1973, D. Birelli, Electa Editrice, photo © Electa Editrice
113 Meledo (Vicenza), Villa Trissino, A. Palladio, *I Quattro Libri dell'Architettura*, II, p. 48 (detail), Centro Internazionale di Studi di Archiettura Andrea Palladio, Vicenza, photo © Centro Internazionale di Studi di Architettura Andrea Palladio, Vicenza
114 Meledo (Vicenza), *Villa Trissino*, ceiling, photo © Titta Rossi Pertile
115 Tivoli, *Temple of Hercules Victor*, RIBA, IX, 8 (detail), Library Photographs Collection Royal Institute of British Architects, London, photo © Library Photographs Collection, Royal Institute of British Architects, London
116 Vicenza, *Villa Almerigo Capra*, known as *La Rotonda*, A. Palladio, *I quattro libri dell'Architettura*, II, p. 19, Centro Internazionale di Studi di Architettura Andrea Palladio, Vicenza, photo © Centro Internazionale di Studi di Architettura Andrea Palladio, Vicenza
117 Vicenza, *Villa Almerigo Capra*, known as *La Rotonda*, photolithograph, 1880, Valmarana Collection, photo © raccolta Valmarana
118 Vicenza, *Villa Almerigo Capra*, known as *La Rotonda*, photo © Pino Guidolotti
119 Venice, *Plan of the stone Bridge of Rialto* with five arches, Gabinetto dei disegni e stampe, Pinacoteca Civica di Vicenza, D. 25 r, photo © Pinacoteca Civica, Vicenza
120 Jacopo De' Barbari, *La pianta prospettica di Venezia del 1500 [Bird's eye view of Venice*, detail], from G. Mazzariol, T. Pignatti, *La pianta prospettica di Venezia del 1500 disegnata da Jacopo de' Barbari*, Venice, Cassa di Risparmio, 1963, 69 × 50 cm, 6 plates, Officine Grafiche Trevisan, Castelfranco
121 Sansovino, *Sketch*, Archivio Bertarelli, Castello Sforzesco, Milano, photo © Castello Sforzesco, Milano
122 Daniele Barbaro, *I Dieci Libri dell'Architettura tradotti e commentati*, Venice 1556, Centro Internazionale di Studi di Architettura Andrea Palladio, Vicenza, photo © Centro Internazionale di Studi di Architettura Andrea Palladio, Vicenza
123 *Draft of a letter and sketches*, RIBA, XVI, 9 v, Library Photographs Collection Royal Institute of British Architects, London, photo © Library Photographs Collection, Royal Institute of British Architects, London
124 Colonnade with doors and windows, *I Dieci Libri dell'Architettura*, Venice 1567, book VI, p. 278 (detail), Centro Internazionale di Studi di Architettura Andrea Palladio, Vicenza, photo © Centro Internazionale di Studi di Architettura Andrea Palladio, Vicenza
125 Rome, *Temples of Saturn and Venus*, RIBA, XI, 20 r, Library Photographs Collection Royal Institute of British Architects, London, photo © Library Photographs Collection, Royal Institute of British Architects, London
126 *Project for the facade of a church* (mirror image on right), RIBA, XIV, 12 r (r), Library Photographs Collection Royal Institute of British Architects, London, photo © Library Photographs Collection, Royal Institute of British Architects, London

127 *Cross section of a church [San Pietro di Castello]*, RIBA, XIV, 1, Library Photographs Collection Royal Institute of British Architects, London, photo © Library Photographs Collection, Royal Institute of British Architects, London (identified by A.F.)
128 *Cross section of a church [San Pietro di Castello]*, RIBA, XIV, 9, Library Photographs Collection Royal Institute of British Architects, London, photo © Library Photographs Collection, Royal Institute of British Architects, London (identified by A.F.)
129 Collage of *Temple of Jupiter Serapis* and *Cross section of a church [San Pietro di Castello]*, RIBA XI, 24, V and RIBA, XIV, 1, Library Photographs Collection Royal Institute of British Architects, London, photo © Library Photographs Collection, Royal Institute of British Architects, London (identified by A.F./collage by A.F.)
130 Marocco (Treviso), Villa Mocenigo, A. Palladio, *I Quattro Libri dell'Architettura*, II, p. 54 (detail), Centro Internazionale di Studi di Architettura Andrea Palladio, Vicenza, photo © Centro Internazionale di Studi di Architettura Andrea Palladio, Vicenza
131 Jacopo De' Barbari, *La pianta prospettica di Venezia del 1500* (*Bird's eye view of Venice*, detail), from G. Mazzariol, T. Pignatti, *La pianta prospettica di Venezia del 1500 disegnata da Jacopo de' Barbari*, Venice, Cassa di Risparmio, 1963, 69 × 50 cm, 6 plates, Officine Grafiche Trevisan, Castelfranco
132 Venice, *Santa Lucia, plan* (edited), drawing from volume F438/IV plate 15, Biblioteca del Museo Correr, Venice photo © Musei Civici Veneziani, Venice
133 A. Palladio, B. Del Moro; surrounding frame by G. Vasari. *Project for a funerary chapel* (detail), Museum of Fine Arts, Budapest, 198, photo © Museum of Fine Arts, Budapest
134 *Project for the facade of a church [Santa Lucia]*, RIBA, XIV, 10 r, Library Photographs Collection Royal Institute of British Architects, London, photo © Library Photographs Collection, Royal Institute of British Architects, London (identified by A.F.)
135 Collage of the drawing *Project for the facade of a church [Santa Lucia]*, RIBA XIV, 10 r and survey by F. Muttoni of the facade of the Church of Santa Lucia, Library Photographs Collection Royal Institute of British Architects, London, photo © Library Photographs Collection, Royal Institute of British Architects, London and Centro Internazionale di Studi di Architettura Andrea Palladio, Vicenza (collage by A.F.)
136 Venice, Church of San Giuliano, facade, 1969, D. Birelli, Marsilio Editori, photo © Marsilio Editori
137 Jacopo Tintoretto, *Portrait of Giovanni Grimani* (detail), Private Collection (formerly London, P. and D. Colnaghi, 1983), photo © Private Collection (formerly London, P. and D. Colnaghi, 1983)
138 Venice, *Church of San Francesco alla Vigna*, facade, survey, Soprintendenza per i Beni architettonici e paesaggistici di Venezia e Laguna, Archivio Fotografico, drawing 2B/1586 (ex 186), photo © Archivio Fotografico, Soprintendenza per i Beni architettonici e paesaggistici di Venezia e Laguna
139 Venice, *Church of San Giorgio Maggiore*, facade (detail), photo © Pino Guidolotti
140 Sebastiano del Piombo, *Portrait of Cardinal Reginald Pole*, 1540, 112 × 95 cm, The Hermitage, Saint Petersburg
141 Jacopo De' Barbari, *La pianta prospettica di Venezia del 1500* [*Bird's eye view of Venice* detail], from G. Mazzariol, T. Pignatti, *La pianta prospettica di Venezia del 1500 disegnata da Jacopo de' Barbari*, Venice, Cassa di Risparmio, 1963, 69 × 50 cm, 6 plates, Officine Grafiche Trevisan, Castelfranco
142 Venice, *Monastery of San Giorgio Maggiore* (detail), Centro Internazionale di Studi di Architettura Andrea Palladio, Vicenza, photo © Centro Internazionale di Studi di Architettura Andrea Palladio, Vicenza
143 Venice, *Monastery of San Giorgio Maggiore* (detail), Centro Internazionale di Studi di Architettura Andrea Palladio, Vicenza, photo © Centro Internazionale di Studi di Architettura Andrea Palladio, Vicenza
144 Anon., *Venezia. Pianta della chiesa di San Giorgio Maggiore* [*Project for the reorganisation of the church and monastery of San Giorgio in Venice, before Palladio's intervention*] (detail), 16th cent., *Miscellanea Mappe* dis. 744/1, Archivio di Stato, Venice, photo © Sezione Fotoriproduzione Archivio di Stato, Venice, concessione n. 58/2010
145 Anon., *Venezia. Isola di San Giorgio Maggiore* [Plan of the church (partial) and

cloisters of the Monastery of San Giorgio Maggiore], 15th cent., 87 × 56.5 cm, *Miscellanea Mappe*, dis. 857/1, Archivio di Stato, Venice, photo © Sezione Fotoriproduzione Archivio di Stato, Venice, concessione no. 58/2010

146 Venice, *Church of San Giorgio Maggiore,* interior, Centro Internazionale di Studi di Architettura Andrea Palladio, Vicenza, photo © Centro Internazionale di Studi di Architettura Andrea Palladio, Vicenza

147 Venice, *Church of San Giorgio Maggiore,* exterior (edited)

148 Paolo Caliari, (Veronese), *The Wedding at Cana,* Musée du Louvre, Paris, photo © Musée du Louvre, Paris

149 Venice, *Monastery of the Carità* (mirror image), A. Palladio, *I Quattro Libri dell'Architettura,* II, p. 30, (detail), Centro Internazionale di Studi di Architettura Andrea Palladio, Vicenza, photo © Centro Internazionale di Studi di Architettura Andrea Palladio, Vicenza

150 Venice, *Monastery of the Carità,* eastern side based on the Palladian design published in *I Quattro Libri dell'Architettura* (collage by A.F.)

151 Giovanni Antonio Canal, called Canaletto, *View of Venice with the Monastery of Lateran Canons* (detail), Windsor, The Royal Collection, Her Majesty Queen Elizabeth II, RCIN 406991

152 Venice, *Monastery of the Carità,* eastern facade facing the canal [now filled in] (edited), Centro Internazionale di Studi di Architettura Andrea Palladio, Vicenza, photo © Centro Internazionale di Studi di Architettura Andrea Palladio, Vicenza

153 Suor Isabella Piccini, *Sepulchre of the Barbarigo Doges in the Church of S. Maria della Carità [Monumental tombs for the Barbarigo Doges],* Gabinetto Stampe e disegni del Museo Correr, Venice, St Cicogna 1551, photo © Musei Civici Veneziani, Venice

154 Venice, *Monastery of the Carità,* location plan showing Palladian project published in *I Quattro Libri dell'Architettura,* with a hypothetical rotunda at the northern end. (The solution of the rotunda church is inferred from drawing D 33 r, Pinacoteca Civica, Vicenza). Based on *I Quattro Libri dell'Architettura,* II p. 30 and Gabinetto dei disegni e stampe, Pinacoteca Civica, Vicenza, D. 33 r, photo © Centro Internazionale di Studi di Architettura Andrea Palladio, Vicenza (collage by A.F.)

155 Rome, *Baths of Agrippa,* RIBA, VII, 4 r (detail), Library Photographs Collection Royal Institute of British Architects, London, photo © Library Photographs Collection, Royal Institute of British Architects, London

156 Venice, *Monastery of the Carità,* cross section of atrium, A. Palladio, *I Quattro Libri dell'Architettura,* II, p. 31, Centro Internazionale di Studi di Architettura Andrea Palladio, Vicenza, photo © Centro Internazionale di Studi di Architettura Andrea Palladio, Vicenza

157 Jacopo Zucchi (attributed), *Portrait of Vasari,* 16th cent., 100.5 × 80cm, Inv. 1890/1709, Corridoio Vasariano, Galleria degli Uffizi, Florence, photo © Gabinetto Fotografico della S.S.P.S.A.E e per il Polo Museale della città di Firenze

158 Venice, *Project for a new layout of the area around the Rialto Bridge,* Gabinetto dei disegni e stampe, Pinacoteca Civica, Vicenza, D. 25 v, photo © Pinacoteca Civica, Vicenza

159 Venice, *Semicircular steps for seating (cavea) in a "half Colosseum",* RIBA, X, 3 (detail), Library Photographs Collection Royal Institute of British Architects, London, photo © Library Photographs Collection, Royal Institute of British Architects, London

160 Jacopo Tintoretto, *Portrait of Alvise Cornaro* (detail), 1560–1562, Galleria Palatina di Palazzo Pitti, Florence, photo © Galleria Palatina di Palazzo Pitti, Florence

161 Venice, Rialto, Squares of the Latins, A. Palladio, *I Quattro Libri dell'Architettura,* III, p. 137, Centro Internazionale di Studi di Architettura Andrea Palladio, Vicenza, photo © Centro Internazionale di Studi di Architettura Andrea Palladio, Vicenza

162 Le Corbusier, *La construction des villes,* 1915, Archives FLC B2(20)645 (detail), Fondation Le Corbusier, Paris, photo © FLC/ProLitteris Zürich, 2010

163 Venice, *Project to rebuild the Rialto Bridge,* A. Palladio, *I Quattro Libri dell'Architettura,* III, pp. 26–27, Centro Internazionale di Studi di Architettura Andrea Palladio, Vicenza, photo © Centro Internazionale di Studi di Architettura Andrea Palladio, Vicenza

164 Above: Andrea Palladio, *Triumphal Arch,* Gabinetto dei disegni e stampe, Pinacoteca Civica, Vicenza, D. 20 r. Below: Antonio Foscari, planimetric reconstruction, photo © Pinacoteca Civica, Vicenza (drawing by A.F.)

165 Dolo (Venice), *Villa Mocenigo,* RIBA, XVI, 2 r, Library Photographs Collection Royal Institute of British Architects, London, photo © Library Photographs Collection, Royal Institute of British Architects, London
166 Dolo (Venice), *Villa Mocenigo,* RIBA, XVI, I, Library Photographs Collection Royal Institute of British Architects, London, photo © Library Photographs Collection, Royal Institute of British Architects, London
167 Dolo (Venice), *Villa Mocenigo,* A. Palladio, *I Quattro Libri dell'Architettura,* II, p. 66 (78) (detail), Centro Internazionale di Studi di Architettura Andrea Palladio, Vicenza, photo © Centro Internazionale di Studi di Architettura Andrea Palladio, Vicenza
168 Quinto Vicentino (Vicenza), *Villa Thiene,* A. Palladio, *I Quattro Libri dell'Architettura,* II, p. 64 (detail), Centro Internazionale di Studi di Architettura Andrea Palladio, Vicenza, photo © Centro Internazionale di Studi di Architettura Andrea Palladio, Vicenza
169 Vicenza, *Project for a palazzo for Giacomo Angarano,* A. Palladio, *I Quattro Libri dell'Architettura,* II, p. 75 (detail), Centro Internazionale di Studi di Architettura Andrea Palladio, Vicenza, photo © Centro Internazionale di Studi di Architettura Andrea Palladio, Vicenza
170 Vicenza, *Project for a palazzo for Montano Barbarano,* A. Palladio, *I Quattro Libri dell'Architettura,* II, p. 22 (detail), Centro Internazionale di Studi di Architettura Andrea Palladio, Vicenza, photo © Centro Internazionale di Studi di Architettura Andrea Palladio, Vicenza
171 Vicenza, *Second project for a palazzo for Montano Barbarano,* A. Palladio, *I Quattro Libri dell'Architettura,* II, p. 23, Centro Internazionale di Studi di Architettura Andrea Palladio, Vicenza, photo © Centro Internazionale di Studi di Architettura Andrea Palladio, Vicenza
172 Vicenza, *Palazzo Valmarana,* A. Palladio, *I Quattro Libri dell'Architettura,* II, p. 16 (detail), Centro Internazionale di Studi di Architettura Andrea Palladio, Vicenza, photo © Centro Internazionale di Studi di Architettura Andrea Palladio, Vicenza
173 Vicenza, Palazzo Valmarana, 1973, D. Birelli, Electa Editrice, photo © Electa Editrice
174 Vicenza, *Project for the Palazzo for Iseppo Porto,* RIBA, XVII, 3, Library Photographs Collection Royal Institute of British Architects, London, photo © Library Photographs Collection, Royal Institute of British Architects, London
175 Vicenza, *Project for Palazzo Valmarana,* RIBA, XVII, 4, r, Library Photographs Collection Royal Institute of British Architects, London, photo © Library Photographs Collection, Royal Institute of British Architects, London
176 Vicenza, *Project for a loggia,* Gabinetto dei disegni e stampe, Pinacoteca Civica di Vicenza, D. 19 r, Gabinetto dei disegni e stampe, Pinacoteca Civica, Vicenza, photo © Pinacoteca Civica, Vicenza
177 Palma il Giovane, *Alvise Foscari* (detail from *The Arrival of Henri III at Palazzo Foscari*), Staatliche Kunstsammlungen, Gemäldegalerie Alte Meister, Dresden (252 B), photo © Staatliche Kunstsammlungen, Gemäldegalerie Alte Meister, Dresden
178 Vicenza, *Loggia del Capitanio* (edited), Centro Internazionale di Studi di Architettura Andrea Palladio, Vicenza, photo © Centro Internazionale di Studi di Architettura Andrea Palladio, Vicenza
179 Vicenza, Plan showing the position of Palladio's Loggia del Capitanio in the pre-existing urban fabric (drawing by A.F.)
180 Vicenza, *Palazzo for Alessandro Porto* (edited), Centro Internazionale di Studi di Architettura Andrea Palladio, Vicenza, photo © Centro Internazionale di Studi di Architettura Andrea Palladio, Vicenza
181 Collage of Loggia del Capitanio and Palazzo Porto, Centro Internazionale di Studi di Architettura Andrea Palladio, Vicenza, photo © Centro Internazionale di Studi di Architettura Andrea Palladio, Vicenza
182 Giovanni Vighi, (Argenta), *Duke Emanuele Filiberto of Savoy,* oil on canvas, 1563, Inv. 110, cat. 18, Galleria Sabauda, Turin, photo © concessione del Ministero per i Beni e le Attività Culturali
183 Venice, F. Bertelli, *The Arrival of Henri III in Venice* [Temporary architecture in the form of a Triumphal Arch for Henri III] (detail), Museo Correr, Venice, photo © Musei Civici Veneziani, Venice
184 Palma il Giovane, *Henri III* (detail from *The Arrival of Henri III at Palazzo Foscari*), Staatliche Kunstsammlungen, Gemaeldegalerie Alte Meister, Dresden (252 B), photo © Staatliche Kunstsammlungen, Gemaeldegalerie Alte Meister, Dresden
185 Alessandro Varotari, known as Padovanino, *Doge Alvise Mocenigo inginocchiato davanti al modello del Redentore [Doge Alvise Mocenigo kneeling before a model of*

the Church of the Redentore] (detail), Collezione Marchesa Olga da Cadaval, Venice, photo © Collezione Marchesa Olga da Cadaval, Venice
186 Isola della Giudecca, Venice, *Church of Le Zitelle* (detail), Tracy E. Cooper, photo © Tracy E. Cooper
187 Maser (Treviso), *Tempietto Barbaro* (detail), Centro Internazionale di Studi di Architettura Andrea Palladio, Vicenza, photo © Centro Internazionale di Studi di Architettura Andrea Palladio, Vicenza
188 Venice, *Plan showing quadrangular solution [Church of the Redentore]*, RIBA, XIV, 16, Library Photographs Collection Royal Institute of British Architects, London, photo © Library Photographs Collection, Royal Institute of British Architects, London
189 Venice, *Plan showing rotunda solution [Church of the Redentore]*, RIBA, XIV, 13, Library Photographs Collection Royal Institute of British Architects, London, photo © Library Photographs Collection, Royal Institute of British Architects, London
190 Venice, *Elevation [Church of the Redentore]*, RIBA, XIV, 15 r, Library Photographs Collection Royal Institute of British Architects, London, photo © Library Photographs Collection, Royal Institute of British Architects, London
191 Venice, *Section [Church of the Redentore]*, RIBA, SB 134, XIV, 14, Library Photographs Collection Royal Institute of British Architects, London, photo © Library Photographs Collection, Royal Institute of British Architects , London
192 *Constantine's Temple of the Holy Sepulchre in Jerusalem, reconstruction by Vincent and Abel* (detail), from P.P. Vincent and Abel, Jerusalem, 1914, vol. II, pl. XXXIII, in Luigi Marangoni, *La Chiesa del Santo Sepolcro in Gerusalemme*, La Custodia di Terra Santa, 1937
193 *[Leon Battista Alberti, Model of Temple for Sigismondo Malatesta, Rimini], hypothesis for reconstruction, C.L. Ragghianti* (detail), 1965, photo © Giorgio Grassi, *Leon Battista Alberti e l'architettura romana*, Milano, Franco Angeli, 2007
194 A. Da Sangallo il Giovane, *Studies for San Marcello, Rome* (detail), c. 1519, U 869 A, Galleria degli Uffizi, Florence, photo © Gabinetto Fotografico della S.S.P.S.A.E e per il Polo Museale della città di Firenze
195 Leonardo da Vinci, CA, f. 733 v (detail), c. 1514, *Codex Atlanticus*, Veneranda Biblioteca Ambrosiana di Milano, photo © Autorizzazione numero F 085/10, Veneranda Biblioteca Ambrosiana, Milan
196 L. Cicognara, A. Diedo and G. Selva, *Plan of the Church of the Redentore* (detail), 1838, *Le fabbriche e i monumenti più cospicui di Venezia illustrati*, V II: c. 237, Fondazione Querini Stampalia, Venice, photo © Fondazione Querini Stampalia, Venice
197 Paolo Veronese, *Marcantonio Barbaro*, Kunsthistorisches Museum, Vienna (PG 29), photo © Kunsthistorisches Museum, Vienna
198 Venice, *The public warehouses on the Terranova*, elevation, drawing from *Piazza San Marco. L'architettura la storia le funzioni, Marsilio*, Padua 1970
199 Venice, *The public warehouses on the Terranova*, Jacopo De' Barbari, *La pianta prospettica di Venezia del 1500* [*Bird's eye view of Venice, 1500*] (edited), from G. Mazzariol, T. Pignatti, *La pianta prospettica di Venezia del 1500 disegnata da Jacopo de' Barbari*, Venice, Cassa di Risparmio, 1963, 69 × 50 cm, 6 plates, Officine Grafiche Trevisan, Castelfranco
200 Domenico Lovisa, *Veduta del Molo di San Marco e dei Granai dal palazzo Grimani* [*View of the Molo at San Marco and the Granaries from Palazzo Grimani]* (detail), engraving, *Volume Stampe* A10, plate 4, Gabinetto Stampe e disegni del Museo Correr, Venice photo © Musei Civici Veneziani, Venice
201 Venice, *A new Palazzo to be built on the Terranova*, Devonshire Collection, Chatsworth © Devonshire Collection, Chatsworth. Reproduced by permission of Chatsworth Settlement Trustees (identified by A.F.)
202 The palace shown in the drawing by Palladio in the Devonshire Collection, Chatsworth, placed on Terranova site. Front view and location plan. The drawing of the façade in the area of St Mark's overlooking the Basin is taken from *Piazza San Marco. L'architettura la storia le funzioni, Marsilio*, Padua 1970 (edited) (collage by A.F.)
203 A. Visentini, *Prospectus a Columna S. Theodori ad ingressum Magni Canali [View of the Column of St Theodor at the Entrance to the Grand Canal]*, (detail), engraving from a painting by A. Canal, for *Urbis venetiarum prospectus celebriores*, plate 12, Venice 1742, copperplate engraving, 27.20 × 42.90 cm, Gabinetto Stampe e disegni del Museo Correr, Venice, photo © Musei Civici Veneziani, Venice

204 Venice, *La Casaria di San Marco,* Cadastral map of 1750 showing all the shops selling dairy products from Campiello dell'Ascensione to the Zecca (detail), Museo Correr, Venice, photo © Musei Civici Veneziani, Venice
205 Venice, Palladian design for the construction of a palace on the Terranova site, RIBA, XVI, 5, (detail), Library Photographs Collection Royal Institute of British Architects, London, photo © Library Photographs Collection, Royal Institute of British Architects, London (identified by A.F.)
206 Venice, reconstruction of the Palladian project for a building on the Terranova site (based on indications given in RIBA, XVI, 5) photo © Library Photographs Collection, Royal Institute of British Architects, London (drawing by A.F.)
207 Venice, Palladian design showing an alternative solution for the construction of a palace on the Terranova site (detail from drawing RIBA, XVI, 5), above, and its location plan, below, photo © Library Photographs Collection, Royal Institute of British Architects, London
207 – Venice, collage (using edited RIBA, XVI, 5, detail, lower part of sheet) (identified by A.F./collage by A.F.)
208 Anon., *Venezia. Isola di San Giorgio Maggiore* [Plan of the church (partial) and cloisters of the Monastery of San Giorgio Maggiore] (detail), 15th cent., 87 × 56.5 cm, *Miscellanea Mappe*, dis. 857/1, Archivio di Stato, Venice, photo © Sezione Fotoriproduzione Archivio di Stato, Venice, concessione no. 58/2010.
209 Venice, *Chiostro dei Cipressi. Monastery of San Giorgio Maggiore* (detail), Patricia Fortini Brown, Princeton University, photo © Patricia Fortini Brown
210 Reconstruction of the Palladian project to build the Doge's Palace, Venice: the ground floor (drawing by A.F.)
211 Vicenza, *Ground floor plan of Palazzo della Ragione,* A. Palladio, *I Quattro Libri dell'Architettura, III,* p. 42 (detail), Centro Internazionale di Studi di Architettura Andrea Palladio, Vicenza, photo © Centro Internazionale di Studi di Architettura Andrea Palladio, Vicenza
212 Rome, *Crypta Balbi (Portico of Pompey),* RIBA, XI, 1, Library Photographs Collection Royal Institute of British Architects, London, photo © Library Photographs Collection, Royal Institute of British Architects, London
213 Jacopo Bassano, *Antonio da Ponte* (detail), Musée du Louvre, Paris, photo © Musée du Louvre, Paris
214 Jacopo Sansovino, Scala dei Giganti (edited), Venice, photo © Soprintendenza per i Beni Architettonici e Ambientali di Venezia
215 Jacopo De' Barbari, *La pianta prospettica di Venezia del 1500 [Bird's eye view of Venice, 1500]* (edited), from G. Mazzariol, T. Pignatti, *La pianta prospettica di Venezia del 1500 disegnata da Jacopo de' Barbari,* Venice, Cassa di Risparmio, 1963, 69 × 50 cm, 6 plates, Officine Grafiche Trevisan, Castelfranco
216 Venice, *Sedime Palazzo,* 1987, from Antonio Foscari, *Un dibattito sul foro Marciano allo scadere del 1577 e il progetto di Andrea Palladio per il Palazzo ducale di Venezia in Quaderni dell'Istituto di Storia dell'Architettura,* Dipartimento di Storia dell'Architettura, Restauro e Conservazione dei Beni Architettonici, Rome 1987 (drawing by A.F.)
217 Vincenzo Coronelli, *Prospetto di Palazzo ducale verso il rio di Palazzo [Facade of the Doge's Palace facing the rio di Palazzo]* (edited), in *Singolarità di Venezia. Venice,* 1708–1709, copperplate engraving, 18.5 × 51.5 cm, Gabinetto Stampe e disegni del Museo Correr, Venice, photo © Musei Civici Veneziani, Venice
218 Reconstruction of the Palladian project to build the Doge's Palace, Venice: the level of the Great Council Hall [Sala del Maggior Consiglio] (drawing by A.F.)
219 Venice, The Doge's Palace, southern elevation, drawing from *Piazza San Marco. L'architettura la storia le funzioni,* Marsilio, Padua 1970
220 Antonio Foscari, Reconstruction of the Palladian project to build the Doge's Palace, Venice: southern elevation (collage by A.F.)
221 Reconstruction of the Palladian project to build the Doge's Palace, Venice: detail of the façade. The basement is an elaboration of the Palladian solution for the courtyard of Palazzo Thiene, Vicenza; the columns are based on the model of the Corinthian columns for the Loggia del Capitanio, Vicenza; the division of the façade between the columns is based on the façade solution in between the pilasters on the façade of Palazzo Valmarana, Vicenza, using the design published in *I Quattro Libri dell'Architettura,* II, p. 17. The design of the windows on the upper

floor corresponds to those in the Chatsworth drawing from the Devonshire Collection. The cornice follows the exemplum of the Temple of Jupiter Serapis, as shown in RIBA, XI, 24. Some acroterial statues are reproductions of figures in RIBA, XVII, 4 r (collage by A.F.)
222 Antonio Foscari, Eastern façade of the *foro marciano* showing the Palladian Ducal Palace, as in our reconstruction. The Doge's residence and the Senate Hall can be seen on the second floor between the Doge's chapel of San Marco and the Palace. A new triumphal entrance (based on the Palladian solution illustrated in drawing D. 20 r, Pinacoteca Civica, Vicenza) has been sited between the church and the Palace. Photo © Pinacoteca Civica, Vicenza, and *Piazza San Marco. L'architettura la storia le funzioni,* Marsilio, Padua 1970 (collage by A.F.)
223 Le Corbusier, *La construction des villes,*1915, Archives FLC B2(20)645 (detail), Fondation Le Corbusier, Paris, photo © FLC/ProLitteris Zürich, 2010
224 Biron, Monteviale (Vicenza), *Villa Loschi Zileri Dal Verme,* Centro Internazionale di Studi di Architettura Andrea Palladio, Vicenza, photo © Centro Internazionale di Studi di Architettura Andrea Palladio, Vicenza
225 Cartigliano (Vicenza), *Villa Cappello,* now Vanzo-Mercante (detail), Centro Internazionale di Studi di Architettura Andrea Palladio, Vicenza, photo © Centro Internazionale di Studi di Architettura Andrea Palladio, Vicenza
226 Reconstruction of the final design by Palladio for the Doge's Palace, showing the façade facing the Piazzetta and the Molo divided into "fourteen bays". The system of vertical connections within the building is based – purely for illustrative purposes – on Palladio's drawing of the ground floor of the Crypta Balbi, RIBA, XI, 1 (drawing by A.F.)
227 Giuseppe (Jakob) Heinz il Giovane, *Processione al Redentore [Procession to the Church of the Redentore],* Museo Correr, Venice, photo © Musei Civici Veneziani, Venice
228 Leonardo da Vinci, Paris MS. B, f. 55 r (detail), Institut de France de Paris. Charles Ravaisson-Mollien (ed.), *Les manuscrits de Léonard de Vinci. Manuscrit A [to MS.M] de la Bibliothèque de l'Institut,* 6 vols., Paris 1881–91, photo © Institut de France de Paris
229 L. Cicognara, A. Diedo and G. Selva, *Facade of the Redentore* (detail), 1838, *Le fabbriche e i monumenti più cospicui di Venezia illustrati,* vol. II: c. 230, Fondazione Querini Stampalia, Venice, photo © Fondazione Querini Stampalia, Venice
230 Venice, Church of the Redentore, view from the south

INDEX OF PERSONS

AUTHOR'S BIOGRAPHY

ANTONIO FOSCARI WIDMANN REZZONICO

Antonio Foscari was born in Trieste in 1938 and graduated in architecture from the University IUAV of Venice.

He teaches History of Architecture at the University IUAV of Venice since 1972, where he specialises in the field of Renaissance architectural history on which he has published and lectured extensively. A list of his works is given in the following pages. Of these, it is worth highlighting his works in collaboration with Manfredo Tafuri, and in particular the book *L'armonia e conflitti* published by Einaudi in 1983.

He began his professional career by successfully taking part in Italian and international competitions (In-Arch. Design competition; international design competition for the Isola del Tronchetto in Venice; international urban planning competition for the city of Varna in Bulgaria; competition for the offices of the Chamber of Deputies in Rome and for an ISES residential complex in Secondigliano).

As an architect he has overseen the restoration of various palaces in Venice, including Palazzo Grassi, Palazzo Duodo, Palazzo Corner Contarini dei Cavalli, Palazzo Bollani, Palazzo Lezze and the Theatre Malibran (after receiving an award for the competition to restore La Fenice). He also built a sports centre for the University of Venice.

Outside Venice, he has built, among other things, a research centre for advanced technology in Urbino, the Valtur Village and the amphitheatre of Pollina and Auchan mall in the Province of Venice. He designed the renovation of the historic centre of Alvisopoli in Friuli. He oversaw the restoration of the Theatre Regina Margherita in Racalmuto (Sicily) and built the Leonardo Sciascia Foundation. He carried out the restoration of the Palladian villa known as "La Malcontenta" (winning a special prize from the Istituto Regionale per le Villa Venete).

He has held various public offices, mainly in Venice. He was president of the City Building Commission, a member of the Technical Committee of the Magistrato alle Acque, a member of the city's Comitato di Salvaguardia, a member of the Board of Directors of the Fondazione di Venezia, a member of the Board of Directors of the University IUAV of Venice and deputy chairman of the Fondazione Scientifica Querini Stampalia. During his term of office as president of the Accademia di Belle Arti in Venice, he promoted the Institute's move into the Renaissance complex of the Ospedale degli Incurabili. He was appointed Commendatore al merito della Repubblica by the President of Italy in recognition of his contribution to cultural affairs.

For many years he has worked in very close collaboration with a number of French cultural organisations. Among other initiatives in this respect, he founded the Alliance Française in Venice which he chaired for twenty-five years. The French Republic recognised this link by nominating him to the Ordre des Arts et des Lettres, awarding him the Légion d'Honneur and, lastly, appointing him through the French Ministry of Culture as a member of the Board of Directors of the Louvre.

OTHER PUBLICATIONS BY THE AUTHOR ON ARCHITECTURAL HISTORY

"La Rocca Pisana a Lonigo di Vincenzo Scamozzi. Rilievo e fotografie" in *L'Architettura Cronache e Storia,* IV, no. 35, September 1958, pp. 342–47

"Disegni inediti dell'archivio Rezzonico. Progetti di Quarenghi, Bonomi, Passalacqua e il piano di Ancona del Vanvitelli" in *Palatino,* XII, no. 2, April–June 1968, pp. 171–78

"Per Palladio: note sul Redentore a San Vidal e sulle Zittelle" in *Antichità Viva,* XIV, no. 3, 1975, pp. 44–56

"L'invenzione di Palladio per un 'sito piramidale' in Venezia" in *Arte Veneta,* XXXIII, 1979, pp. 136–41

"Ricerca sugli 'Accesi' e su 'questo benedetto theatro' costruito da Palladio in Venezia nel 1565" in *Notizie da Palazzo Albani,* I, 1979, pp. 68–83

"Un altare di Andrea Palladio nella Chiesa di San Pantalon (1555)" in *Architettura e Utopia nella Venezia del Cinquecento,* Venice 1980, pp. 255–56

"Le Zitelle", in *Architettura e Utopia nella Venezia del Cinquecento,* Venice 1980, pp. 269–70

"L'invenzione palladiana di un palazzo a Venezia. Due ipotesi sul 'sito': Un'ipotesi per San Samuele" in *Architettura e Utopia nella Venezia del Cinquecento*", Venice 1980, p. 270

"L'allestimento teatrale del Vasari per i Sempiterni (1542)" in *Architettura e Utopia nella Venezia del Cinquecento,* Venice 1980, pp. 273–74

"Schede veneziane su Jacopo Sansovino" in *Notizie da Palazzo Albani,* I, 1981, pp. 22–34

"Un progetto del Sansovino per il palazzo di Vettor Grimani a S. Samuel" (with M. Tafuri) in *Ricerche di Storia dell'Arte,* no. 15, 1981, pp. 69–82

"Un progetto irrealizzato di Jacopo Sansovino: Il palazzo di Vettor Grimani sul Canal Grande" (with M. Tafuri) in *Bollettino Civici Musei Veneziani d'Arte e di Storia,* XXVI n.s., nos. 1–4, 1981, pp. 71–87

"Evangelismo e Architettura. Jacopo Sansovino e la Chiesa di San Martino a Venezia" in *Bollettino Civici Musei Veneziani d'Arte e di Storia,* XXVII n.s., nos. 1–4, 1982, pp. 34–51

"Sebastiano da Lugano, i Grimani e Jacopo Sansovino. Artisti e committenti nella Chiesa di Sant'Antonio di Castello" (with M. Tafuri) in *Arte Veneta,* XXXVI, 1982, pp. 100–23

"Palladio a Feltre" in *Contributi su Andrea Palladio. Nel Quarto Centenario della morte (1580–1980),* Venice 1982, pp. 33–56

"Accordo per la Facciata della Chiesa di San Pietro di Castello in Venezia" in *Contributi su Andrea Palladio. Nel Quarto Centenario della morte (1580–1980),* Venice 1982, pp. 57–78

"Tre appunti veneziani per Palladio" in *Contributi su Andrea Palladio. Nel Quarto Centenario della morte (1580–1980),* Venice 1982, pp. 79–90

"Il 'Cursus Honorum' di Zuan Dolfin (Committente di Michele Sanmicheli e di Jacopo Sansovino)" in *Ateneo Veneto,* XX n.s., nos. 1–2, 1982, pp. 205–36

"Palladio a San Pantalon" in Lionello Puppi (ed.) *Palladio e Venezia,* Florence 1982, pp. 89–93, figs. 80–81

L'armonia e i conflitti (with M. Tafuri), Turin 1983

"Giambattista Piranesi da Venezia al Campidoglio" in A. Bettagno (ed.) *Piranesi tra Venezia e L'Europa,* Florence 1983, pp. 269–92

"Altre schede veneziane su Jacopo Sansovino" in *Notizie da Palazzo Albani,* nos. 1–2, 1983, pp. 135–52

"Tra la lezione di Carlo Lodoli e il Neoclassicismo: Federico Foscari e Antonio Battisti" in *Bollettino. Civici Musei Veneziani d'Arte e di Storia,* nos. 1–4, XXVII n.s., 1983–84, pp. 35–40

"Il Cantiere delle Procuratie Vecchie e Jacopo Sansovino" in *Ricerche di Storia dell'Arte,* no. 19, 1983, pp. 61–76

"Festoni e putti nella decorazione della Libreria di San Marco" in *Arte Veneta,* XXXVIII, 1984, pp. 23–30

"Appunti di lavoro su Jacopo Sansovino" in *Notizie da Palazzo Albani,* no. 2, 1984, pp. 35–56

"Un dibattito sul foro Marciano allo scadere del 1577 e il progetto di Andrea Palladio per il Palazzo Ducale di Venezia" in *Quaderni dell'Istituto di Storia dell'Architettura,* 1987, pp. 323–32

"Introduzione a una ricerca sulla costruzione della Libreria medicea nel Convento di San Giorgio Maggiore, a Venezia" in Ranieri Varese (ed.), *Studi in onore per Pietro Zampetti,* Ancona 1993, pp. 226–36

"Un conflitto sulla scena veneziana" in A. Piva and P. Galliani (eds), *Lo spazio virtuale della rappresentazione. Contributi per un sistema museale del '700 veneziano",* Venice 1993, pp. 51–67

"Tommaso Lombardo da Lugano nella bottega di Jacopo Sansovino" in *Venezia Arti 1995,* 9, 1995, pp. 141–45

"Un arco trionfale per la facciata della Cappella Ducale. Qualche riflessione sui silenzi di Jacopo Sansovino" in Renato Polacco (ed.), *Storia dell'arte marciana: l'architettura – Atti del Convegno Internazionale di Studi,* Venice 1997, pp. 255–76

"La costruzione della Chiesa Agostiniana di Santo Stefano. Innovazioni e conformismi nell'architettura veneziana del primo Quattrocento" in *Gli Agostiniani a Venezia e la Chiesa di Santo Stefano: Atti della Giornata di Studio nel v Centenario della Dedicazione della Chiesa di Santo Stefano,* Venice 1997, pp. 121–58

"Floriano Antonini, Andrea Palladio e la 'bellissima fabbrica' da loro costruita a Udine" in L. and M. Asquini, *Andrea Palladio e gli Antonini,* Mariano del Friuli 1997, pp. XIII–XXIII

"La veneranda habitazione dei dogi Barbarighi, rifatta poi sul modello di Sansovino" in *Venezia Arti 1997,* 11, 1997, pp. 35–42

"Michelozzo, Donatello e la Signoria di Venezia" in Gabriele Morolli (ed.), *Michelozzo. Scultore e Architetto (1396–1472),* Florence 1998, pp. 61–66

"Per Jacopo Sansovino. Una interpretazione della vicenda edilizia della Ca' di Dio" in *Studi in onore di Elena Bassi,* Venice 1998, pp. 15–28

"Il piacere dell'armonia. La Malcontenta" in *L'Architettura cronache e storie,* XLV, no. 523, 1999, pp. XXI–XXVIII

"Silenzi e parole di Le Corbusier" in *Hôpital de Venice Le Corbusier. Testimonianze,* in Renzo Dubbini and Roberto Sordina (eds), Venice, 1999, pp. 120–25

"Sul nartece della Cappella Marciana" in *Scienza e tecnica del restauro della basilica di San Marco. Atti del convegno internazionale di studi,* Padua 1999, pp. 219–25

"La casa di Jacopo Sansovino a Oriago, 'luogo amenissimo e bello'" in *Quaderni di Studio della Riviera del Brenta,* no. 1, 2000, pp. 20–21

"Un altro 'gran quadro di basso rilievo' di Jacopo Sansovino" in *Venezia Cinquecento,* no. 22, XI, 2001, pp. 5–13

"Enea Vico e Jacopo Sansovino. Due visioni antagoniste della sistemazione di Piazza San Marco" in M. Piantoni, L. De Rossi (eds), *Per l'arte, da Venezia all'Europa. Studi in onore di Giuseppe Maria Pilo, I, Dall'antichità al Caravaggio,* Gorizia 2001, pp. 191–96

"Magnanimi monumenta ducis domus inclyta salve. Un'ode sulla costruzione di Ca' Foscari" in *La casa grande dei Foscari in volta de canal,* Venice 2001, pp. VIII–XXXIV

"Rerum Venetiarum Fragmenta" in *The Venice International Foundation,* no. 10, 2002, pp. 17–20

"Diego de Siloe e la definizione del modello per la Sacra Capilla de El Salvador in Ubeda. (Una eco spagnola del modello di Leon Battista Alberti per il tempio Malatestiano)" in I. Chiappini di Sorio, L. De Rossi (eds), *Venezia, le Marche e la civiltà adriatica. Per festeggiare i 90 anni di Pietro Zampetti"* Gorizia 2003, pp. 312–17

"Attorno alla fabbrica palladiana 'sulla Brenta', alla Malcontenta" in *Manovre di fantasia controllata,* Rome 2004, pp. 40–43

"Per Michele Sanmicheli e per Paolo Veronese. L'organo e l'altare della chiesa di San Sebastiano" in L. Caselli, J. Scarpa, G. Trovabene (eds), *Venezia Arti e storia. Studi in onore di Renato Polacco,* Venice 2005, pp. 118–31

"La casa veneziana" in *The Venice International Foundation,* no. 17, 2005, pp. 9–15

"Prima di Ca' Foscari, La 'casa delle due torri' e il doge" in G.M. Pilo and L. De Rossi (eds), *Ca' Foscari. Storia e restauro del palazzo della Università di Venezia,* Venice 2005, pp. 22–37

"Il doge e la costruzione della sua 'casa granda'" in G.M. Pilo and L. De Rossi (eds), *Ca' Foscari. Storia e restauro del palazzo della Università di Venezia,* Venice 2005, pp. 52–67

"Tra Giulio Romano e Tiziano. Il duplice supplizio di Marsia e altre metamorfosi" in Lionello Puppi (ed.), *Tiziano. L'ultimo Atto,* Milan 2007, pp. 129–34

"Michelangelo secondo lo IUAV" in Franco Mancuso (ed.), *Lo IUAV di Giuseppe Samonà e l'insegnamento dell'Architettura,* Rome 2007, pp. 105–17

"Sulla riva del Canal Grande, a San Simeon Piccolo. La 'struttura teatrale' in cui ha debuttato a Venezia il Ruzzante" in M.A. Chiari Moretto Wiel and A. Gentili (eds), *L'attenzione e la critica. Scritti di storia dell'arte in memoria di Terisio Pignatti,* Padua 2008, pp. 101–13

"Germanicis Dicatum. Il fondaco dei Tedeschi a Venezia" in *Viaggi in Italia* Milan 2008, pp. 186–223. Republished in *Ateneo Veneto. Rivista di Scienze, Lettere ed Arti. Atti e memorie dell'Ateneo Veneto,* CXCV, terza serie 7/II 2008, pp. 7–17

"Le Corbusier a Venezia nel luglio del 1934. Un *Entretien,* Giuseppe Volpi e altri incontri" in *Ateneo Veneto. Rivista di Scienze, Lettere ed Arti. Atti e memorie dell'Ateneo Veneto,* CXCIV, terza serie 6/II, 2007, pp. 217–42

"La *Trasfigurazione* veneziana di Giovanni Bellini" in *Arte Documento. Rivista e Collezione di Storia e tutela dei Beni Culturali,* no. 25, 2009, pp. 70–83

"À Venise en 1934" in *L'Italie de Le Corbusier: XVe Rencontres de La Fondation Le Corbusier,* Paris 2010, pp. 200–9

ACKNOWLEDGEMENTS

This study, which was prompted by the celebrations to mark the fifth centenary of Andrea Palladio's birth, could not have been carried out without the help of many organisations: the Royal Institute of British Architects, the Victoria & Albert Museum, the Musei Civici di Vicenza, the Venetian State Archives, the Soprintendenza per i Beni Architettonici e Paesaggistici di Venezia e Laguna, the Fondazione Querini Stampalia, the Biblioteca del Museo Civico Correr, and above all the Centro Internazionale di Architettura Andrea Palladio. I would like to thank Charles Hind, Maria Elisa Avagnina, Renata Codello and, in particular, Guido Beltramini for their generous help and for the kindness and promptness with which they dealt with my requests. I am immensely grateful to them all, as well as to Francesco Buranelli of the Pontifical Commission for Cultural Heritage.

Among the owners of Palladian buildings, my thanks go to Vittorio Trettenero, Carl Gable, Manuela Bedeschi, Titta Rossi Pertile and Lodovico Valmarana who allowed me to spend time in their *fabbriche* while completing my research.

I also wish to acknowledge the expertise of Alberto Torsello, Tommaso Masiero and in particular Marco De Lorenzi and the willingness with which they helped to give graphic form to my ideas for the reconstruction of some of Palladio's unfinished works.

I am also profoundly grateful to two others: to Lucinda Byatt who has translated my words with insight and fluency, and to Carmela Donadio who has followed my work with such patience and efficiency that, in the end, its completion owes much to her.

As always, a book is the work of not only its author but also its publisher. Without Lars Müller's friendship and expertise this volume could not have been produced with such impeccable editorial quality. And if it were not for Giulia Foscari's love and support, also in terms of organisation, in all likelihood this book would have never seen the light. For this reason, I will not even attempt to put into words what I feel for Lars and Giulia.

ANDREA PALLADIO – UNBUILT VENICE

ANTONIO FOSCARI WIDMANN REZZONICO

Design: Integral Lars Müller/Lars Müller and Res Eichenberger
Editorial Advisor: Giulia Foscari
Translation from the Italian: Lucinda Byatt
Copyediting and proofreading: Ishbel Flett
Lithography: Lithotronic Media GmbH, Dreieich
Paper: Munken Pure, 130 g/m², Allegro 150 g/m²
Printing and Binding: Kösel, Altusried-Krugzell, Germany

Lars Müller Publishers
Baden, Switzerland
www.lars-muller-publishers.com

ISBN 978-3-03778-222-4

Printed in Germany

9 8 7 6 5 4 3 2 1